DRIVEN TO RIDE

THE TRUE STORY OF AN ELITE ATHLETE WHO
REBUILT HIS LEG, HIS LIFE, AND HIS CAREER

MIKE SCHULTZ

WITH MATT HIGGINS

TRIUMPH
BOOKS

Library of Congress Cataloging-in-Publication Data available upon request.

This book is available in quantity at special discounts for your group or organization. For further information, contact:
Triumph Books LLC
814 North Franklin Street
Chicago, Illinois 60610
(312) 337-0747
www.triumphbooks.com

Printed in U.S.A.
ISBN: 978-1-62937-913-5
Design by Sue Knopf
Page production by Patricia Frey

To my wife and No. 1 teammate, Sara, for always standing by my side through the triumphs and challenges since the beginning. To my daughter, Lauren; you make us so proud and I can't wait for all the future adventures we will have together.

Contents

Section Three: Operation

Foreword

I met Mike Schultz for the first time in the athlete lounge at X Games in January 2016. We were both competing at that X Games, so the athlete lounge was the simplest place to meet up. In my career as a professional halfpipe skier, I've been lucky enough to win every title available in my sport and rubbed elbows with the A-list elite from various realms. Some celebrities are excellent humans, and some of them are people you could not pay me to spend time with. Fame does not impress me much, but when I met Mike, I felt like a giddy fanboy. We all have our sports heroes, but I admired Mike for a lot more than just his accomplishments on the world stage.

My sister Christy was a few months out from an accident which resulted in an above-knee amputation. I had been doing research on sports alternative prosthetics for Christy and stumbled across a company called BioDapt that made motocross-inspired prosthetics with Fox Shox and even ski-specific prosthetic feet and ankles. The deeper I dug into the company and its founder, the more impressed I was. Many professional athletes start their own brands, but most of those companies are focused on profit or self-glorification. BioDapt was clearly focused on helping adaptive athletes by offering something that was not available. BioDapt is filling a hole created by the prosthetic industry's relationship with insurance companies, and athletic amputees all over the world benefit. I was excited to meet the man behind the Moto Knee that I hoped would help my sister ski like herself again.

Christy is a very active person, and I can attribute a lot of my success to her and her twin sister, Jessica, pushing me as a youngster. I could always count on Christy to be willing to try any sport or adventure. I knew one of the most difficult parts of her injury was going to be the limitations on activities. Early on as an amputee, Christy had to face the sense of loss surrounding things that she would not be able to do anymore. My goal as her brother and lifelong adventure buddy was to try to keep her focused on what she could do. Because of Mike and his prosthesis, Christy was able to add carving turns on skis to that list. We went out skiing as a group and I will never forget the look on my sister's face as she and Mike finally got the settings right and she was able to link race-quality turns again.

I have had the good fortune to spend some quality time with Mike since that first X Games, and my admiration for him has only grown. I think that the best way to measure the true depth of a man is to watch how he interacts with his wife and kids. Mike has a list of accomplishments that could easily fit on the résumé of two or three people, yet he hasn't accomplished those things at the cost of his closest relationships. Many of the competitively dominant sports figures and businesspeople that I know put their career before their family; they see it as the only way to get ahead in a fast-paced world. What Mike and Sara have accomplished together is the opposite of that. Rather than turn away from each other to get ahead, they chose to lean on each other and build something meaningful together.

Not only have Mike and Sara survived a traumatic injury and the resulting financial duress that would have put any marriage to the test, but they have also learned to thrive together through it. Together they have started a company that is making permanent change in adaptive athletes' lives and in the prosthetic industry. They have built a professional adaptive motocross career, a professional adaptive snocross career, and now a professional adaptive boardercross career. How can one guy do so many things? Mike obviously has a titanium force of will and a work ethic that could put anyone to shame, but he also has a partner with strengths and qualities to mirror and complement his own. This is not just a story of one man overcoming adversity; it is a saga of a young couple banding together and persevering in spite of the odds. Believe me when I tell you that we can all learn a lot from the story between these pages. Prepare to stretch your sense of gratitude, grow your threshold for what adversity is, and expand your concept of what selfless love looks like.

Few people understand how difficult competing for Team USA in the Olympics or the Paralympics can be on the athlete's family. Baseball, football, and hockey athletes and their families are treated like royalty everywhere they go, but Olympic athletes are often lucky if they get a discount on lodging or food. No journey to the Olympics or Paralympics can happen without immense sacrifice by the athlete's family. (My wife sometimes comments that she feels like a military wife because it's as if I am deployed while traveling the world when the snow is falling.) When the athlete wins a gold medal, people will view the sacrifice as worth it, but what if the athlete doesn't even make finals or has a bad race during the medal round? Our families support us knowing that there is no guarantee that we will win gold. They support us because they know that going out there and doing what we were made to do is necessary for us. Not doing so would be like denying a large piece of us. People like Mike are born with an exceptional need to compete. You could call it a competitive fire. What Sara exemplifies is how to support someone with that fire without resentment. With Sara's support, Mike has the freedom to shamelessly be Monster Mike, and he is a much better man for it.

Whether it is on a snowboard, a snowmobile, or a dirt bike, watching Mike ride shows me that racing is his calling. Mike is the perfect embodiment of the word *adaptive*. Mike doesn't look "disabled" when he races; he could still smoke me in most races (though I haven't seen him in a halfpipe yet). When I see Mike race, I can tell that he just loves to go fast and fly high, the same way I do. The machines or boards that he rides are just mediums to help him go faster and fly higher. The fact that he is missing a good portion of his leg isn't a limit, it is just an adjustment that needs to be overcome. What Mike proves to me is that I need to reassess what I see as a limit or what I might feel like is impossible. Most of the things in life that we believe are impossible are that way because someone said so, or because no one else has done it yet. I am sure that Mike and Sara heard plenty of things were not going to be possible post-injury. I am thankful that they chose not to listen and decided to find out what they could do together.

—David Wise
Olympic freeski halfpipe gold medalist, 2014 and 2018
Reno, Nevada
September 2021

Prologue

Good timber does not grow with ease
The stronger wind, the stronger trees
                    —"Good Timber," Douglas Malloch

IT'S DECEMBER 2008, AND I'M LYING IN A BED AT ST. MARY'S HOSPITAL in Duluth, Minnesota, with my entire family gathered around me. Groggy and stunned, I try to concentrate on what a doctor is telling me.

Through a drug-induced haze, I hear him say that circulation in my left leg has been compromised, and blood is pooling in my foot. I look down at my toes, plump and discolored. I can't move them, not even a millimeter, no matter how hard I try. He tells me that my kidneys are shutting down. He tells me that, best case scenario, I'm looking at 20 surgeries in the next year, and I *still* might never use my leg again.

He tells me he wants to amputate. In order to save my life.

I'm totally blindsided. I cannot believe it. *Amputate my leg?* Just three days ago, I'd been competing in the high-octane realm of professional snocross, a snowmobile discipline in which competitors roar on 170-horsepower machines through a course of tight turns, bumps, and jumps, launching 100 feet or more through the air. I'd been "Monster Mike," a nickname earned because of my aggressive forward stance on a racing sled, the way I leaned my muscular 5'10", 190-pound frame over the handlebars to wrangle my way through difficult terrain with brute force and determination. I'd been strong, a professional athlete with two healthy legs who charged through any obstacles put before him.

True, I'd recently hit a rough patch in my competitive career, but after changing teams, I'd been ready to get back on a winning track. I'd approached the starting line at a racecourse on a ski hill in Michigan's Upper Peninsula blinded by snow and flat light conditions but ready to give them hell, to signal to my competitors that I was still a contender. But during the race I'd lost control and crash-landed, shattering my left leg and all my life plans. Paramedics shuttled me from the tiny hospital in Ironwood, Michigan, across two states to the ICU here in Duluth, where I've endured three surgeries in three days, with my wife, Sara, a professional nurse, by my side. My mom, dad, and brother stand with her around my bedside as the doctor soberly delivers the news. My dad, a construction worker and farmer, the toughest guy I know, fights back tears.

Slowly, it sinks in. Amputation will save my life, but it will kill the dream I've been chasing since I was 13 years old, when I lined up for my first race on a BMX bike back in rural Minnesota. I'd graduated to buzzing around the farm on my dirt bike. By the time I'd turned 16, I'd been attending high school during the day and working the evening shift at a metal fabrication shop to fund my racing dirt bikes on weekends. Initially, my dad had disapproved, thinking racing was too dangerous, but eventually he came around. He has always been a fan of riding snowmobiles, so helping me get into racing snocross was a great way for him to support and be part of what I loved to do most—go racing. Each winter, he, Sara, and I trekked across the state for weekend races. By age 19, I'd begun making some money as a professional snocross racer, imagining myself someday standing atop the podium as the undisputed fastest in the world. It hadn't always been easy, hauling a trailer containing my 400-pound sleds across the frozen highways of the upper half of the U.S. from New York to Montana, but Sara and I had lived for the sport. We'd loved the travel, the competition, the camaraderie with the other riders and their wives. We'd never really known life together without racing at the center of it.

Now, in a hospital more than 100 miles from home, I'm confronting a life without racing, without my leg. The doctor gives us time to talk it over, but there isn't much to say, and we agree to the amputation. Because I'm under the influence of pain medication, Sara must sign a consent form, just like she did when I was a high-school racer and she was 18 and acting as my guardian at the track. She's always taken responsibility for my care, and once again the responsibility rests in her hands.

Doctors immediately begin prepping me for surgery, a whirlwind of tools and beeps and commands. In that moment, unsure about what lies ahead, I want only to survive. I don't yet know how my resolve will be tested. How losing my leg will inspire in me a creativity and drive I didn't know I possessed. How I will reinvent myself as an athlete, against all odds, in a different sport, traveling around the world in pursuit of greatness. How my injury will inspire me to help others, to revitalize the futures of countless fellow amputees. I don't know hard it will be, how I will endure pain even greater than this, or how my relationship with Sara will be tested and come out even stronger on the other side. I don't know the people I'll meet, the new person I'll become.

I think it's the end of it all; it's only the beginning.

SECTION ONE: PARTS

No pessimist ever discovered the secret of the stars, or sailed to an uncharted land, or opened a new doorway for the human spirit.
—Helen Keller

1

Monster Mike

Saturday, December 13, 2008
Ironwood, Michigan

ON THE MORNING OF THE RACE, IT IS BITTER COLD, MAYBE 15 DEGREES Fahrenheit. Clouds coming off Lake Superior carry snow flurries and a cast of light that flattens all the features on the track until they resemble a sheet of blank paper. This particular course winds up and down Mount Zion ski hill, a modest 300-foot-high bump in westernmost Michigan, where the north woods of the Upper Peninsula abut the Wisconsin border. When the sleds begin to tear up the track in a couple hours, white granules fine as dust will fill the air and a field of nine riders will be racing inside the most intense snow globe imaginable. Being fast and consistent will come down to memorizing the course. Visibility will be so poor, we won't be sure whether we're about to plunge into a hole or hit a four-foot mogul that will launch us airborne. These weather conditions, the poor performance of the sled at practice, all of it weighs on my mind. These are forces outside my control, much like the direction of my life and career lately.

I'm 27 years old, toward the end of my peak as a professional athlete in a career that has carried me from my home in Central Minnesota all across the globe on a snowmobile—Canada, Iceland, Sweden, through the snowbelt of the States. I've got a lot of good riding left, but it's critical for me to prove it today with a strong finish on the second stop of the International Series of Champions (ISOC) tour, the world's top level of snowmobile racing. I'm one of seven riders on the only team that offered me a position at the beginning of the season. Another poor result will not only mean less incentive-based pay in my pocket; it will mean I cannot afford to continue racing while piling up expenses lugging my sleds; myself; and my wife, Sara, across a frozen landscape in pursuit of the professional snowmobile circuit. If I can't turn things around soon, I'll be finished.

For 10 years, I've raced snocross, a supercharged discipline that takes place on a tight course of twists, turns, bumps, and jumps that resembles a motocross track. For the past four years, I've made it a career. Competing at the elite level, each race I'm pitted against a dozen or more riders astride snarling 400-pound machines capable of reaching an ear-pinning 9,000 RPMs (engine revolutions per minute). We ride clad in full-face helmets and armor, wrapped in thick boots and suits meant to ward off the chill of snowbound locales like West Yellowstone, Montana; Duluth, Minnesota; and Lake Geneva, Wisconsin. When the green flag flies to start a race, a dozen 170-horsepower engines scream, and every nerve ending tingles while riders try to launch off the starting line and pull from the pack on finely tuned machines racing over a frozen track. The speed, the strategy, that high-flying thrill of fear when your heart sinks into your stomach and your mind is so tuned to the moment that there's no space for stray thought—these sensations keep me going through inevitable sacrifices, including injuries and the stress of income that depends entirely on my most recent race performances. It's an emotional investment that, when all goes right, finally pays off on the podium with hugs and high-fives from your peers, a nice-sized paycheck, and the knowledge that on that day you were one of the fastest snowmobile riders in the world.

I've been chasing that thrill since lining up for my first BMX race at 13 years old. This dream I bought into at an early age has sustained me through racing bikes, motorcycles, and snowmobiles and given me the strength to overcome failure, several concussions, and a half-dozen broken bones. But by early winter of 2008, I haven't been seeing those results that make it all worthwhile. My stepdad, Rick, has offered for me to return to work with his construction company, digging in utility lines, a job I've dabbled in each summer. Rick is nearly bald with a handlebar mustache. He rides a Harley and looks like a badass, but he's a kind person with a positive attitude. He and my mom got together in my early teens and created CNR Contractors, an underground utility installation company, building it from scratch into an outfit that employs 15 people. After I graduated from high school, Rick hired me but never acted like a traditional boss. He would present me with a task and let me figure out the best way to tackle the job. These work experiences really challenged me and prepared me to become a great problem-solver. Being part of a crew, operating earth movers, digging trenches, it's like playing in a giant sandbox. The pay is good. Why scrape by on the meager income of a racer, facing the threat of further injury?

Why continue racing? Rick asks each summer as we drive together to job sites. *Why continue doing this to yourself?*

These are fair questions, and I'd be lying if I said I hadn't started to reconsider my future. But could I really give up? What *was* keeping me going, day after grueling day, the nonstop physical training, the mental roller coaster of emotions, hauling this machine across the country and the world in pursuit of greatness? There's the chance for a Winter X Games gold medal and a championship trophy, obviously. But more than that, it's the community of racers, mechanics, and owners that keeps me going. There's camaraderie among these people, *my* people, an energy when we're unified in committed pursuit of a common goal.

I don't know, I say. *Because it feels so good when things go right. There's just no other feeling that compares when it all comes together.*

NONE OF US DREAMS OF BEING AN UNDERDOG. We racers, each of us in our minds, we're top guns, separated from a podium finish and the rest of the pack by a stretch of bad luck, an injury, maybe a mechanical breakdown or a snafu with sponsors.

You need a lot to break right to be consistently among the fastest. You need a team with money, sure, but also a fast machine and the right mechanics, plus a crew chief to create conditions for success. It's not just about navigating hairpin turns and making bold moves on the course; you need support behind you. The quest for the right team conditions—that's kept me going, too.

For three years, I raced for Team Avalanche, a new outfit out of Glyndon, Minnesota, just across the state line from Fargo. The team is funded by Mike and Bonnie Glefke. Mike is a businessman from Chicago, an alpha male who's accustomed to calling the shots. His interest in racing comes from his son, and at first he seemed tickled just to be along for the ride, having some laughs while playing owner. One year after putting together a team from scratch, he recruited me to be a pro class rider during the 2005–06 season. I was an up-and-comer, the perfect fit to lead a fresh team competing in only its second season.

By 2007–08, my third season with Avalanche, I ranked fourth in the standings, with a handful of podium finishes on the Amsoil National Championship Snocross Tour, the pinnacle professional circuit in the world. I was a half-step from the top of the podium and the elite men I'd been chasing for years. It was my best performance yet, and the best yet for Team Avalanche. The machines ran well. Morale was high, and we concluded the season confident that we belonged on the podium. Anything less would be a disappointment.

When Sara and I married the following summer, all my teammates, mechanics, crewmen, and even the Glefkes gathered outside Brainerd at a golf resort on picturesque Gull Lake surrounded by stately oak trees. My mechanic, Chad, was one of the groomsmen. I wore a black sling to match my tuxedo. The previous weekend, I had sustained a broken collarbone and a concussion from a crash on my dirt bike. I suggested postponing the wedding until I was healed, but Sara wouldn't stand for a delay. She said, "I've already waited nine years!" Rather than a honeymoon, I was scheduled for surgery on my shattered left collarbone. When the pastor said, "For better or for worse, in sickness and in health," Sara laughed out loud. Team Avalanche was a happy family—which only magnified the hurt when things went sour so fast.

In every race the previous season it seemed as if the sleds broke down, or I'd make a mistake or suffer bad luck. Pressure to get on the podium, as one of the top three finishers in the pro class, ratcheted up. We'd also added two new riders on Avalanche, and the increased budget meant Mike Glefke was spending nearly seven figures to run our team for the season. Most team owners on tour are wealthy businesspeople looking for a tax write-off or a chance to break even. "Want to know how to make $1 million racing snocross?" Mr. G would ask with a chuckle. "Start with $2 million."

When I failed to produce results in the pro class, the fun for him— for all of us—drained from the enterprise. Stressed, he was no longer the laughing, jovial man who recruited me to the team. Team morale plummeted. He played mind games to try to motivate me. When Mr. G questioned my heart and stripped me of my mechanic, Chad, replacing him with a rookie wrench, he and I had it out. By season's end, I felt like a team pariah and was looking to exit my contract.

After reaching out to the top half of the 10 pro teams on tour to find my ride, Warnert Racing from St. Cloud, Minnesota, was able to squeeze me in last-minute before the season start. The team is operated by two brothers, Ron and Mark Warnert, businessmen who own real estate and franchises for auto parts stores, and are known for working hard to promote snowmobile manufacturer Ski-Doo. The Warnerts are in racing to make money; their reputation among riders is that they don't pay very well.

I'm one of seven racers on the team, and the oldest by six years. (Oh, and I've also had to settle for a 60 percent pay cut.) But I'm part of one of the bigger outfits on tour, three times larger than Avalanche. With Warnert, we are a major operation, rolling into each race weekend with two semi-truck rigs and a fifth-wheel trailer. If the other riders are bummed that Warnert brought on another racer, diluting the resources and budget, they don't show it.

THE INTERNATIONAL SERIES OF CHAMPIONS (ISOC) operates the Amsoil Tour, which is the NASCAR of snowmobile racing, where the world's best compete every year from late November to mid-March. The pro class consists of approximately 25 competitors. Any given event can draw around 200 to 300 riders between all the classes, from pros on multi-million-dollar programs all the way down to novices, weekend warrior types who treat racing as a hobby. We all ride on the same tracks, which can vary at each venue from bumpy oval-shaped courses situated inside massive outdoor stadiums to twisting natural terrain with high-flying jumps and high-speed straightaways. This weekend in Ironwood, we are on the latter, a long track traversing a ski resort, which is a new venue for our race series.

Tour workers travel to race sites up to a month in advance to ready the courses, using snow guns like those at ski resorts to augment whatever Mother Nature has provided. Big semi-truck rigs belonging to the pro race teams—eager for fast results to help spur sales for snowmobile manufacturers—arrive the week of the race to begin setup in the pits. The pros, like me, arrive a day or two before races to get acquainted with the track and begin practice.

The social circle in snocross is small. Some top pros erect walls, but mostly we are all cordial. Competitors can come from Canada, Scandinavia, or Finland, but most hail from Midwestern states like Minnesota, Wisconsin, and Michigan, and we are bound by family and friendship. On the road, we all tend to stay at the same budget hotels because there isn't enough money in the sport to create much of a status hierarchy. At the breakfast buffet in the hotel lobby, we catch up and make conversation. In Ironwood, Sara sneaks into my room to spend the night. Normally I have a roommate, but one of my new teammates lives in Ironwood, so he's sleeping at home. Warnert team rules don't allow wives or girlfriends to stay in the shared hotel rooms. If I want to stay with my wife, I have to foot the bill for my own room. I smuggle Sara in with me, and we talk over my feelings about the new team and the old one. I'm not in the best headspace.

The teams I've raced for in the past were smaller, tighter-knit. Everyone felt more emotionally invested. Sure, we had our share of arguments, but when one of us landed on the podium, it was the ultimate rush, with high-fives and hugs, powerful, proud moments for the entire team. Together we rode a roller coaster of emotions. I have a good relationship with the Warnert team, but the atmosphere is more business-oriented. If you land on the podium, you're more likely to get a handshake and a "Good job!" Sara and I miss the sense of family of my former teams. We miss the friendships we had on Team Avalanche. But the way it all went bad has left us feeling betrayed.

Earlier in the day in Ironwood, Sara and I spotted the Avalanche crew in the hotel lobby. We were headed to the track for practice, bundled in jackets and caps, when we caught sight of some of my old teammates. They clearly saw us, too.

We didn't exchange words, but the encounter stirred raw feelings.

"It's like breaking up with a girlfriend and then seeing her at a party," I said.

"Riiiight," said Sara, with an eye-roll, "because you broke up with a lot of girlfriends over the years, Mike. We were 16."

I first met Sara when she was a ski instructor at Powder Ridge, back home in Kimball, Minnesota. More molehill than mountain, Powder Ridge rises 350 feet like a small island in a sea of corn and soybean fields surrounding St. Cloud. I was a lift operator, flirting in 15-second snatches of conversation until the next chair swung around to sweep her away. Her smile, the fit of her tight ski pants, got me thinking about what I would say the next time she appeared in line. A mutual friend set us up on a first date. At this point in time, we've been together 10 years.

Powder Ridge is a place that's as central to our lives as family. Sara's grandparents sold a portion of the land to the developers of the resort with the stipulation that members of the family would receive lifetime season passes to ride the lift. She and I celebrated our prom at the lodge, and my mom and my stepfather, Rick, held their wedding reception there. Growing up in a small country town, Sara and I have enjoyed support from family, friends, and community. So when I was able to sign a contract with Warnert, it was a chance to return to what we knew in St. Cloud, the perfect place for me to restart, refocus, and make a strong push to the top.

MY COMEBACK HASN'T EXACTLY UNFOLDED according to plan, though. At practice in Ironwood, my confidence took a hit while buzzing around the course under the lights at night. I will be racing two different snowmobiles this weekend. My mod sled was feeling really good (we can modify the engine and chassis in this machine for more horsepower and better handling). The stock sled (which we can't modify from the stock orientation) bounced around wildly on downhill sections, stirring doubts and worries. When I hit the brakes or let off the throttle, the sled often swapped side-to-side, nearly out of control.

Every few laps, I pulled to a staging area of dirty, tracked-out snow along the course, a place thick with sponsor flags, semi-rigs, trailers, all-terrain vehicles, and team personnel, where the mechanics hang out in their long coats, tool kits in a backpack or roller cart. Between practice sessions, my mechanic, Nathan, and my suspension tech, Tim, hauled out the skid, a rear suspension component, experimenting with the calibration of shock valves, trying varying spring rates based on my feedback. I watched as my machine was torn apart, oily metal components strewn around the makeshift garage in the back of the rig. Nathan and Tim keep the space immaculate, their tools organized in metal drawers lining the workshop. Tim takes pride in ensuring my suspension is set up for optimal performance. Big and strong, he's from Western Canada and raced professional motocross before becoming a mechanic. He understands my concerns as a rider and could see in my face that I was deflated. We tried a dozen chassis configurations. With my age and experience, the mechanics respect my input. "Do we need to tow out the skis more?" I asked. "Do we need to soften the front end? Stiffen it?"

These questions remained unanswered when I roared out on the reassembled sled for another lap and a race official waved the checkered flag. "Practice was over 10 minutes ago," he said.

In the staging area, the mechanics and I were overcome by a gray feeling. "There's nothing else we can do," Nate said.

I gave them credit for trying to fix the sled, but acknowledged that, yeah, this was going to be a tough one to race.

We'd run out of time to continue tinkering, and I knew I was going to have my hands full trying to wrangle my machine in the morning, especially on the gnarly high-speed downhill section where I was bounced around like a rodeo cowboy clinging to a wild bronco. I always like to leave practice sessions confident. But this time, I was unsure how I would hang on and keep the machine from tossing me. Standing silently with Nathan and Tim in the harsh artificial light of the pits, generators humming in the background, our breath issued puffs of gray vapor. The temperature had plummeted on another frigid Michigan winter night, along with my self-assurance.

THE NEXT MORNING BEFORE THE RACE, I flip through my goggle case for the right color lenses to give the terrain some definition in flat light. I have four sets of goggles with four lens options for each— blue, rose, smoke, and clear. None of them will work real well in these conditions, but I settle on the rose.

Snow flurries continue to fall as I run through adjustments and strategies in my head, but it's impossible to craft a reliable contingency plan for an unruly machine. At 10 AM, I sit at the start line with eight other riders, engines idling, waiting for the first heat in the pro class to begin. We are delayed while medics tend to an injured rider on the track from a semi-pro race that's just finished—it's Derek Ellis, from Team Avalanche, barely visible through the blowing snow.

I need to finish in the top five to advance straight through to the final. If I miss out, it will mean a long, exhausting day of qualifying heats. When the green flag flies to start the race, all nine of us in the opening heat will burst into a 70-yard holeshot heading uphill into a left-hand corner. I'm planning to just put my head down and charge for the front of the pack.

Finally, the green flag waves. I hit the throttle. The engine burps, or the rubber track spins on the sled without gaining traction. Either way, I don't move for a split second as the other riders lurch forward, engines screaming, shooting 20-foot rooster tails of snow. My visibility is instantly fouled to nothing. The race has just begun, and I'm already in last place.

I arrive to the tight left-hand corner at the top of the hill, filing in behind the others, eating their roost of ice chunks and snow dust, my sled bouncing violently. Instinct takes over. I have been here before; I will be patient but aggressive, and work my way up in the field.

The race consists of 12 laps. I strategically pass a rider or two every lap, and halfway through, our mechanics raise a pit board, a dry-erase tablet, showing our position and lap time. One more pass and I'll be in fifth, good enough to salvage my disastrous start and earn me a trip to the final.

The course features two main downhill sections—one steep with sharp holes that forces riders to slow down as they descend, the other a high-speed downhill with a rhythm section of bumps. On the high-speed downhill, you can double these bumps, launching over two at a time or, better yet, skipping over the tops like a flat stone on water. I grit my teeth each time on this bumpy downhill because when I push the pace, just like in practice, my sled gets unpredictable. In these whiteout conditions, each hole or bump tries to toss me.

Bobby LePage, the fifth-place rider, is just ahead of me heading into the sketchy downhill section, the longest on the course—and an optimal place for me to make my move.

I push hard on the throttle, accelerating into a cloud of snow dust from Bobby's machine. It's time to punch my ticket to the final.

Bouncing and ricocheting through the rhythm section blindly, I fly over a hole and then get jarred by a bump. The machine swaps from side to side. I grab a handful of throttle to accelerate and increase traction in the hope of straightening out. Instead, the swapping gets worse. Moving at 40 miles an hour, the sled drifts left at a 45-degree angle when I'm bucked hard by the next bump, instantly separating man from machine. Momentum sends me sailing through the air in an upright posture. I kick my feet out to break my fall, spotting my snowy landing. I've learned to tuck and roll to absorb the impact.

My left foot meets the hard-packed snow with violence. The force hyperextends my knee, despite braces I wear to prevent such a scenario, snapping it 180 degrees in the wrong direction. Slamming into the ground face-first, I tumble onto my back, my left boot swinging up and kicking me in the chin of my helmet.

The most intense pain I've ever known radiates through my knee as I'm lying flat on my back, and my boot lies across my chest in a place it should never be. Staring at the sole, I freak out, fling the boot away, and when it hits the ground there's no sensation in my foot; it doesn't even feel like it's mine. I feel only excruciating burning in my knee joint. Stretched out on my back, I scream through clenched teeth, confused, staring through snow flurries at the dull gray cloud ceiling overhead.

Gary Walton arrives first, running toward me and sliding on his knees, camera swinging from his shoulder. He's a race photographer, a friend I've known for years. He looks me over.

"Mike, are you all right?"

"My knee is all jacked up," I manage to choke out.

"Yeah, I know!" he says. His tone startles me. "I'm here," Gary reassures me. "We've got you. The EMTs are on their way."

Sleds buzz past where I lie on the infield of the course, halfway up the hill, on a plateau 150 feet from the bottom. The race continues on.

Gary tells first responders my leg is broken. The medics want to take a look, pulling a zipper open on my pant leg. There's a loud splash, as though someone has dumped a gallon of water from a pail. No one says anything. They don't need to. I know that sound is blood, which has been pooling in my pants. The seriousness of the accident finally hits me: I'm bleeding out on the racetrack.

The paramedics load me up, yelling in agony, and cart me to the base of the hill, where Sara meets me, kneeling, face close, her blonde hair peeking out from underneath a knit cap, while we wait for an ambulance. "I'm here, Mike," she says. She is a nurse, a pro. She is calm in a crisis. Sara has seen blood. She has delivered babies. She's a comfort, telling me to breathe, like I'm an expectant mother in the delivery room. I try. Between screams.

Sara says it's going to be all right. Her blue eyes are more and more nervous, though, with each glance at my leg.

THE HOSPITAL IN IRONWOOD IS SMALL, and the emergency room consists of one double room with two curtains separating beds. A lone doctor, with one nurse, wheels me in, slipping and sliding on the floor that's slick with my blood. The nurse stabs at my arm to start an IV and misses. More blood streams forth. Sara's jacket, snow pants, and boots are crimson. In nurse mode, Sara grabs the oxygen mask from the wall, cranks it full throttle, and places it over my mouth. She squeezes my IV bag to speed flow, and encourages me to breathe.

My blood pressure is too low for pain medicine. Paramedics removed my boot earlier, nearly wrenching my leg off in the process, and there's no pulse at all in my bone-white foot, even though the doctor and nurse keep checking with a Doppler machine in the hopes of hearing something.

My leg flops around as if held together with dental floss. An X-ray reveals that it's severely broken...obviously. There's nothing more the doctor and nurse here can do. I need a surgeon to stop the bleeding. The doctor and nurse haven't applied a tourniquet. They keep swapping out fresh gauze pads when I soak them with blood. I need a bigger hospital with a trauma center. Outside, the weather has worsened. Flurries have morphed into a serious snowstorm, grounding all flights—including the medevac helicopter. Sara and I grow more worried when we hear that we cannot fly. The only option is for an ambulance to drive me to Duluth, two hours and two states away.

Facing my own mortality, I can't hold it together any longer; the tears start to come, and I let them run.

"I'm done," I tell Sara between sobs. "I'm done racing."

"Don't say that," she says, trying to reassure me. "Don't worry about it now."

For the past nine months I've been grinding to hang on to my dream of racing, doing little but worry—about sponsors, team owners, mechanics, teammates, my performance, making a living. My stepdad, Rick, was right. Why submit to all that anxiety and hardship, especially with the risk of such serious injury?

The tears, and the thought of no longer having to fret about racing, bring unexpected relief.

"Just done," I say.

No more anxiety. No pressure to perform. My mind is now focused on one thing: getting through this. Nothing else matters. I begin to breathe a little easier as the paramedics carry me away.

THE AMBULANCE SPEEDS WEST on U.S. Route 2, "The Highline," one of the northernmost highways in the country outside Alaska, barreling the 108 miles toward Duluth at 80 miles an hour. Sara refuses to be left behind, fighting her way into the ambulance, and rides shotgun. An EMT and I sway in the rear with the accelerating and braking. Pain sears my knee, and I'm wracked by a feeling of throbbing pressure. As I stare at the ceiling, time ticks slowly, each second excruciating. I concentrate on breathing to distract from the pain. I can't help thinking, *Why do I keep putting myself in these dire positions? Why do I keep doing this? I'm done.*

When the doors swing open at St. Mary's Medical Center in Duluth, a half-dozen doctors and nurses are waiting outside the emergency room entrance, clad in yellow gowns. They roll me into the hospital, and more than five hours since my crash, I'm in good hands, at last. I finally breathe easy.

Time warps as they pump me with pain medicine. They scan my leg. The room grows hazy. Blood loss has left my hands pale and yellow. I drift in and out of consciousness.

At the double doors to the surgical unit, Sara kisses my forehead. "They're going to bolt you back together," she says, "and you're going to be just fine."

A breeze on my face tells me the four nurses and doctors flanking the gurney are moving fast down the hallway. They talk over me, occasionally asking how I'm doing. Their expressions are serious, fluorescent bulbs flashing past as I fade out.

WHILE I'M UNDER SEDATION, Sara creates a profile on a social media platform called CaringBridge to provide regular updates on my condition, and to deliver messages to family and friends. Her first entry:

Journal entry by Sara Schultz — Dec. 14, 2008

During Saturday afternoon's surgery, the vascular surgeon needed to harvest a section of artery from Mike's right thigh to repair the damaged artery in his left leg. The surgeon was unable to find the main nerve at this point. No reconstruction of the bones, muscles, tendons, or ligaments was done during this surgery. They've kept him ventilated so they can better administer pain medication and keep him sedated. Sunday morning, they weaned him off some of the pain meds. He was drifting in and out of sleep, but somewhat coherent. Good to see him make eye contact, ask for H2O by pen, and make gestures. Mike has required a lot of blood. At 11:30 AM Sunday they took him back in to surgery to clean up the wound site and look for bleeding in the vascular repair site, as he is still losing blood in this site. We're now waiting for him to come back. The staff at St Mary's has been amazing. They have been very informative on his prognosis, treatments, current stats, and are doing all they can to keep Mike comfortable. It is very comforting knowing that he is in the best capable hands in the area for his injuries. Please keep Mike and Sara in your prayers. They have a steep road ahead.

For three days, and three surgeries, I'm intubated, in an induced coma, as doctors try to save my leg. My tibial plateau—the top of my tibia, and the thickest, most solid piece of bone in the human body—has been pulverized into dozens of pieces. My main (popliteal) artery is severed. Surgeons remove an artery from my right leg, my good one, and transplant it to my left to get blood flow to my foot. They cannot locate the nerve. Rods and screws fixed to my shin and femur create an external metal framework. The calf muscle is severed, blown out the back of my leg on impact. They've placed three devices called wound vacuums—two on the back of my leg, another on the bottom of my foot—to promote healing and blood flow to my wounds.

The problem: blood flows into my leg but does not return. Dying muscle releases toxic levels of the protein myoglobin, overwhelming my kidneys, causing them to shut down. I've received 47 units of blood, three times the normal amount in the human body. I'm swollen, my skin yellow, leaving me looking like a bruised banana.

There's little of my knee left to salvage. Surgeons work to put me back together again as my severed, frayed nerves send confused, painful signals. *Phantom pain*, they say. But the pain is real—and excruciating.

MY DAD AND HIS GIRLFRIEND, PAULA, were at the race in Ironwood, and they've driven to Duluth, arriving while I was in the emergency room. They're staying in a hotel provided by Warnert Racing. By Saturday night, while I was undergoing my first surgery, my mom had driven up from home outside Brainerd, and she's been sleeping in the ICU waiting room. She arrives just ahead of a snowstorm that shuts down travel on Sunday. By Monday, December 15, Sara's mom, Deb, arrives. She and my mom are good friends; Deb can give my mom the emotional support she needs. The waiting room quickly grows crowded as riders and team owners from the races begin to drift through Duluth on their return home to Minnesota. Snocross is a tight-knit family. Maybe 100 racers travel the national tour consistently weekend after weekend, from 11 years old up to the professional ranks. There are only 25 pro riders plus another 30 semi-pro tour regulars. You become friends and get to know their families. All of our visitors are crammed into the general waiting room with my family, and the families of other patients, and Sara says it's getting too close for comfort.

Fellow racer Levi LaVallee, one of my good friends on tour who lives near Brainerd, and some of my teammates fight their way through the snowstorm to visit me in the hospital. Sara doesn't want any riders to see me busted up because she's concerned it could mess with their heads as they prepare for the next races.

One of my teammates on Warnert Racing won't take no for an answer. Tim Tremblay is adamant and about to barge into my room. "I need to see Mike," he says in a thick French Canadian accent. Tim and I have become close friends in just a few months. He's in his early twenties, in his second year on Warnert, an up-and-coming racer. He's a tall, strapping kid, clean-cut with a strong Type-A personality. He's motivated to make the most of his opportunities in racing.

Tim comes from Drummondville, Quebec, and he has learned to speak English with help from team owner Mark Warnert's wife, Paula. Tim usually means business when he talks in a voice that is reminiscent of Arnold Schwarzenegger from *The Terminator*: "I'm here to race snowmobiles. Don't get in my way."

He and I share a race trailer. His gloves and goggles are always stacked perfectly. His cabinet and gear pack are organized meticulously. He's talented and has a great work ethic. He's eager to learn from my years of experience. Whenever I offer a piece of advice, he listens. Tim sustained a serious knee injury two years earlier and he's worked hard to return to racing. Whenever the riders on Team Warnert get together for a session with a fitness trainer, he's the overachiever. Most of the guys lollygag, lose focus, or give half-effort. They act like kids. Not Tim. He and I have forged a fast bond.

Sara enters with Tim and another teammate, Darrin Mees. Darrin hangs back in the corner, looking as if he might choke up any second. "Hey," she says, "Tim and Darrin are here. Can you give them a thumbs-up?"

I extend my thumb. I'm intubated. It's the best I can do.

For those who cannot make it to Duluth, and for those huddled in the hospital waiting room who haven't barged in to see me, Sara provides an update on Monday.

Journal entry by Sara Schultz — Dec. 15, 2008

Good Morning—this is Sara—Mike was able to rest comfortably thru the night. I also finally slept. I went into Mike's room at 6:30 and he opened his beautiful blue eyes when I said his name and squeezed my hand. He is still intubated, and he tries to talk, but can't. I had to leave the room at 7:00 to let the doctors and nurses complete their morning assessments. When I told Mike I had to leave he started pouting, making it harder to leave. The plan for today is to remove the tube this AM, keep his pain under control, and finally get to talk to him. His HGB is 9.1 this morning. He received another 2 units of blood last night. His left foot is "PINK" and very swollen. His output is improving slowly. He will have surgery again tomorrow (Tuesday). I will update this afternoon and promise to tell Mike about all the people that love and support him. THANK YOU so much for all the thoughts and prayers they are helping!!! Love Sara

ON TUESDAY MORNING, my fourth day in the hospital, doctors reverse the sedation and remove my breathing tube. My throat is too ragged to talk, so I write "wife" on a piece of paper. I want Sara, who has left the hospital for the first time since I've been admitted. She needed to clear her head. I want water. I haven't had a drink in three days. The nurses say I can suck on a wet sponge. When Sara arrives in the ICU, I'm holding a suction catheter, a pen-like device dentists use to vacuum saliva from your mouth.

"It needs more power," I whisper to try and lighten the mood.

Sara starts to cry. She has a lot on her mind.

Sara brings me up to speed on the procedures performed while I was under sedation. Yesterday afternoon I underwent surgery to relieve pressure in my leg and foot. Surgeons removed more tissue and placed a third wound vac on the bottom of my foot to aid with healing. She tells me about the visitors who've made their way through a snowstorm to the hospital in Duluth: the entire Warnert Racing Team—Mark, Ron, all the mechanics and crew. The majority of the Avalanche Race Team, including my old mechanic, Chad Kyllo; previous teammate, Andrew Johnstad; and crew chief, Jamie Cheney. Scott "Juddy" Judnick of Judnick Motorsports, who runs the Factory Polaris Race team, is among a handful of others from the race tour. There are also several friends and family from back home that have made the more than two-hour trip north to show their support, give a quick hello, and wish us well. Sara's mom and good friend Rachel have made plans to stay as long as needed.

There are things Sara isn't telling me, too. I don't know it yet, but she and doctors have been talking about my condition. Yesterday, an orthopedic specialist had a conversation with Sara, her mom, and my parents about my prognosis for recovery. It doesn't look good. He's told them he's never seen a knee injury as bad as mine. My fractures are some of the worst he's ever seen. This morning she has had a separate talk on the phone with the ICU doctor coordinating my care, and the conversation weighs heavily on her.

Sara asks me to look at my leg. It's covered in bandages with hardware holding it together. "Can you wiggle your toes?" she asks.

They are so swollen they resemble breakfast sausages. With every ounce of power I can muster, I try to flex my toes. Nothing. I try again, and again. For two minutes. "They just feel numb," I say.

When the doc arrives, he puts me through the same battery of tests, asks the same questions Sara has. He asks me to wiggle my toes. I try again. Nothing.

He pokes my toes with a sharp tool. They are plump, discolored, and blistered, not healthy at all. I watch my skin yield to the tool, but feel nothing. It's as if the doc is poking some object sitting on the table, not part of my body. I'm freaked out watching my foot move. The reality of the injury hits me. *Shit*, I think. *This is serious.*

When the doc summons my mom, dad, and older brother, Chris, to join us in the ICU, I know it's *really* serious. My parents have scarcely said a word to each other since they divorced 20-plus years ago, let alone been in the same room. My mom is a very emotional and caring person but a bit fragile in tough situations. But my dad, a construction worker and farmer, is a hard man, not given to emotional displays. I see in his face he's torn up seeing me mangled. I've been hurt many times through my career but nothing nearly as serious as this. I've hurt my family; the thought of all this emotional pain I've caused really gets to me, and that knot in my throat leads to tears running down my face.

ON OUR FATHER'S FARM, MY BROTHER, CHRIS, and I grew up riding three-wheelers and four-wheelers. Tooling around on BMX bikes in town with friends led to racing at local tracks when I was 13. One of my BMX friends was into motocross, too. I accompanied him to a race, and afterward begged my dad nonstop for a dirt bike. He agreed, but I would have to buy it myself, earning the money by performing chores on the farm. My dad always emphasized with Chris and me the importance of respect and a strong work ethic. Farm work came before play, but Dad would pay us for our labor or reward us with a trip to the races.

Once I had a dirt bike, I wanted to try racing. My dad told me I would hurt myself. As if to prove him right, I broke my ankle at 15 while hot-dogging on the street, hanging wheelies to impress friends. Dad encouraged me to rip around the farm instead of the racetrack and helped me buy parts when needed, but my dream of racing wouldn't die.

We had a shop on our farm where I created go-karts from lawn mower engines, welding metal pieces together to fashion a frame. My dad taught me the basics of welding and cutting metal. He showed me how to repair motors. I learned on my own, too, by obsessively tearing machines apart and reassembling them and tinkering to coax better performance out of my bike. It wasn't long before I could rebuild the motors and every other component on my bikes.

Chris raced snowmobiles and dirt bikes, too. Together we built a motocross track at the farm, clearing trees and putting up lights so that we could ride whenever we wanted. It became a cool gathering place for friends, and I pushed myself to improve, putting in more time each summer to be faster than the others. I loved the competition.

At 15, I was granted a farmer's exemption to get a driver's license early. Driving around, I found a part-time job at Powder Ridge working the lift. That's where I met Sara. My dad still wouldn't help fund my motocross ambitions. *If you want to do it, pay for it yourself*, he said.

So I did. My junior and senior years of high school, I attended school each morning and worked from 1:30 PM to 11 PM four days a week at a metal fabrication shop, building car crushers for scrap yards. I was utilizing some of the lessons from my high-school drafting class—one of my favorites—calculating how pieces of machinery fit together. On weekends I would race, Sara at my side. By my second year of racing, my dad started to come around. He could see my commitment.

"What do you think about racing snowmobiles?" he asked. His favorite pastime was snowmobiling, and he wanted to connect with me in a shared interest.

"Heck, yeah," I said.

I was a typical 16-year-old, and didn't necessarily want to hang out with my parents. My dad had always taken Chris and me fishing and hunting, but I would get bored sitting in the boat or fish house if the fish didn't bite. When I was 13, I shot a bear while bow hunting in a tree in northern Minnesota. I spent about four hours with other bears prowling around on the ground. I absolutely loved growing up in the outdoors. My dad taught my brother and me so many things about hunting, fishing, and camping. But as exciting as all this could be, I spent my time in the woods thinking mostly about riding and racing.

My dad and I raced snowmobiles together for three up-and-down seasons. He bought the sled and the trailers, paying our way as he, Sara, and I rambled across Minnesota to races on weekends. At my first race, in Duluth, I qualified for the final against competitors with years of experience. I was hooked. All of us—including the parents—made friends, huddling together in a heated trailer, dipping into a communal Crock-Pot at mealtime. Dad ran the show, and although I was grateful for his support, I eventually chafed under his control. He and I didn't always see eye-to-eye. Each weekend I would ride my snowmobile and a roller coaster of emotions with my dad. I was the typical teenager trying to gain my independence.

Motocross had always been my first love, and I continued riding in the summers, on my own program, with Sara, and without my dad. Snowmobile racing would hold more promise, though, with its smaller industry and talent pool than motocross. The best in motocross come from the South, and West, where they ride year-round. Living in Minnesota, my future in racing would be on snow.

I graduated high school, and went to work in construction for my mom and stepdad, Rick, at their company outside Brainerd, an hour north of St. Cloud. My mom has always supported my passions. When I was 13, she would drive me over an hour from home to my first season of BMX races, which opened the door to my competitive career. She guided me through my first bank loan to purchase a new motocross bike, a 1997 Honda CR125R. I was so pumped to load it up and bring it home from the dealership. My mom is a superfan of mine, but you have to be careful if you're standing next to her during a race. She gets a little emotional and dramatic every time my machine twitches more than a couple degrees one way or another. She shrieks louder than a mod sled revving at 9,000 RPMs, but I know it's because she's worried about my well-being and doesn't want to see me fall.

My mom and Rick gave me a great opportunity to work for their construction company, allowing me to grow as a young adult. I knew I wanted to race, though, competing on the weekends and training in my spare time. By my third season racing snocross, I moved up to compete in the semi-pro class, where, at last, everything started to come together. I won one national event and placed third in another, drawing interest from sponsors. At the end of the season, Tom Rager Sr., Polaris race manager (the guy who you really want to notice you), asked me to join. This was a true dream come true; the door into becoming a pro had just opened. I signed a contract as a rider for Polaris (one of the big three snowmobile manufacturers) and was one of three riders backed by the race team at Bristow's, a large dirt bike and snowmobile dealership in St. Cloud. They provided the snowmobile and mechanics and facilitated travel. A check for $10,000 from Polaris arrived in my mailbox that year. I was 19 years old, thrilled to be part of an official race team with factory support. My racing career had officially begun.

As a pro, you're part of a team where everyone shoots for the same goal. I wanted and needed that support and camaraderie, especially when I was first starting out. There's a motivation and passion I didn't see in a typical occupation, where workers showed up for their shift, punched in, performed a job, and punched out. We were actually getting paid to race snowmobiles. It was our job.

Not everyone understands that riding is more than a hobby. In addition to farming, my brother and dad hang Sheetrock and work in housing construction together, a daily grind that both of them hate. "It must be rough to get to go riding again," Chris would say, as if all I ever do is play. I'll admit I have a kick-butt lifestyle, but it's easy to overlook the work and preparation required to ride at the professional level— and the compromises, too. Riders relinquish control while operating within a larger program, relying on others for the resources necessary to be successful. My entire career I've devoted myself single-mindedly to chasing a position on a team with a better wage so I can reach my potential as a rider and not have to supplement my income with part-time work.

Another downside: injuries are part of the bargain you make as a professional athlete. If you're racing, eventually you're going to get hurt. My dad had been right about that.

THE DOCTOR AT ST. MARY'S in Duluth takes his time talking to me, but I'm still groggy from medication. He's thoughtful, trying to make me understand my condition without sugarcoating things. He says circulation in my leg has been compromised—blood in my foot cannot find its way back out, pooling, causing swelling. Dead tissue poisons my kidneys. They are shutting down.

"You can't move your toes," he says, while my family looks on. "You can't feel what I'm doing to your foot. Even if we do fix your leg, you're not going to be able to control anything. You're facing 20 surgeries during the next year or two, and we may never get your leg to work again."

If I cannot feel my foot, how will I use it? I've been through three surgeries already. It dawns on me that I may not be able to endure another 20.

"We think it's best to amputate your leg," the doc says finally, "in order to save your life."

I consider what he's saying, stunned. I entered the hospital with a knee injury; now they want to take my leg. I want to survive. I want to move on. I want to be healthy again. When I've been hurt before, I've always focused on recovery. If we keep trying to save my leg, that's not moving on. This time, amputation will be the next step in my recovery.

I look to Sara to interpret what the doctor is telling me. I trust her 100 percent. She's a nurse; she knows about these things. *Is this right? To take my leg?* I know that it is.

I look at the dismal expressions on the faces of my family, grimly quiet while listening to the doc. What is there to say? I'll lose my leg, but I won't lose them. They'll stand by me.

My mom has taken the possibility of amputation better than I could have anticipated. She's holding herself together, posting on the CaringBridge site today.

> Please please please keep Mike in your prayers as this will not be an easy decision for him and hard to deal with for him and all his family—this truly will be a life changing decision for him. We know Mike is strong and otherwise very healthy. And, he'll be designing some high tech prosthesis that will be way better than any known to mankind. We all know he is very talented, determined and has a ton of great friends and family that will help him through this.

How will I react when I wake with a chunk of my body gone? This is a realistic concern for Sara and me. Once it's gone, it's gone.

"Look at it as only 25 percent," Sara says. "We get to keep the rest of you."

I'll be done riding a dirt bike, done competing. What will my life be like when I don't have two legs anymore? Will phantom pain torment me?

The doctor doesn't give a straight answer. He explains that some people have bad phantom pain, and some don't have much at all. I'll just have to wait and see.

I have a few hours to consider my future while waiting for surgery. A big window in my room looks out on Duluth, which provides some distraction. The city resembles a dream, shrouded in fog and snow from the storm that created the conditions leading to my crash. I glimpse the waterfront. A ship on Lake Superior appears to be floating on the clouds, and piles of snow line the streets as a car's wheels lock, sending it sliding through an intersection down a hill, out of sight.

A nurse finally arrives with a consent form for Sara to sign. Sara wants me to make an X, or a smiley face, any mark so that the decision to amputate does not come down to her signature alone. The hospital administrator won't budge. I'm under the influence of pain medication, she says. I lack legal authority over my own body.

I'm okay with it, I tell Sara.

Clipboard in hand, her teeth gritted, Sara signs the form.

It's done.

Sara and I have time alone. We look at my two legs, knowing this will be the last time. She cries and, when the time comes, has a hard time parting, finally kissing me good-bye and stumbling dazed into a private waiting room, where 15 of our family and closest friends will wait out my surgery. I'm whisked away, wheeled into a cold, bright operating room, fans humming with white noise. The table, tools, and carts are all gleaming stainless steel. I'm loaded onto the chill, hard operating table, flat on my back. Nurses buzz around, eyes visible behind caps and surgical masks, hooking me to tubes and monitors, strapping my arms down, immobilizing me. I'm cold, scared.

"Do you have any questions?" an anesthesiologist asks.

I don't know. *Do I?* When I wake, my leg will be gone. *Will the pain be gone, too?* That's all I want to know.

"You'll want to count down from 10," he tells me. "You'll be out before reaching one."

Ten...

Nine...

Eight...

I'm exhausted—from the anesthetic, from the effort, the constant grinding pressure of pushing ahead, as if I've been riding a bicycle uphill for years, knowing that the second I let off the pedals, I'll roll backward. I'm plain tired of getting beaten up by this sport.

Seven...

Six...

Five...

When I wake, my leg will be gone. My dreams of being a top athlete, one of the fastest names standing atop a podium, will be gone, too. With one leg, I won't be able to pedal uphill anymore. I won't be able to race.

Am I really prepared for what's next? For this new life? Is this the end of Monster Mike?

Four...

Three...

Two...

2

13 Days

SARA AND I HAVE A PLAN TO PULL BACK MY BLANKET AFTER SURGERY
and unveil my stump so we can experience my new reality as an
amputee together. That's not what happens. By the time I come out
of surgery after 9 PM, return to my room in the ICU, and reunite with
Sara, I'm in excruciating phantom pain. I feel as though a giant nail
is being driven into the arch of my missing foot, and pliers wrench
at my big toe. My calf muscle is seized by the worst cramp I've ever
felt. I cannot stop thrashing, and the pain does not let up. My leg is
gone above the knee, leaving only a stump crisscrossed with the tracks
where surgeons stitched up my incision. Doctors have removed 15 to 20
pounds of bone and tissue, leaving my limb feeling weightless, another
really weird sensation.

"What hurts?" Sara asks. "What's wrong?"

I tell her about my phantom pain. In the hours after my leg injury,
on a scale of 1 to 10, my pain was 10-plus. Now, my hurt is off the
charts, 30 to 40 percent worse and relentless. I'm about to begin the
longest night of my life.

Doctors pump me full of as much pain medication as possible without killing me, allowing me to relax a little. When I finally begin to drift off, I stop breathing, setting off alarms in the ICU and waking me up. Watching my oxygen levels on a monitor, Sara and I concentrate on breathing. I had been on a ventilator while in an induced coma, compromising my lungs, and I'm swollen with 65 pounds of fluid, making it even more difficult to breathe. Everywhere I've been stuck with an IV or a needle, I weep fluid, leaving puddles on the bed. When my oxygen begins to return to normal, I relax and drift off. When I do, I stop breathing again, setting off alarms and waking me up to concentrate on my breathing once more. I try different medications to bring sleep, and Sara helps move me into more comfortable positions. Still, this cycle of drifting off, setting off alarms, and resuming my breathing repeats for 12 hours, in which I get maybe two hours of pain-wracked sleep.

Once the morning comes, a new shift of doctors and anesthesiologists arrives and they try ketamine and an epidural to block the pain signals. They relieve my pain some but create a new problem: hallucinations. They are a side effect of the drugs I'm taking. As I stare at a one foot by one foot air vent on the ceiling above my bed, I begin to imagine I'm trapped in a dungeon. Voices come from the vent, and I imagine doctors are performing experiments on me. I begin to freak out when a doctor enters the room. In my mind, I'm on the psychiatric ward at the mercy of a mad scientist with a fluffy white beard. I start swinging to protect myself before Sara can calm me down.

My nephew, Tucker, has given me a yellow teddy bear with the racing bib No. 199 of motocross rider Travis Pastrana, one of my favorite pros. The bear sits in my room on a cabinet, staring at me. When I shut my eyes, I see a Christmas tree decorated by hundreds of these bears. It's freaking me out, so Sara hides the bear in the cupboard. Once the bears disappear, I now find myself backstage of a play. I have no idea what the play is about but I'm behind the big curtain listening to the actors on the other side of it babbling about something. The worst part is that I know I'm hallucinating but I just can't figure out what's real and what isn't. I request to get off the ketamine. Soon I'm on a regimen of morphine and methadone, which barely blunts the pain and leaves me drooling, staring at the wall till finally I succumb to sleep for a few hours. By Wednesday evening, 24 hours after my amputation, the pain is manageable enough that I'm able to swallow orange juice and some ice cream. It's a struggle to bend my arm to reach my mouth with the spoon because I'm so bloated with fluid that my skin is stretched tight. I fall asleep and wake up at 4 AM when Sara gives me a sponge bath.

Steadfast, devoted, Sara has stuck by me through many ups and downs. Sara's small stature belies an inner strength that she has demonstrated while tending to my injuries, supporting me physically and emotionally, all while urging me toward ever greater challenges. Sara is sharp and unafraid, with superhuman patience and calm. She checks me when I'm being too stubborn and living on the edge, encourages me when she knows I need an extra push, and inspires me with her unflappable willingness to make it work. An organizational dynamo, my best friend and confidante, Sara has been an indispensable presence whether I'm hauling a trailer with my snowmobiles and motorcycles across the country to races, or down and out in the hospital. Our life together has been a love story, navigating unlikely challenges together, overcoming impossible obstacles and coming out stronger on the other side. I need her more than ever as I simply try to endure another day, one day closer to normal.

ON THURSDAY, I'M TRANSFERRED from intensive care to a private room on the orthopedic floor. My hallucinations are over. I have control of my thoughts again. I can sit up and eat. There's a cot in the room for Sara. Someone has brought in a small plastic Christmas tree. Cards from friends, family, and fans crowd every available surface and balloons bob from strings. Just when I'm beginning to feel normal, I must go back into surgery on Friday to close up an incision on the bottom of my stump. In preparation, I cannot eat all day. The anxiety of another surgery leads to panic. Any beep from monitors sets me off. "What's that?" I ask Sara.

The surgery takes only two hours. Once out, I'm in constant pain and struck stupid with a cocktail of oral and IV medication. Still, I'm getting better. By Saturday, December 20, one week following my accident, I'm trying to lose 40 pounds of fluid so that I can begin physical therapy to prepare me for going home. I have exercise bands and begin an upper body workout in bed. My mentality as an athlete has always been to focus on fitness and diet. I look at the options on the menu from the hospital and worry about gaining weight. Sara chastises me for being so picky. "Dude, eat food!" she says. "It's been a week."

My body remains a wreck, all my systems out of whack. I had pneumonia from being intubated and being on a ventilator, unable to breathe on my own. My kidneys have been working overtime. I'm getting insulin to control my blood sugar. Nurses regularly prick my finger to draw blood and it's annoying. I'm fed up with needles.

On Sunday, December 21, I lose 13 pounds of water weight, peeing it out through my catheter with such frequency that it sounds like a Zen fountain. Sara gets tired of calling in the nurse to empty the catheter and does it herself. On Monday, December 22, I lose another 15 pounds.

Exercise has always acted like therapy, making me feel productive by doing something to improve my situation. Returning to a normal weight (well...my new normal, minus the 15 pounds of leg I'm now missing), I've been rising out of bed, and into a wheelchair, to use the commode regularly. But on December 22, I leave my room for the first time to go to physical therapy.

Gripping the walker and standing for the first time since the accident, I'm struck by the weightless feeling of my stump. I realize what has been an abstraction so far—there's nothing attached to it. It's just hanging in the wind. Balancing is difficult as I hobble a few steps, trying to catch my breath. I'm fatigued and winded easily, shuffling with my walker down the hallway from my room, trailing tubes and cords for my IVs, catheter, and wound vac. Everywhere I go, I'm followed by Sara and a nurse, and an entourage of equipment rolling behind.

I make it two rooms down and return feeling weak, which is a major bummer. Walking 20 to 30 feet has left me exhausted. Over the coming days, I will graduate to crutches, which I'm familiar with from my many injuries, allowing me to move quicker.

ON TUESDAY, DECEMBER 23, a prosthetist visits my room. He's a tall, slender man, and he's carrying an elastic shrinker, a compression sleeve that you roll over the stump to get it to stabilize and shrink to a size that can fit into a socket for a prosthesis. He tells me how a prosthetist will choose what kind of equipment I'll be using and will fabricate a leg for me. No one had really mentioned prosthetics before my amputation, and now I'm considering what they will mean. From now on I'll be walking around on a mechanical replacement for the limb surgeons removed.

The prosthetist shows me how to turn the shrinker inside out and roll it over my stump. It's tight and my incision is sensitive. Unrolling the shrinker hurts so damn bad. The prosthetist can tell I'm in pain and senses that I'm wondering whether I will find any comfort in the future. He assures me that it will get easier, and just before he departs, he reaches down and rolls up his pants leg, revealing that he's a below-knee amputee. When he's gone, I turn to Sara. "I would never have known he was an amputee from his gait."

THE NEXT DAY IS CHRISTMAS EVE, and I'm discharged from the hospital just after lunch. My dad has driven up from Kimball to bring Sara and me home. Sara sits in the bed with me and "I'll Be Home for Christmas" plays on the radio. "We're going home, Mike," she says brightly, adding: "This is going to be tough. It's going to be hard on our relationship. These moments make or break a couple. We have to maintain good communication. You have to tell me how you're feeling. We have to be a team, because this isn't going to be easy."

A team of nurses in the hospital helped get us through the past weeks. We've developed a routine. Now it's up to Sara and me. Some patients in my circumstances would be sent to a nursing home. The doctors have told Sara to take me home instead.

He's strong, the doctor told her. *You're a nurse. Go home.*

Still, I'm not prepared for the harsh world that awaits outside the hospital. After two weeks in a warm bed, the cold winter air outside cuts right through me. Temperatures have plunged below zero. From the rear of the cab of my dad's truck, I glimpse the world again, frozen and snow-covered, going about its business in final preparations for Christmas. I'm cold and uncomfortable, sweaty with a case of the chills. Halfway home, we stop at a gas station along the highway. I climb out of the truck and crutch across a frozen parking lot to use the bathroom, bitter cold knifing through me. The snow crunches under our every step as my dad stands at my shoulder to keep me from falling. My next challenge: using a urinal while balancing on crutches. If my dad weren't here, there's a possibility I would collapse onto the floor of this gas station restroom. A new reality of being vulnerable and living in the world dawns on me.

In the mini-mart, I have my dad grab me a slice of pizza, my first meal outside the hospital in 13 days. It feels like a triumph to order a normal snack, and I love pizza. The heat and aroma hit my face as I wolf it down in the back of my dad's truck during the final hour's drive home to Brainerd.

We arrive at home at 4 PM, unprepared for the radically different phase of life that lies ahead. We live on 10 acres, in a region dotted with lakes 10 minutes west of Brainerd, in a three-story log-sided house with a big porch surrounded by oak and pine trees. There's a hay field to the east and a berm on the north side of our horse pasture, beyond which lies a gravel pit. An active gravel pit with trucks hauling in and out and asphalt mixers making noise may not seem like an ideal neighbor, but the workers have never complained about the racket I make riding on my motocross track. A deep blanket of snow covers the land and four-foot snowbanks flank the narrow road leading to our property as my dad pulls up to our door. It's going to be a white Christmas.

Four steps lead to our front door, tall rickety planks slick with ice from runoff from our roof. I crutch up and inside. Sara's mom, Deb, has bought a new bed for the main floor guest room and a recliner for the living room with help from family and Warnert Racing. Our moms have pitched in to decorate our Christmas tree and help prepare our home for my arrival and the holidays. Our dog, Zeus, who's been at the kennel for two weeks, is waiting for us. The bedroom Sara and I normally share is on the second floor, and with my mobility limited, I'll stick to the main level.

You'd think being home for Christmas would be great, but everything is shut down. That includes clinics and doctor's offices. The only way I can see a doctor is by going to the emergency room. I'm not exactly well, either. I'm sweating, soaking through my clothes constantly, losing water weight, leaving me chilled and shivering. I also have a fever and pneumonia. Plus, I'm in pain, my nerves sending nonstop white-hot electrical signals to my brain.

Sara keeps track of my antibiotics, inhalers, and pain medicine. She changes the dressing on my incision. In bed I quickly soak the sheets with sweat and excess water weight, forcing her to change the linens frequently. I'm running her ragged with my care.

On Christmas Eve, I sleep downstairs in the brand-new bed set up for me in our extra bedroom. I just want to sleep in my own bed. On Christmas night, as we get ready for sleep, I crawl upstairs on my hands and knee into our master bedroom and haul myself into bed. I hear Sara calling from downstairs. "Where did you go?"

"I'm up here. I'm sleeping upstairs. I just want to feel normal again."

Sara is annoyed. She has all my medications and water to wash them down set out next to the bed downstairs and now she must transport all of it upstairs. It takes about 30 minutes, three times a day for Sara to organize my medication regimen. I just take a handful of whatever she hands me, although I'm beginning to doubt the effectiveness of the meds for managing pain. I have some discomfort from surgery, but my phantom pain really drives me mad. I tell Sara I don't want to take the meds. "They're not working," I say. Also, narcotics leave me constipated.

"You have to take it, or it could make it worse," she argues.

It's hard to imagine the pain could be worse. It feels as though my missing toes are being torn off with a vise grip and there's a nail being driven into the arch of my foot. I cannot sleep. To disrupt the pain, I lie on my stomach and kick my good leg all night long as a distraction. I slam my foot down again and again. Now Sara cannot sleep either.

In the morning, I rock and knead my hands together. Making my way down to the kitchen, Sara catches me banging my head on the cabinet to disrupt the constant pain signals. I'm in a cycle of agony and I don't know how to get out of it.

THE DAY AFTER CHRISTMAS happens to be my nephew Tucker's seventh birthday. He's my brother Chris' son, and I haven't seen him since my accident. Tucker and I are buddies, and he often came out to cheer me on at the races. He wants to come up and see me for his birthday. We're not sure how to show him my amputation or how he will react. When he arrives in the afternoon, he seems to handle the fact that I'm missing my leg really well. He wants to do what we usually do together and watch a motocross video, this one starring Travis Pastrana called *199 Lives*, basically a biopic about his racing and freestyle moto career.

Together we dim the lights in the living room as the DVD documentary action and racing images play across the TV screen. Seeing them makes me emotional, tears streaming down my face, a knot forming in my throat. Across the darkened room, Tucker hears me sniffling back sobs.

"Sara," he says, "what's wrong with Mike?"

"He's just sad he won't be racing anymore," she explains, tearing up herself, articulating feelings that I've suppressed. I flash back to moments from my career. For a decade, I'd ordered my life in pursuit of getting faster, and now I'm feeling purposeless and lost while confronting a harsh reality in which I'm no longer a professional racer—no longer an athlete, even. I plan to sell my dirt bikes; we'll need the money to pay for my medical care. I'll never compete or chase a championship again. I'm without a team and already miss the camaraderie of life on the ISOC tour. Despite all the well-wishes I've received, I feel abandoned from the lifestyle I loved so much. Watching the video has me flashing back to memories of my career, and it hurts like hell to think I'm now just a *has-been*, another regular guy lamenting the future that could have been.

OVER THE NEXT TWO WEEKS, I spend many long hours trying to rest in a recliner that Team Warnert has bought for me, surrounded by bottles of medications and liquids to wash them down, a walker stationed at my side. Zeus, my little rat terrier, curls up with me, where my leg used to be. When Zeus was about a year old, he broke his leg while running loose in the woods. The vet recommended that we amputate his leg. He said Zeus would be better off. Sara and I immediately said no. We couldn't imagine amputating his leg. We didn't want a three-legged dog. We had the vet put a plate on the leg to mend the bone, but Zeus broke the plate right away. He didn't know he needed to recover. He simply wanted to run. Next we had the vet put a rod in Zeus' leg. For a year, we tried to fix his leg but it never fused properly. His femur remained broken in the middle, leaving him looking like he has an extra joint. Zeus has simply adapted. He can barely put weight on the leg, and it flops around when he moves. Now, he hops on the footrest of my recliner and snuggles where my leg used to be. He's my buddy, and I reach down and pet him. I remember when we were in the hospital talking about amputation, I told Sara I didn't want to end up like Zeus. He's been hurt his whole life, and it's left him irritable.

When Sara drives me to yet another doctor's appointment, I ask, "Do you think we made the right decision?" Maybe, I start to wonder, amputating my leg wasn't the best option after all. I'm in complete agony; how could it possibly be worse if we had tried to save my leg? Sara purses her lips and doesn't respond. I know the decision is weighing heavy on her mind, as well. It's one of my lowest moments, but there can be no going back.

Fidgety and uncomfortable, I use crutches to visit my workshop in the garage to tinker, or hobble down to the basement, where I have a home gym, for an arm and chest workout. I cannot focus for more than a few minutes at a time, and I always find myself back in my chair. I'm irritable and wracked by maddening phantom pain in the arch of a foot that is no longer there and a constant sensation of an extreme cramp in my missing calf muscle. I try mirror therapy, in which you hold a mirror on your remaining leg in an attempt to trick your mind that you have two legs. It works, instantly reducing the pain. As soon as you remove the mirror, the pain returns. Sara has a portable electrical stimulation (e-stim) device, hooking up the contacts to my stump to try electric pulse massage to disrupt my nerve signals. Every night I put it on and watch my limb dance around, making me laugh and drawing my attention from the pain a little. I'm treated with acupuncture several times a week. These interventions provide temporary relief, at best.

I'm beginning to realize that if I can occupy my mind, really focus 100 percent on something else, the pain will disappear. It always returns in waves, but the greater the distraction, the less my pain intrudes and occupies my thoughts. When I stop whatever I'm doing, the pain returns instantly. I'm beginning to think that controlling phantom pain is a mental game.

ON NEW YEAR'S EVE, Sara and I agree to meet friends out. Though family drops by from time to time, mostly it's been Sara and me alone together. I get dressed up for the first time in weeks. We head into Baxter to a higher-end restaurant called Prairie Bay, with a farm-to-table menu. It's awkward crutching in public without a leg. I wonder whether people are looking at me. *Yeah, I'm different. I'm not the physical person I used to be.* I've lost weight and muscle mass, too. It starts to bother me. I'm fidgety and cannot relax. All through our meal, my phantom pain intrudes. As I sit there with friends, I'm unable to enjoy myself the way I used to.

Before the accident, Sara and I lived blissfully in our house in the woods, among the oaks and pines and lakes that give Minnesota the nickname "Land of 10,000 Lakes." In the summer, boating and fishing prevail. In winter, it's ice fishing and snowmobiling. A half-mile to the south, the Crow Wing River funnels into the Mississippi, and in the fall I would paddle my kayak for cardio training, spotting whitetail deer along the banks and bald eagles in the trees scanning for fish. When we weren't on the road at a race, Sara spent time hanging out with friends from the hospital where she works. She rode her horse, Ivan, that we keep on our property. I tinkered with my sled and dirt bike in my workshop and hung out at Brothers Motorsports, a local dealership, chatting up the salesmen while coveting the latest toys. Together Sara and I would load up on feed and supplies for Ivan and the pony, Buster, we board to keep Ivan company. We'd walk through town, window shopping, and wind up at Grizzly's Wood-Fired Grill & Bar for dinner and drinks.

When we traveled, we operated like a well-oiled machine. Sara would cook up dinner in a Crock-Pot and occasionally act as pit crew. She enjoyed the work and the travel, the time together, and the friends she made on tour. And I couldn't have done it without her. But in the dark days following my amputation, acting as my primary caregiver puts Sara under a terrible strain. I am a miserable patient.

In bed at night, phantom pain causes me to thrash, leaving both Sara and me sleep-starved. In my agony and frustration, I'm short-tempered, sniping at Sara, who's weighed further by our fragile household finances and the eye-popping medical bills from the hospital that have begun to arrive in the mail.

In one of our most strained moments as a couple, doctors encourage Sara to call on her nursing experience and remove the more than 200 staples used to close the incision on my stump. We've been home for 10 days when she tells me, "Okay, time to take your staples out." I remove my shrinker. Scabs have begun to form where my skin has grown around the bits of metal. Removal will require finesse on one of the most sensitive parts of my body. Sara instructs me to lie back on our bed. Staple remover in hand, she begins plucking the metal fasteners as gently as possible. The pliers pinch and twist my tender flesh. My fists gripping the bed sheet, I grit my teeth and try to be as strong and quiet as I can. I begin to sweat. By the time Sara has removed only four staples, I'm punching the bed, profanities pouring from my mouth.

"This is not helping me get these out," she pleads.

We are both short-circuiting emotionally. I have been in too much pain to acknowledge the impossible position I've put her in. In the end, I use Neosporin and lidocaine to soften the skin on my stump and remove the staples myself. Teeth gritted, I fill a plastic bag with the twisted bits of metal. Sara remains by my side the entire time. The stakes are much higher than just my own personal recovery and competitive career; the once-steady dynamics of my marriage have dramatically shifted, and Sara and I will have to adjust and grow along with them. Removing the staples lets me know I'm ready to manage on my own. I tell Sara that she needs to get out of the house and get away from me—for her sake, not mine.

She's used up all her vacation time already, and I'm not earning any money. Our health insurance comes through Sara's employer, and we have bills to pay. After four weeks off, it's time for her to think about returning to her job as a labor and delivery nurse at the community hospital in Brainerd.

ON JANUARY 7, SARA RETURNS TO WORK, and I'm home alone for the first time since my accident. I'm bored, and by the afternoon I look out the window at a four-foot-high snowbank and start to think that if I can fire up my snowmobile, I can ride to the end of the driveway and collect the mail from the box. I'm excited to finally have a purpose, a task, and a reason to get outside. I get myself dressed and crutch to the garage and open the door. My snowmobile rests on a set of rollers and I muscle it around the best I can, but I don't have much strength. Finally,

I get it pointed out the door, and pull-start the engine. I push the heavy machine out of the garage, rotating it the best I can in the direction of a big snowbank. I hop on, eager to move again, and push the throttle, accelerating up the snowbank, not aware that beneath lies a sheet of ice. My skis plow into the snow and the track spins but the sled doesn't go anywhere. I'm on my race snowmobile and it doesn't have reverse. I'm stuck. *Shit, how am I going to get out of this?* I think about how Sara will come home and see the sled stuck on a snow pile, and start asking a lot of questions. Kind of like when you were young and you broke the rules while your parents were gone. I don't want that, so I start twisting the handlebars, yanking and jerking to maneuver the machine off the snow pile. Once free, I cruise up and down the driveway a few times. The cold air on my face, the familiar vibration of the handlebars from the motor, and the smell of two-stroke exhaust revive me. The sense of regaining my independence is a small triumph. I retrieve the mail and cruise around a little before parking in the garage.

When Sara returns from work that evening she's not thrilled to see the snowmobile tracks. "What if something happened?" she said. "What if you had gotten stuck or tipped over?" She points out how I had to leave my crutches behind to climb on the machine.

"If I would have gotten stuck down the road, I would have crawled back to the house," I say, unable to hide my delight from the ride. "Everything was fine," I tell her with a smirk. "I am a professional, you know."

THE NEXT RACE ON THE ISOC TOUR will be January 10, just over a month from the Ironwood stop—and my accident. Sara and I have begun feeling stir-crazy at home, and we decide to drive two and a half hours to the next stop on the snocross tour, at Canterbury Park, a horse racing track with a 16,000-capacity grandstand in Shakopee, Minnesota, near Minneapolis. Canterbury is always the biggest event on tour, drawing the largest crowds and competitive field. Fans come out for the weekend or spend a day, bringing their families, all bundled in winter gear. They grab a meal and drinks inside, gawk at the riders and the latest snowmobiles and equipment on display, and settle in for a series of racing heats. The paddock is thick with sponsor trucks, team trailers, and RVs, humming generators keeping the lights and heat on. Team owners crowd together, forming their own private club, each clutching a hot cup of coffee, chit-chatting, catching up on the latest gossip during race weekend. Riders, mechanics, and their families wend their way through a village of utility cords, muddy slush, and whining sleds, activity running all day and late into the night under the harsh glare of floodlights.

I'm instantly heartened by the energy of the event. Using crutches, I slowly make my way around the snowy pits, tracked with mud, relieved to be back around racing, friends, the sleds, the crowds. Making my way in front of the stands, I slip on a patch of ice and tense up, feeling a pop internally where my muscles have been sutured together. It hurts like hell, and I know something is wrong. Still, I'm back around racing again and I'm determined to gut it out.

Sara and I join my teammates in the Warnert Racing trailer. We sit with Tim before his final in the semipro class. He's unusually quiet, but it's understandable. He probably wants to get in the zone before a big race. "I win this one for you, Mike," he says finally, in his thick Quebecois accent. He's been my closest buddy on the team, and I'm moved by his gesture. He's been a contender all season but has never won a final at the semipro level. I want him to win, but I don't want him to feel additional pressure to prove anything for me.

By the time the semipro final rolls around, Sara and I have made our way to the third floor of the grandstand, a viewing area with tables behind glass, where you can watch the race out of the cold, in comfort, and get a bite to eat. We're both exhausted. We haven't slept much since my accident, and I'm still in constant pain. I've stopped taking narcotics because I'm tired of the side effects and they don't seem to help much with my phantom pain. As we watch the races, we are swarmed by friends, fans, and acquaintances from the world of snowmobile racing who offer their condolences and best wishes or simply want to talk. It's been wonderful, but I'm worn out as I settle in to watch Tim race the final.

The course at Canterbury covers the front stretch and part of the infield of the horse racing track, and it's ideal for viewing. There are no blind spots, and from my perch three stories up, I can see all the action, the jumps and turns, the close calls and wrecks. The final doesn't start well for Tim. He gets caught in the middle of the pack, unable to break free. It's an exciting race, though, and as the laps add up, Tim charges his way through the field. I can tell he's on a mission as he passes one rider after another, within striking distance of the leaders. Sara and I are so pumped for him. He's running a great race and when he finally passes for the lead, we go bonkers and cheer as loud as we can, while watching him cross the finish line for his first win.

I can't wait to congratulate him. Hopping up, I crutch to the elevator and take it down to track level, fighting my way through a crowd around the podium to give Tim a high-five and hug. I've never been this excited or emotional about someone else on the racetrack. The announcer interviews Tim as he stands atop the podium. Toward the end of his comments, Tim says in his kindest French Canadian Terminator voice: "I wanted to win this race for my teammate Mike, who is still recovering from a bad injury." I am so proud of Tim's accomplishment and honored that he would mention me in *his* moment on the podium.

INSPIRED BY BEING BACK AROUND RACING, I arrange a deal with the Warnerts: they will continue to pay my salary; it's not much. I'll get a monthly paycheck that will add up to maybe $12,000 for the entire season. In exchange, I'll help with practice track preparation, training, and coaching. I will coordinate with the team trainer, Drew, to design some drills to keep the team sharp. It's not racing, but it's a reason to get out of bed in the morning and keep me involved with competition. The chance for a new routine brings some relief—not only for me but for Sara. Coming home from a full day of treating patients to take care of a gloomy, ailing husband had begun to wear on her.

I've remained in pain most of the time despite acupuncture treatments a few times a week. On January 14, Sara and I visit a doctor in St. Cloud, and she prescribes Lyrica, which can be used for pain. The doctor explains that it's also an anti-depressant. "I'm not depressed," I snap. "I'm dealing with this."

"It's used for other things, too," Sara says. "Please just try it."

I fill a prescription and begin taking Lyrica for my phantom pain, hopeful that something will finally work.

TWO TO THREE DAYS A WEEK, I rise early, toting a clipboard and stopwatch. Using my good leg, I work the accelerator and brake of my truck while my left hand massages my stump to disrupt phantom pain signals. It's an hour-and-fifteen-minute drive to our team practice facility at Quadna Mountain, in Hill City, Minnesota.

A former ski resort, Quadna Mountain has been converted into a snocross training course by Team Warnert, with a small garage containing a woodstove for getting warm between sessions on the track. From the cab of the groomers—big-tracked machines you see at ski resorts with multidirectional blades mounted on the front—I plow the snow into a practice course for the race team to train on. I imagine the kind of course I would want to ride, with big jumps and some fun but difficult rhythm sections. I time the riders' practice laps, afterward conveying to younger teammates some of the wisdom and experience I've acquired over the years. I quickly realize that I enjoy working with my teammates and become invested in them and their performance.

One day during practice, I can't resist: being around snowmobiles and racing inspires me to give one of the sleds a spin. I borrow a helmet and climb on my teammate Darrin Mees' sled for a ride, hanging on for dear life with only one foot to grip the machine. I'm accustomed to gripping with both feet and both legs. Now my stump just dangles. It's a crazy feeling trying to adjust to hanging on with only one leg. A slight bump, scarcely big enough to lift the sled off the ground, nearly tosses me. Startled, I let out a laugh, thrilled to be back astride the familiar thrum of the machine. I take a few laps, faster each time, and incredibly awkwardly compared to what I'm used to, but it feels amazing. I get off the machine and my hands are trembling with excitement. This brief ride makes me feel more alive than I have any other time since my accident.

3

The Next Step

ON A BONE-COLD DAY SIX WEEKS AFTER MY ACCIDENT, I CRUTCH into the office of my prosthetist, Chip Taylor. Chip is part-owner of Prosthetic Laboratories, located in a small multi-unit building in the center of Baxter, on the west side of Brainerd. This is my second trip to see Chip. I was out a week earlier to meet him for an evaluation, which served as my introduction to the world of prosthetics. He spent hours discussing the details of prosthetic equipment functions and options. During the first visit he also formed a plaster cast of my stump in order to build a plastic socket for my prosthesis called the check socket. The socket must fit perfectly to distribute my weight through the soft tissue and the ischium, the curved bone forming the base of the pelvis, also known as the "butt bone." Chip filled the mold with liquid plaster in a separating agent to get a plaster positive that looks just like my limb, with all the contours, soft tissue, and areas where the bone comes close to the surface.

As he cast a mold of my limb, Chip and I got to know one another. A tall, conservative man in his late thirties, with thinning hair, Chip possesses a friendly reserve and an abiding interest in hunting and outdoor sports. Chip strikes me as measured and analytical, a by-the-book personality. He's well established in the industry with more than a decade of experience as a prosthetist. Chip began in the prosthetics business as a technician, building and fabricating prostheses before transition to fitting and adjustments. He and his colleagues epitomize the up-north Minnesota ethic, often visiting snowbound clients at home in some of the smaller, remote towns. Most of their clients are older, often diabetics. Not all are amputees. Some need braces for broken ankles or support systems for their extremities because they have no feeling due to neuropathy or have developed ulcers on their feet. In many cases, Chip and his colleagues treat clients in the hopes of salvaging limbs and preventing amputation.

With me, Chip is enthusiastic about having a young, active client for a change, and he has embraced the challenge of getting me back to my former activities. Chip follows the snocross circuit. He knows some of my fellow racers personally, and he's heard about my accident. I can tell from the excitement in his voice that my case could be an opportunity for him to test what's possible in prosthetics with a healthy, high-level athlete. "What's your goals?" he asked during our initial meeting. "What do you want to accomplish? What kind of activities do you want to get back to?"

For starters, I just want to be upright again. That's all I'm thinking about. Once finished with the casting process, we set a date for the fitting, and on January 23, Sara and I arrive at the clinic for the second time. Beyond the reception desk, there's a hallway. The first two rooms on either side are reserved for patients. In the back, beyond the reception desk and examination rooms, there's a technical lab, essentially a workshop with all the parts and pieces where the prostheses are built. It's not as high-tech as you might expect. It's like a woodworking shop, only it's for leather, plaster, fiberglass, and carbon fiber. Chip uses hand tools—sanders, grinders, vices, and a cobbler's bench—to resole shoes. He attaches buttons and snaps while hand-building sockets to attach prostheses, orthotics, knee braces, ankle braces, and inserts for shoes. For someone like me, who's interested in fabrication and hand-crafted components, Chip's tool bench and hardware components represent a kind of heaven. Down the hall, there's also a room with a set of parallel bars and benches, where Chip evaluates his creations while patients try out their new limbs.

On this day, I take a right, crutching into the patient room, Sara at my side. My leg leans against the wall, a shiny robotic part with a carbon-fiber pylon and foot and a mechanical knee. It looks so cool, and I am excited to try it on.

Chip has chosen a prosthesis that my insurance company would be likely to approve quickly so that there will be no delays in fitting. It's a versatile model, but one designed for everyday activities. He could have tried for more advanced components, but there's a possibility it would be tied up for months awaiting paperwork to be cleared by insurance.

I change into a pair of shorts. While I'm admiring the prosthesis, Chip walks in and begins discussing the process of trying on the socket he's made for me. Threads attached to the top of the knee joint and the socket allow the two components to be screwed together. During the past week, he's been fine-tuning and shaping the socket to get it just right for me. This is the moment of truth—the fit.

There are three steps to the fitting. First, I slide an airtight silicone rubber liner over my stump, turning it inside out and unrolling it slowly to minimize the pain. The silicone sticks to my skin, tugging at it. When surgeons sawed off my femur, it left my leg feeling like the jagged edge of bone would stab into my stump when under pressure. The sleeve is tight and with each roll of the rubber, the sharp bone jabs into my tissue, sending electric jolts of pain up my leg. Once the sleeve is fitted, I slip a cotton sock over my stump to get an exact cushioned fit. Finally, it's time to fit my leg into the clear, hard plastic socket, the top half of the prosthesis. I thread a Velcro strap at the bottom of the sleeve through a slot at the bottom of the socket and pull. The socket slides over my limb. With the prosthesis attached, I rise, uncertain, to stand on two legs again for the first time since the morning of my accident. I had been on crutches for so long that I wasn't sure how it would feel.

It hurts.

Chips says this is normal. The socket is made of thermal plastic. He asks where it hurts, and we remove the socket. Chip fires up a heat gun and holds it over the plastic, pushing, altering its shape to minimize pressure points. I try the socket on again. It still hurts. "You want to kiss the bottom," Chip says about my limb, "but not the bone bearing on the socket. You want a total contact fit that enhances stability and gives a feeling that the prosthesis is part of you. It's the difference between a pair of nice-fitting running shoes versus running in a pair of loose rubber boots."

Having the right sock helps. Slipping on a thicker one, or an extra one over a limb, can make for a better fit. "Most patients will lose volume," Chip says about muscle mass. Their muscle atrophies because they aren't using it as much, or in the same way. "A patient is a moving target," he explains. "I don't care if you're active or sedentary. The human body changes constantly." Socks and liners compensate for changes and offer flexibility in fitting.

We repeat the fitting process with the heat gun for more than an hour until finally I stand, resting my 190 pounds in the socket with no discomfort.

I look down and see two shoes underneath me. For the first time since the accident, I feel whole. For a split second everything seems normal. I start smiling, feeling better than I expected. I'm upright again. I've got hope. I'm ready to begin walking.

Chip leads me to a set of parallel bars, where I slowly learn to balance on my new leg. I'm not sure how any of this is going to feel. "Alright," he says, "take a step with your good foot. Pull your limb forward, and that's going to make the knee flex, then kind of flick it out in front of you. That's going to extend the prosthesis all the way, and then you can put weight on it. You've got to be very careful to extend the prosthesis completely before you put weight on it, or it's going to collapse."

Hands gripped around the parallel bars, I follow Chip's instructions. I'm smiling because I'm walking again on two feet again, slowly stepping my way between the parallel bars. After a few steps, I've got the hang of the mechanics involved, and I try to accelerate. "Hold onto the bars," Chip reminds me. "That thing can buckle if it's not straight."

I make more than 10 passes, back and forth, before I'm ready for the next challenge. I graduate to crutches, walking up and down the hallway of Chip's office. "This is the fastest I've ever had someone in a leg," he admits.

Speaking of fast, I try to walk more quickly, and Chip urges me to slow down. He's in unfamiliar territory with how rapidly I've taken to my prosthesis.

I switch to one crutch, and soon I try a few steps unassisted before Chip reels me back in. I'm growing emotional, wanting to push the boundaries the way I've always done in racing, or with any challenge. Chip remains measured and restrained. I sense our relationship defining itself as one where I'll be in a rush and Chip will want to keep me in check.

"I can do this," I tell Chip with a big smile, walking around the clinic with minimal assistance from one of my crutches, basically using it as a safety net if I stumble. The mechanics feel somewhat natural. I flick my weight forward and shift onto my prosthesis, then back to my right leg, then back to my prosthesis. It feels so good to be upright.

Chip has told me that most patients require some physical therapy. Most will not be able to bear weight so quickly after an amputation. Most will utilize a walker for a couple weeks before transitioning to crutches or a cane. It takes a lot more effort to walk with a prosthesis than with two sound legs. Some patients, particularly the elderly or those who are out of shape, will set a goal of walking perhaps 30 feet. Those in good shape may immediately pursue their goals, whether it's riding a snowmobile or carrying their kids. Chip says he can tell within the first five minutes if a patient will be a success story based on their attitude. If they prioritize getting upright and getting moving, they will achieve their goals. He says having a positive mental attitude makes all the difference.

I've healed faster than any patient Chip has worked with, owing to being healthy and an elite athlete prior to my injury. He's wanted to get me back on my feet because it's a huge psychological boost for those who've lost a limb. The sooner patients are upright, able to be eye-to-eye with loved ones again, able to resume normal activities, the sooner their mind can shift from their missing limb. I've been in Chip's office almost four hours and gone from crutching in with my limb swinging beneath me to being able to take a few steps unassisted. "I've never had anyone walk out of here on their first day with a prosthesis," Chip tells me.

Back in the patient room, I pull on my jeans again, barely able to stretch the denim over my test socket—a bulkier temporary unit I'll use until my permanent carbon fiber socket is molded and completed by Chip. Chip explains that my pants will fit better once he delivers my slimmer permanent socket. Standing there, pants covering my prosthesis, I look... normal. "Wow..." I say to Sara, feeling triumphant as I walk out of Chip's office on my new leg, using only one crutch for assistance.

RIDING A HIGH FROM MY APPOINTMENT WITH CHIP, the next day Sara and I drive down to St. Cloud for a party at the Warnerts' to watch the Winter X Games. On the way, we stop off in Kimball to visit my mom at a cabin she and Rick own. We haven't told anyone that I've gotten my prosthesis; I want it to be a surprise. I get out of the car and with the help of one crutch, climb the steps and ring the bell. My mom answers the door and welcomes Sara and me inside, giving me a big hug. She's always been a hugger. It feels good to have two hands free finally, to be able to wrap my arms around my mom while standing. I had taken for granted little things like having my hands free to carry things. She asks how I'm doing. It takes her a moment to notice the obvious—that I'm on two legs. "You got your leg!" she shouts finally, and everyone laughs.

I sit down in a chair and demonstrate how to put on my prosthesis, explaining how it works. I remove everything, revealing my stump to show her how to put the liner on my limb. I'm excited to share with her all the activities I'll be able to resume, and she seems genuinely thrilled, but then she starts crying. Not out of happiness, but sorrow. Sure, I can stand now, my arms free to hug her. I may be upright, able to look her in the eye. But it's not the same. Seeing the remains of my amputated leg is a painful reminder. Her child isn't whole. He's handicapped. He's in pain and will never be the way he was.

She exits the room to try and hide her tears, leaving Sara and me alone. This is a major comedown moment. It hurts me to see how fragile my mom remains at this point during a happy moment, a milestone when my prosthesis has made me upright again. I wish she could get past her feelings, toughen up, and see the bigger picture and the progress I've made in such a short time. I know I'll be okay. I want my family to focus on the positive of me making a huge step forward in my recovery, and she's stuck on negative thoughts. I'm reminded how much my injury has hurt my family.

Sara and I depart my mother's after trying our best to leave her with positive thoughts. We drive to the home of Paula and Mark Warnert in St. Cloud, where the rest of the team has gathered to watch the snocross event at the Winter X Games. Held in Aspen, Colorado, Winter X is a highlight of the season, an event I've competed in for the past six years. Still, I've never performed well there and seldom enjoyed the experience due to all the added pressure of the "big show." Broadcast on ESPN in prime time, X Games is the biggest platform for our sport. All the riders take it seriously, and the teams place a premium on performing well, pumping money into sending racers, sleds, and mechanics to the Rockies. The pressure from sponsors on teams to finish well and get TV exposure places enormous stress on the riders. This year, Matthew Morin is the only Warnert racer invited to compete, and the team has sent a skeleton crew to support him.

I surprise the dozen people gathered at the Warnerts' when we arrive. They have a beautiful home a few miles outside St. Cloud, and I hobble downstairs to the basement, an area set up for entertaining with a couple tables laid out with food. Some of the riders who haven't earned an invitation to X Games are there with girlfriends, plus a few mechanics. Everyone offers hearty congratulations, immediately noticing that I'm walking with my prosthesis. The good vibes buoy me.

My phantom pain continues to come in waves, but it's somewhat manageable compared to the previous several weeks. Having a prosthesis acts sort of like mirror therapy. I look down and I have two legs. The pressure of the socket on my limb desensitizes the nerve endings and tricks my brain into thinking I've got two feet again. I still sense that my lower leg and foot are present, but that they end at my kneecap. It's a gnarly feeling; I don't know whether I'll ever grow accustomed to this new reality.

We all gather around the television, cheering Matthew during his race, but it doesn't go well. He's knocked from contention early, and the mood at the party abruptly shifts. The gathering turns out not to be the celebration I had been anticipating. We sit around eating popcorn and cake, making idle chit-chat while watching the rest of the competitions. I'm thinking about how, although maybe I never enjoyed it as much as I would have liked, I would be thrilled for another chance to compete at X Games. I should be in Colorado now, gunning for a medal. Sure, acquiring my leg and learning to walk again has been a triumph. Yet as I stand among friends and teammates, reality sets in, causing tears to well in my eyes. It's a plunge from my moment of victory in Chip's office a day earlier as I realize I won't be competing at Winter X Games again, not ever. From now on, I'll be watching from home.

4

Helping Hands

EACH DAY I'VE BEEN GETTING BETTER ACQUAINTED WITH MY prosthesis. It's a rudimentary model designed for daily use—the kind covered by most insurance companies—and its shortcomings are apparent when my artificial knee gives out suddenly, without warning, just as Chip had warned. My daily tumbles leave me bruised, picking rocks from the palms of my hands after bracing another fall. The problem is in the mechanics: the knee of my walking prosthesis consists of a hinge that must be loaded properly to bear weight. I must swing the leg out ahead with each step, straightening the joint so that it locks. Then I step with my left leg in a vaulting motion. On an incline or decline—any uneven terrain, really—the hinge mechanism fails regularly. The limitations are even more pronounced in a seated position—say, on a snowmobile. With my knee bent, I cannot load the joint. I've taken a few spins on borrowed snowmobiles up at Quadna Mountain during training sessions and my prosthesis tends to flop around. When I'm on my feet, getting around snowy, ice-covered ground presents its own challenges. I've graduated from a crutch to a cane to now walking on my own, but I still take spills regularly, routinely stubbing the toe of my prosthesis on the ground, buckling the knee, causing me to crash. It's a hard reality check. *How should I take this?* I try to make light of it. Falling on your face in public every day gives you a dose of humility. I can get upset, but it only makes other people feel awkward. If I can't accept my situation for what it is, how can I expect other people to accept it? *Yes, I have a mechanical leg. It buckled. I fell over, and that's it.* Each time it's frustrating and a little embarrassing enduring the startled stares of concerned witnesses wondering what has just happened.

Still, I refuse to remain home. I need to get out of the house, accompanying Sara to the grocery store or on a run to Target. Sara gives me a wide berth when we walk together so I don't take her down, too. I must concentrate on every step. Some stores have scooters for customers and I'm quick to hop in the one I think will be fastest. I'm always racing, even while shopping. *Beep! Beep!* I'll jam on the horn and watch people's reactions as they see a young man zipping by on a scooter, not aware of my wonky prosthesis under my pants.

Some of the top prosthetics companies produce legs with advanced microprocessors that make minute calculations by the millisecond, allowing amputees to not only walk easier, but go for a hike and even climb ladders. Chip has strategically put me in a cheaper prosthesis because he knew insurance would approve the model quicker, allowing me to get upright and on my feet and continue my recovery. Microprocessors may take months to approve, which would have left me crutching around nearly till summertime. For all its faults, my leg has taught me the fundamentals of walking with a prosthesis. Maybe I'm not ready to resume sports, but my goal has been to perfect my gait to the point where I can be mobile on my own two feet and maybe even fool the public when I'm wearing pants.

MY ACQUIRED WALKING SKILLS will be put to a test when the professional snocross tour stops in Brainerd on February 5—an event that will give me another whiff of competitive racing. The night before the races begin is a Thursday, and a local car dealership on Highway

371, north of town, hosts a benefit to raise money for my medical and living expenses. The Dondelinger dealership is under renovation, so all the cars have been moved out. The race teams pull their semis into the parking lot and display their sleds. I've been out of the loop, and I'm completely blown away at the scale of the event and the amount of community support when Sara and I pull up and see thousands of people on hand to help me. As we drive through and find our parking spot, I do everything I can not to tear up as the knot in my throat grows. "I don't even know what to say..." I tell Sara.

In the parking lot, race teams show off their semi-trucks and sleds to fans. Riders sign autographs and display their medals. There's Tucker Hibbert, a dominant young racer and the reigning Winter X Games champion from Pelican Rapids, Minnesota, about an hour west of Brainerd. There's Robbie Malinowski, an Amsoil Tour champion from Canada. These are my rivals, guys I've been chasing on the track the past few years, and I'm grateful for their support. Inside the dealership, hundreds of items for auction fill rows of tables.

I'm overwhelmed as people file through the dealership, signing up for items as part of a silent auction. The crowd is composed of locals, race fans, tour bigs, and my fellow racers. Brainerd is invested in outdoor sports. In the summer, it's water sports. Come winter, it's snowmobile season. I've been sponsored by Brothers Motorsports, a snowmobile dealership down the road from Dondelinger, and they've played a leading role in organizing the benefit. I've been part of the snocross tours for 10 years and become well-known in the community as one of the nicer guys who's willing to meet and chat with fans and enthusiasts about snowmobiles.

My injury has sent shock waves through the entire tour, and they've all come out to help. The event has been spearheaded by my good friend Brian Bleeke and Joanie Ebert, the wife of the crew chief for Team Arctic Cat, with added help from Paula Warnert. A charter bus filled with friends and family from Kimball has driven up. I'm embarrassed and uncomfortable by the outpouring, and a knot once again forms in my throat.

I watch in wonder during a live auction when a jersey belonging to hotshot up-and-coming motocross racer Ryan Dungey becomes the object of a bidding war. Malinowski and my former team owner with Avalanche, Mike Glefke, go back and forth, driving the price to $1,500.

The purpose of the benefit is to raise money for me to pay for my staggering medical bills, which have Sara worried. Insurance will cover most of the costs of my prosthesis, but I will have to pay, too. Chip and his company, Prosthetic Labs, have donated a socket. The generosity and compassion of so many leaves me in tears on and off through the night. Sara and I feel overwhelmed with gratitude when we learn the benefit alone has raised nearly $37,000.

When it's all over, and the last items have been auctioned, the tables are packed up and hauled away. The semi-rigs rumble to life in the frozen parking lot, and the teams and riders roll into the darkness a mile up Highway 371 to Brainerd International Raceway, where the first motos of the weekend begin tomorrow.

AT THE RACES THE FOLLOWING DAY, the sun shines on the speedway, exploding in blinding light off the snow and the grandstands, decked out in colorful sponsor banners. The speedway hosts NHRA drag races and a handful of other types of auto races during the summertime, and the snocross course has been built on the drag strip between the two grandstands, creating an intimate setting for the event, packed tight with thousands of fans. All weekend, they have had a chance to buy raffle tickets for a brand-new model of my No. 5 Ski-Doo race sled donated by Brothers Motorsports. The proceeds will be put toward my medical bills.

All weekend I make my way around the pits, careful not to take a spill on any patches of ice. I've adjusted to the reality that I'm not a racer anymore. I'm a coach now. Still, I miss the nervous anticipation of sitting in the trailer before a race, the routine of getting my mind right before another moto. On Sunday, the weekend winding down, the stands at Brainerd International Raceway are thick with fans bundled in parkas, hats, and gloves under an orange winter sun. That's when the starter calls me up to the racecourse, explaining that they want me to make a lap on the sled being raffled off to benefit me. The starter hands me a checkered flag. "Go, do a lap!" he says. I'm excited to be on the racetrack, with a chance to ride on the playing field of my sport in front of a huge crowd again. I shove the flagpole down the back of my jacket. I'm clad in my helmet and mirrored goggles to block the bright sunshine. Trembling with emotion, my good knee bobs like a sewing machine needle from nerves. The crowd roars along with the engine as I rev the throttle and take off, careful to control my speed. I want to go fast but not too fast, and I nearly fall off the machine when my knee collapses beneath me. How embarrassing would it be to wipe out while taking a lap in front of all these people? I'm reminded that my prosthetic knee is not designed for riding snowmobiles. With my knee bent, I cannot load the joint, preventing me from standing. Unlocked, the prosthesis collapses, flopping around from the hinge, causing me to nearly fall off again, but it doesn't even matter. I'm on a snowmobile, on a racetrack, and I can't help but smile under my helmet.

Buzzing along on my bright yellow sled, the No. 5 racing plate on the handlebars and side, the checkered flag flaps behind me in the wind. I cannot ride my fastest, but I give a good account of myself and approach the finish line tabletop jump, where my entire team and family have gathered to greet me. Surrounded by a crowd of two dozen friends and loved ones, the race announcer conducts a surprise ceremony in which my No. 5 will be retired forever. It is a bittersweet moment. No one will wear the No. 5 again—including me.

AT MY NEXT APPOINTMENT, Chip is alarmed to hear I rode a snowmobile at the races with the plastic socket on my everyday prosthesis. "Mike," he says, wrinkling his brow, "you can't be riding with that. It's plastic, brittle in cold weather, and liable to break apart."

"Yeah, yeah," I tell Chip, dismissively. "I've got to."

I'm excited to meet with Chip and look at his tool bench and hardware components. We're both interested in fabrication, so when he removes my socket to bring it back to his workshop, he invites me to hop down the hall on one foot from the patient room. Standing in the doorway, I watch him with my leg as he ponders how he's going to make this temporary socket hold up to riding. He begins by wrapping another layer of fiberglass around it, which is the same hardening fabric used for making casts when you break a bone. He also adds a layer of foam on the ischium support to reduce a pressure point. Finally, he makes fresh nylon straps with Velcro using an old-fashioned sewing machine and finishes them with buckles. Studying Chip while he works at his craft, I want to know how prostheses function, and how they don't, especially after my experiences walking and riding my snowmobile. I'm not only getting an education in fabrication, but I'm also learning about the business of prosthetics.

Chip explains that the attitude of insurance companies limits development of prostheses. "Insurance will sometimes pay for more of a basic design rather than a higher profile, without a lot of justification," he says. "It slows the progression of development in technology in our componentry."

The economics of prosthetics mean components are simply one part of the equation. Research and development, fabrication, and the costs of running a business all add up to a significant dollar amount. "People ask me why this piece of plastic costs so much," he says about the socket. "You're paying for the service if not as much as, or more than, the piece of plastic, plus follow-up care. The piece of plastic won't do any good if you don't have people with the background to make it successful."

Chip and the more than 6,000 other working prosthetists cannot bill insurance companies for follow-up office visits, like the one I'm at now. Prosthetists must bill up front, no matter how many further tweaks and adjustments are required later.

Now Chip wants to ask me some questions, namely about how I want to live my life as an amputee. *What are my ambitions?*

The taste of roaring around on a track beneath a grandstand at the races has inspired me to return to riding, even if only recreationally, and that will require better performance from my prosthesis. Chip has wrapped extra fiberglass around my socket for strength so that it can withstand the cold weather and the inevitable abuse it will take while riding a snowmobile. He's added more substantial components with the highest ratings for the kind of punishment riding dishes out. "You'll want to wear this one if you're ever going to be in a bar fight," Chip cracks.

The socket will be sturdy, but I'll still need a leg that doesn't flop around while riding. Chip shows me the specs for a couple legs designed for recreation. The first is called the XT9. Designed for skiing, the XT9 features a spring coil–over–shock design. The knee flexes 90 degrees, which is fine for skiing, but I need a greater range to be able to sit on my snowmobile. "I don't know if this would really work," I say. "I need more range than that."

The other model is called a Bartlett Tendon, which uses a similar-sized shock to the XT9. It looks like it would be good for riding a bicycle. But it doesn't appear to have enough spring tension and durability for what I need.

I've ridden mountain bikes as cross-training for years. I'm familiar with the suspension components used. The wheels in my head begin turning as I think about the mechanics of riding my snowmobile. Obviously, I need a suspension system with components that will support me and absorb the impact as I'm bouncing through bumps. I've spent nearly 10 years tuning my own equipment, learning how it works so I can better communicate with my mechanics and suspension techs to get the needed performance.

I leave my appointment with Chip wondering if, by using a mountain bike shock, a leg could be fabricated that would permit more than 90 degrees of flex. I don't know how to do what Chip does, but growing up in the shop around farm equipment—and the complex machines of snowmobiles and dirt bikes—means that I'm used to coming up with creative solutions to mechanical problems. Whether tinkering with a bike or a farm machine, I've always embraced the process of learning by doing, taking things apart again and again until I learned how they worked. I find now that I'm doing the same for my leg, building a blueprint for a suspension assembly in my mind.

I'M STILL MULLING THE POSSIBILITIES when Sara and I visit her mom, Deb, back in Kimball, three months removed from my accident. Sara and I are Minnesotans through and through, and we're close to both our families, who mostly live just a short drive away. While there, we run into Sara's 22-year-old brother Luke, who bears little resemblance to his big sister. Sara has fair hair and light eyes, and Luke has darker features, like their late dad. What they have in common is a friendly, outgoing personality. Luke has two older sisters, and ever since I started dating Sara he's treated me like his surrogate big brother. A ski racer and motocross rider, Luke shares my interest in competition and also in design and fabrication—he's enrolled in college, studying to be a technology/agriculture teacher—and has begun taking an interest in trailing me to the track and offering to help out any way he can at the races.

The week of my wedding, Luke and I attended a "guys' weekend" racing motocross in southern Minnesota at Spring Creek MX Park. This is one of the favorite venues for the pros as the Motocross Nationals come through Minnesota in mid-summer. It's an incredibly exciting and challenging course to ride with its varying terrain, big jumps, rutted corners, hill climbs, and steep descents, and the event always draws max capacity rider attendance. I had been planning to come home on Saturday, but I was having so much fun I elected to stay an extra day and race on Sunday. During the second moto of the races, I went down in a high-speed whoop section when another rider veered hard right, took out my front end, and slammed me to the ground before I could react. My helmet smashed into the ground and my shoulder took a heavy hit, too. I sat up with a dazed look on my face, and I knew it right away. *Damn it! I just broke my collarbone again!*

I knew I was supposed to get married, but I couldn't remember the day, and I was mad at myself for getting busted up. Luke phoned Sara for me and explained things. "Sara, sorry, sorry, sorry!" I pleaded. I asked if we were getting married next month. "No, it's next weekend," she said.

A CT scan revealed I had a concussion. An X-ray of my shoulder showed the bone had been shattered and required surgery. Sara said it would have to wait until after the wedding, so I put on a sling and gritted my teeth through the ceremony.

Luke's a good guy to have around in an emergency, but we simply haven't had many other opportunities to grow close. He knows how much fun I've been having being back around snocross at Quadna Mountain, working as a coach. Now he wants to show me a route back to motocross.

"Check this out," he says, pulling out his laptop. He shows me an online article about the ESPN Summer X Games adding an adaptive Supercross race to the lineup for the coming competition in Los Angeles in the summer. A dirt bike discipline similar to motocross, Supercross takes place in the fan-friendly environment of a stadium. "This would be great for you," Luke tells me. He encourages me to get back on my dirt bike and offers to work as my wrench. Brimming with self-confidence and a willingness to do anything for you, Luke just wants to be part of the action.

Before my accident, I stayed in shape for snocross by racing motocross in spring, summer, and fall, competing in a class one rung below the professional ranks. Motocross is my favorite sport. I like the feeling of riding in warm weather, on natural terrain, along a course traversing hills and valleys with high-speed straightaways and long jumps. On 450cc gas-powered engines, you can hit 50 to 60 miles per hour within a blink of an eye. With as many as 40 racers lined up elbow to elbow in the start gate, things can get hairy real quick. Staying nimble on a 250-pound dirt bike requires more precision than it does on a 450-pound snowmobile. It's easy to lose your balance on two wheels and topple over, and harder still to stay upright with only one good leg.

For months, I've been planning to sell my dirt bike on the assumption that I would never ride again. Seeing it parked in the garage has been a painful reminder of something I've lost, and Sara and I could use the money. But now I've got reason to reconsider. I'm so excited. All I can think is that I need to find a way to get back on my dirt bike in order to compete at X Games. I call out to Sara to tell her what we've discovered.

"Whoa," she says, "Whoa! Let's put the brakes on and think this through." Sara has always been practical. She has hardly gotten used to me on my prosthetic leg; to imagine me racing again so soon after my accident is too much, too fast. All I can think about is how to make it happen.

If I had a leg with more flex in the knee, could I compete at X Games on my dirt bike against other amputees? I don't know the answer. But I think I know where to look for help. While I was in the hospital recovering from my amputation, Sara fielded a phone call from Jim Wazny, an amputee motocross and snocross racer who saw news of my accident. Wazny offered help if I ever wanted to resume racing. I thought nothing of it during my pain-wracked recovery. I was finished racing; what would Wazny and I have had to talk about? But now I'm thankful for the call.

JIM WAZNY IS THE MOTOCROSS ORGANIZER for the Extremity Games, a competition for adaptive athletes held in Michigan over Memorial Day weekend that will serve as the qualifier for adaptive Supercross at X Games. I'll need to compete at the Extremity Games in order to punch my ticket to X Games. First, I'll need to get my dirt bike ready to compete.

I figure Wazny can help with some questions I have about adaptive equipment for my motorcycle. When I finally phone Wazny, the voice on the other end of the line is loud, excitable, belonging to someone who speaks as if he's just eaten a pound of sugar. I learn that Wazny is a former expert motocross racer who lost his left leg in a gruesome practice accident. Wazny has been in my circumstances. He's endured a devastating injury and the inevitable doubts that come with it, wondering whether he would resume riding and racing again. His success as an adaptive rider offers an alternative vision of life, and our conversation ignites the first stray sparks of a dream. Wazny possesses endless energy, an extensive knowledge of motorsports, and infectious confidence. He knows from firsthand experience that returning to the track is an important part of recovering a sense of self and purpose. The more he talks, the more excited he gets, and the more confident I am that a return to racing is more than a pipe dream.

We bond while talking about the challenges of riding dirt bikes while missing our left legs, the ones we use to shift gears on a motorcycle. The shifter is a foot-activated mechanism located near my left peg. My prosthesis won't allow me to shift gears with my foot since it doesn't have the ability to rotate up and down on demand. Wazny has modified his dirt bike with an electric shifter that's controlled by push buttons on the handlebars, near the left handgrip. He tells me he uses a bungee cord to tether his prosthesis to his foot peg so that his boot doesn't slip. Over the course of the call, Wazny gains my trust and mentors me as I start to plot my return to racing. He imparts practical information like where to order an electronic shifter for my bike. Wazny also encourages me to come out and compete at Extremity Games. By the time I hang up the phone, I know what I'll need to do. My vision of stress-free retirement, tinkering in my garage, goes out the window. I've still got some fire left in me. With newfound inspiration, I'll have three months to prepare and train.

First, I'll need a prosthesis better suited to riding a dirt bike. Chip hasn't been able to find any on the market. I figure that with my knowledge of suspension components from all the years I've spent working on my snowmobiles and dirt bikes, I can build something superior to what's currently out there. I focus on how mountain bike shocks provide about the right size and travel for what I'll need. Thinking back to my high school drafting class and my experience in metal fabrication, the wheels in my head begin turning, and I grow excited mulling design ideas.

Meantime, I've learned to manage my phantom pain. My prosthesis has played a part, mentally and physically. My socket has desensitized my nerves by putting consistent pressure on my limb. I'm also not thinking about my leg as much because I'm up and walking. Mentally, I've made a shift: if I think about nerve pain, it returns. If I'm not thinking about it, the pain disappears. And I have plenty else to think about to occupy my mind as I prepare to return to riding my dirt bike.

With the sun higher in the sky, and a spring breeze delivering a breath of warmth to northern Minnesota, I feel winter fading and the snowmobile season coming to an end. April will bring a familiar sense of renewal, and I'm already starting to feel more like myself again.

5

Rebuild

THE FINAL RACE OF THE SNOCROSS SEASON WILL TAKE PLACE IN Lake Geneva, Wisconsin, at the end of March. Up at our team training center at Quadna Mountain, I've been working with our physical trainer to design riding drills on the practice track. I'm giving the racers structure through their practice days. With the weather warming, and another winter coming to an end, everyone is in a good mood.

I'm looking forward to the final stop on tour, too. I've committed to competing in the mechanics' race, a competition at the end of each season featuring a field of retired racers and mechanics testing their rusty skills on a pro track. This year the race will include a one-legged former pro with something to prove. The race usually includes dramatically decreasing lap times with each pass, and a few entertaining crashes from riders who are past their prime, or never reached it in the first place. There will be bragging rights at stake for those who place. Still, no one's taking it too seriously. No one, that is, except me. I'm starting to take practice as seriously as when I was able-bodied, becoming a slave to the stopwatch.

The race is held on a ski hill at a resort, and several thousand people attend. Less than four months since my accident, I'm back on a track, in front of fans and friends, anticipating the thrill of racing again. I've followed Jim Wazny's advice and lashed my prosthesis to the machine using a bungee cord. I'm shaking with nerves.

When the green flag flies to signal the start of the race, we hit a track heavily rutted and holed out from a long weekend of racing. Picking my way through four-foot-deep moguls and holes, I bounce wildly. Hanging on tight, my prosthesis flies all over, maintaining minimal purchase on the running board. The race lasts a mere three laps, less than one-quarter of what I'm used to in the pro classes. By the end, I'm physically spent, but I cross the finish line first, earning an interview with the race announcer, who recaps my season for the fans who've stuck around to watch the closing race. Early in my career, I was shy, preferring to let my riding do the talking. When a microphone was stuck in my face, I'd clam up or stammer, *Uhhh, umm...* Through practice and classes given by my race teams, I've learned to embrace speaking while in the spotlight, and I take the opportunity to thank the fans and the rest of the racing community for all their support through what have been the most difficult months of my life.

At the end of season banquet after the races, hundreds of racers, mechanics, crewmen, and owners fill a ballroom at the host hotel, the Grand Geneva Resort. Warnert Racing has a lot to celebrate; Tim Tremblay has won his first championship in the semi-pro Open class. When it's time to hand out awards, I'm the recipient of the first True Grit Award. As the night wears on, many in the race community will cut loose and party hard. I linger a long time, too. Having gotten a taste of racing again, I don't want the season to end.

DESIGNING A PROSTHESIS TO GET ME BACK on my dirt bike and racing again offers me a way to actively control an aspect of my recovery. With the snowmobile season concluded and Sara at work, I'm alone in the house with no distractions. Calling on my high school mechanical drawing classes, I spend my days sketching the image of a prosthesis that I've formed in my head. I'm familiar with fabrication from all my jobs outside snowmobile racing, and the first step is always to draw a sketch and work out the dimensions. Full of hope and excitement, armed with pencil and paper, a ruler, a compass and protractor, and a lot of eraser, I begin to sketch and work out the dimensions. This will be far more detailed and intricate than anything I've ever done and involve difficult geometry problems I won't be able to solve overnight.

I set up in our spare bedroom, which one of the previous owners of the house painted pink. Sara and I each have a desk, but I want an upgrade and buy a massive fancy corner desk. For hours at a time, I sit at my desk, drawing obsessively, calculating, erasing, and redrawing, to get all the angles right. I have 15 vertical inches to work with—the length of my leg from the knee to the floor. I want to use a Fox mountain bike shock because it's small, compact, and lightweight, and has a high range of adjustability. I want the range of motion of a normal knee. The shock itself is 7.5 inches long and it travels two inches in and out. I'm stumped as to how to create 130 degrees of angular motion. I try cams and multi-link connections and continually return to a simple scheme using a track rolling system. But I don't know if it will be durable enough, whether debris will cause it to lock up, or if there will be too much free play between the rollers and track surface.

I'm obsessed with the project, which helps distract from my injury and any lingering phantom pain. Frequently I'm alone. Sara has picked up extra shifts at the hospital. She's on day and night rotations, working labor and delivery. Babies come at all hours. She works double shifts to help out because I have no income now. I have a financial cushion from the money raised at the benefit, enough to cover our monthly bills for now, and I want to make the most of the time to build a knee that will allow me to get back on my dirt bike.

Once I've drawn the arcs, curves, and dimensions that I think create the proper geometry, I set out to build a two-dimensional model out of cardboard, employing thumbtacks as hinges in order to rotate the moving parts. It's a slow process. Whenever I've done metal fabrication involving complex bends or building a box shape, I've always used full-size cardboard models first to cut down on mistakes. Corrugated cardboard doesn't bend easily, and paper doesn't hold its structure. I've found that manila file folders work best. The process reveals that a roller slot allows the design to work. Finally, after five weeks, I'm settled on the design, dimensions, parts, and assembly. It's time to start cutting.

AT THE FINAL RACE OF THE SNOCROSS SEASON in Lake Geneva, I'd run into Ricky Strobel, an old friend who works for Fox Shox, a leading shocks manufacturer. I had mentioned to Ricky that I had an idea to use one of the company's shocks in a prosthetic leg I'm designing.

Later, while working at home on the design of my leg, I made a trip to Brothers Motorsports and saw the Arctic Cat truck in the lot. Ricky was in the rig, and he asked how my prosthesis was coming along. "Whatever we can do to help your project, let us know," he offered.

"I need to do some machining," I said. "Would you be willing to help?"

Fox has a small research and development shop for their powersports division, belonging to Ricky's family, located about 20 minutes south of Brainerd. He offered me use of the shop and two Fox mountain bike shocks. "Go ahead," Ricky said. "You're not going to hurt anything."

With my design work finally done, I head to the shop for lessons on machining. I've bought $150 worth of materials—two quarter-inch-thick aluminum plates that will serve as side frames for the knee, and an assortment of small shafts and bushings that I intend to make on the lathe to hold all the components in place. I have no experience machining parts. I've never used a mill or lathe. Luckily, I'm friends with Ben Hayes, who works at the shop. "Hayzer," as he's known, was a mechanic with Polaris, based in Wisconsin, when I lived there while on the snocross tour. We had become great friends while spending hours and hours at the Polaris Factory race shop and traveling the national tour over the last few years. He's close to my age and also into riding moto. He's a clean-cut, precision-thinking guy, always contemplating how to get the best performance out of everything. "I can teach the basics of running a mill and lathe," Hayzer says. "I can get you started."

I arrive at the shop on a Monday morning when the workday shift of the three employees starts. The shop is little more than a small garage, basically a 40-foot by 50-foot pole shed in Ricky's backyard. It's a small prototype shop specializing in research and development, where Fox performs all its custom development for snowmobiles and ATVs. There's a mill, a lathe, and a couple tables.

Set up in the corner on a mill and lathe, I begin machining away by myself. The process is slower than I expected. I'm accustomed to grabbing a grinder and grinding metal away, welding pieces together, or bending and pounding pieces into shape.

I quickly learn from the workers at the shop that machining parts is a slow, precise task; you measure, cut, and measure again to get the size and shape just right. Machining requires incremental adjustments on spools, shaving tiny layers, measuring and double-checking. With the shafts and bushings, tolerances must be perfect or there's sloppy play in the assembly and you must start again with fresh components. I've never worked on an assembly that must be so precise. I begin working on the parts on Monday, and continue full-time, 8 AM to 5 PM, for five days, clocking in and out with the Fox employees. Once the parts are machined, I must assemble them. I finish late on a Friday. The shop grows tense with anticipation, and my hands shake with excitement during final assembly as the employees gather around to see the final product.

The result is not pretty, resembling a boat anchor more than a human—or even a robot—leg. The prototype looks bulky, blocky, and heavy. Hayzer and the others watch as I screw the knee to my socket and slide it over my stump. I see the skepticism on their faces. They've got to be thinking, *Is it really going to work?* The knee doesn't look fancy, but I know the geometry is right. Standing, I bounce a few times to test it, flexing the knee. The shock needs a better calibration, but the mechanics feel more natural than I could have imagined.

Everyone is quiet, waiting for my reaction. "What do you think?" one of the workers finally asks.

"Oh, hell yeah," I announce. "I can work with this."

I DRIVE HOME IN THE DARK. Sara knows I've been working on this prototype. When I arrive at home, I see her car. She's recently returned from work, but I stop in the garage first to tune the shock. When I walk in the house, I place the knee on the kitchen table with a resounding *thud* and announce my arrival. "Check it out," I say, anticipating that she will be thinking, *What is this heavy, bulky-looking thing?* She looks skeptical and a little shocked. "What are we getting into?" she asks. "Are we racing again?"

Sara and I built the foundation of our relationship on the road during race weekends. She was not only my high school girlfriend but my teammate and pit crew. Once upon a time, it was just the two of us, before I made the big teams. If I'm going to race dirt bikes again, it will likely be just the two of us again, at least once we start out.

Ten years earlier, in 1999, when I was 17, Sara and I chased the motocross series every weekend, all summer long. Sara would wash my dirt bike with a power washer, making the motorcycle sparkle. My brother, Chris, had always been the clean-cut one. His bedroom was always spotless and organized. Mine was a mess. His car was clean. My truck was covered in mud. With my racing equipment, I was always self-conscious about how it looked, but I was limited financially and would ride till things wore out or I had the funding to replace them. During races, though, I always showed up to the start with a clean bike. Sara had a lot to do with that. My mom and dad divorced when I was four and I lived with my dad and brother. Sara had started to notice that maybe it was time to get new sheets on my bed or wash my jeans once they got grubby. Living with two other men, sometimes these details got overlooked. Plus, my family didn't have a lot of extra money. If I wanted something new, I needed to work for it. Most of my money was stuck into my truck and my dirt bike. Birthdays and Christmas were for new clothes. Sara started to get me thinking a little differently about my appearance.

She had arrived in my life at a time of transition. My first years of high school I was hanging out with guys who were a year or two older. They had their driver's licenses, and I would hitch rides with them. We were a bunch of country boys who liked to drive trucks in the mud and climb hills and ride our dirt bikes. On weekends, we all got together to drink some beers, getting trashed in gravel pits around flaming bonfires.

Once I started racing dirt bikes, I couldn't stay out all night drinking and still get up at 5 AM to get to the racetrack, and this created a schism with my friends, who would all be hungover. "Come on, guys," I said. "Give it up for one night." I tried talking my best friend into working as my pit man at the races. "Nah," he said, "I'm going out." So it was just Sara and me. She was 18 and acted as my legal guardian at the track because as a minor I had to be accompanied by an adult. Sara got flak from her friends, too, about spending all her spare time with me at the races. But we shared a sense of mission.

My dad didn't like me on the road at motocross events all the time, and he didn't like me spending so much time with Sara. He felt I was losing my way, or maybe he felt he was losing me. He took the keys to my truck so I couldn't race. He would glare at Sara, and sometimes harsh words were exchanged. "You've got your head so far up your ass, you don't know what day it is," he said to me. "You're missing out on things." I was love-blind. All I cared about was working, dirt bikes, and my relationship with Sara. Sara got pressure from family and friends, too. Even while living at the College of Saint Benedict, in nearby St. Joseph, Minnesota, earning a degree in nursing, Sara would always hit the road with me on weekends. Family and friends told her that when she went off to college, she needed to date other boys. But we never broke up. Not once. Things came to a head between my dad and me when he took away my truck keys during my senior year of high school in the spring of 2000. I responded by telling him I was moving up north near Brainerd to live on one of the properties my mom and Rick own. It was one of the hardest things I've ever done. I felt sick to my stomach. My dad and I were close as I grew up, but I felt it was time for me to choose my own path. I told him I was going to move out as soon as I graduated and I would begin work for my mom and stepdad. My dad didn't like it one bit. My parents couldn't stand one another, and my dad no doubt saw my choice to live with my mom as a betrayal. He threatened to take my truck away. "I worked my ass off for that truck," I said during a heated argument. "No, you're not taking that away!"

We didn't talk for four days afterward. The following months were rough. As soon as I graduated, I packed up my stuff and moved out. Sara was also having a terrible start to the summer and was in need of a change. One month earlier, her dad had died of pancreatic cancer. She moved in with me for the summer up north, where my mom and Rick had a house deep in the woods. Hard by Highway 371, down a long driveway through a stand of trees, the Mississippi River a couple hundred yards west, we set up a temporary summer home. We lived in a fifth-wheel camper until a workshop on the property was converted into a three-room living space. I was 18 and she was 19. I lived there for three years, Sara joining me when she wasn't at school. We were half a mile from Ricky Strobel's house and his shop for the power sports division of Fox Shox.

Sara has remained by my side ever since, on the road, at the track, in the pits, at the hotels, the hospitals. I trust her opinion more than anyone else's because she knows what makes me tick. She's formed lasting friendships with the other wives and girlfriends of the riders and team owners on tour. Neither one of us had wanted to change our racing lifestyle. On the circuit, traveling the country in the company of people motivated for a single purpose, to be a top racer, has been everything for us. It may sound crazy, but I want that again. I need Sara to want it, too.

First, I need to try out the knee. As I bolt my new leg onto my socket, my heart races and my palms sweat from excitement. I hop on my dirt bike, fire it up, and head for a trail at the base of a ditch that runs along my property. Buzzing back and forth, I'm hit with an overwhelming feeling of accomplishment and excitement as I realize how great my new creation performs. When I hit a jump, the shock on my prosthesis absorbs the impact. I don't feel as though I will tip to my left, the way I do with my peg leg.

When I return inside, Sara sees me beaming and smiles back. I haven't been this happy in six months, or maybe an entire year. My mind turns to getting on the racetrack and dreams of Summer X Games, totally forgetting about nearly losing my life and how it has affected Sara and me.

"We have to talk," she says, initiating the first of a series of dynamic conversations about safety, ambition, and risk versus reward. Maybe someone else would simply tell me *no way,* scared off forever after my traumatic accident and what it put us through. But Sara isn't like that. She just wants to be sure we're making smart decisions that fit our new reality.

"It really sucked," she says about my injury, admitting that it's still fresh in her mind six months later. "It was a perfect storm, and if we're going to move forward with racing, we have to put it behind us. If I'm always worried—don't get me wrong, I'm worried—I get butterflies. If my complete focus is a chance of injury, you can't race. You can't race if all *you're* thinking about is getting hurt."

"Be prepared," I say, anticipating her concerns. "Don't rush into it."

"Don't expect somebody else to take care of you," Sara says.

It's a shift in our mentality. We'd always put responsibility for safety or medical treatment on the team and race organizers, or just didn't even think about it. It's sobering to hear this, but she's right. The days of being part of a large team ended with my accident in Ironwood. She and I are on our own now in a way we weren't before—but that just means we need to be even stronger.

"If we go forward with this," Sara says, "we're going to be as safe as we can and ease into it and really make smart choices."

I trust Sara's judgment, and her words make me realize I need to analyze risk versus reward more seriously. I've been so caught up in the all-consuming task of designing a knee to get back on my bike, I haven't spent much time considering whether racing in my current condition is worth risking further injury—or even my life. Sara and I haven't had this conversation before, except casually, and it makes me uneasy. Neither one of us is ready to be finished with racing, though. We agree on that much.

6

Extremity Games

I SPEND MAY AND MOST OF JUNE RIDING DIRT BIKES WITH MY new prosthetic leg, what I've dubbed the "Moto Knee." I adopt the hand shifter that Wazny recommended and experiment with modified foot pegs. I've traded in the bulky boot for a lighter-weight shoe. (I don't really need to protect my foot anymore. If it gets run over, it's not going to hurt!) I fasten my foot in place using a bungee cord, the way Wazny does. I don't like the setup. I'm connected to the bike, preventing an ejection in the event of crashes, which have been happening a lot as I experiment and try to find my most comfortable methods of riding and, I hope, racing.

In preparation for the Extremity Games, I load my dirt bike in my trailer and head to a local Brainerd racetrack, where the corners are tight and the course sandy, creating challenging conditions. I'm riding a Yamaha YZF 450, a beast of a bike that weighs nearly 250 pounds, with a kickstart on the right side. When the bike falls on me, I must wiggle free, performing the "croppy flop" so I can get my leg out from under the bike, stand up, and try to restart the engine. I put one of the wheels in a hole for stability or find something tall to stand on for better leverage. Sometimes the bike back-kicks when restarting, and I tip over again. *Damn it! Is this really worth it?* Even while roaring around on the bike, my left foot continually walks off the peg, creating a distraction. Looking down continually at my foot will cause me to lose focus, a situation that could end badly during a race. Worse, when turning left at low speed, unable to use my leg to brace my weight, I continually topple over and must shake sand out of my gloves and gear.

It's bittersweet being back on my bike. Riding on a track has been my happy place, and I enjoy the familiarity. For months I thought I would never ride my motorcycle again, and now I'm training and prepping for a chance at X Games. But it's a buzzkill to think that I'm no longer the fast guy flying around the track. *What if I'm not able to keep up?*

The worst incident comes in the start gate at an open practice when I lose my balance and fall on the rider next to me. No one gets injured, but it's embarrassing. Do I still fit in with the racers in the A-class, the top class? I'm accustomed to being one of the fastest guys on the track. I don't want anyone looking at me wondering, *What is he doing out here? He's going to get hurt, or hurt somebody else.* Not that anyone will ever say as much to me. Most folks at the track know my story, and they congratulate me on my return. Yet some don't know I'm an amputee. They only see a guy out there tipping over repeatedly. In my mind, I'm still the same, a professional athlete. I know how to perform mentally, but deep down I'm worried about accepting the fact that I'll likely never recapture my physical form.

After a month of riding at home, I enter a local Friday night race as a tune-up for Extremity Games, competing against six other amateurs in the top class. I'm unsure if I'll be able to break away from my old killer instinct and adjust to the slower pace I have to keep as I learn to balance with my new equipment. Is it worth riding if I'm going to be so slow and accident-prone? These thoughts echo while I prepare for the race. I don't topple in the start this time, but I will go down in the corners a couple times. Finishing in the back of the pack during both heats leaves me dead-last in the standings. Still, I finish the race. The biggest surprise? Not feeling terrible about my placing. I had resisted a return to racing knowing I would never be as fast as I had been before losing my leg. I had doubts I would enjoy riding at a slower pace. Now I'm realizing my relationship to racing has never been about lap times. I've always been attracted to the challenges of the sport. And riding fast with a prosthesis provides plenty of challenges. It feels good simply to be back on a dirt bike again.

Still, I can't help but think what it will be like at Extremity Games riding against other adaptive racers. I don't know any of the competitors I'll be going up against. I've talked to Jim Wazny a few more times on the phone and the racetrack he's described sounds fun, but nerve-wracking, too. The stakes are high: this will be my shot at X Games. Here I am, in a racing scenario again, only a few months after my accident. "Are we really doing this already?" I say to Sara. The excitement grows as the days count down to my return to competition.

SARA AND I PACK UP THE RACE TRAILER on the eve of Memorial Day weekend, 2009, just over five months following my amputation. We are about to embark on a 12-hour drive to the Extremity Games in Millington, Michigan, a town of about 1,000 midway between Flint and Saginaw, at the base of the thumb, if you think of the state's shape as a mitten. It is my first real race following my traumatic injury—and my first with my new prosthesis. I've spent May riding dirt bikes with the Moto Knee. I'm slower than before my accident, and I continue to take my share of falls. I worry whether I'll fit in with the racers in Michigan, and whether my competitive nature will allow me to live with a diminished version of myself on the track.

On the upside, preparing for a race provides a comforting, familiar routine. I slide behind the wheel of my half-ton pickup, pulling a 20-foot enclosed trailer equipped with a foldout couch to sleep on, plus a TV and work bench, all powered by a generator. We've packed food to last four days, plus parts for my bike and my prosthesis. I've arranged my trailer as efficiently as possible, with a tire rack and a vise clamp for tuning up my suspension. I like knowing that everything has its place, and I've come to despise messes. This setup is how Sara and I roll while on the road. This time we've brought along Luke to act as my pit man. When we pull into the track, I unpack the rig, pulling out awnings and setting up sponsors' flags for the likes of Amsoil and Prosthetic Labs. Being professional is not just about riding fast on the track. It's about looking fast in the pits, too. I take pride in that.

THE SCENE AT THE TRACK RESEMBLES a typical district or regional amateur-level race. There are a few fastidious setups with clear sponsor backing, but most are the weekend warrior types who are just pumped to get out on the track and race. Also, the competitive atmosphere you can cut with a knife at a pro event is absent. No one treats me like a threat, at least not right away, sizing me up the way I'm accustomed to being treated.

We arrive two days ahead of motocross competition, time enough to check out some of the other events, such as wakeboarding and mountain biking. I meet Dan Gale, who runs Adaptive Action Sports, an organization based in Copper Mountain, Colorado, dedicated to introducing people with disabilities to action sports, especially skateboarding and snowboarding. He's accompanied by Kep Koeppe, a big and burly snowboarding coach based in Crested Butte, Colorado. A mountain man straight out of central casting, with a beard to match, Kep disarms with a friendly demeanor and offers to help me any way he can. He and Dan assist Jim Wazny with organizing the motocross event at Extremity Games. Neither of them has a motorsports background. They are bros from the board sports world, but we all hit it off, and I cannot anticipate the transformative roles they will play in my future.

The fascinating new realm of adaptive sports is populated by determined and devoted characters. The other competitors—more than 20 in all from around the world—comprise amputees and paraplegics. Some have sustained spinal cord injuries and must use wheelchairs. On the track they employ crash cages, one-and-a-quarter-inch tubing that goes from their handlebars down around their knees and foot pegs to prevent their legs from getting smashed in the event of a crash. Seatbelts strap them to their bikes, and two or three helpers, right-hand men, haul them from their wheelchairs onto their bikes. These helpers hold the bike upright until it's started, and the riders take off. Watching these paraplegics perform is an eye-opener, both inspiring and nerve-wracking. Despite our differences, our common bond is a love for motocross and the sacrifices and adaptations we've made in a stubborn refusal to give it up.

Another one of the riders named Jason Woods is missing all his digits, fingers and toes, the result of a bacterial infection. With the stubs of his fingers, he's able to hang onto the handlebars with the help of Velcro straps. All motocross riders use tear-offs, clear sheets of plastic placed over your goggles held on by a small peg on each side. We wear them stacked on top of each other, as many as a dozen, so when we get roosted by mud spit from the tires of competitors, fouling our vision, we can peel off a dirty layer for fresh vision. With no fingers, Woods can't use tear-offs in the traditional way. His solution: tying a string to his handlebars, with the other end attached to a tear-off. When his vision gets muddy, he leans back, stretching the string to remove a tear-off. (Unfortunately for him, this only works one time per race.) Another rider in the field is missing an arm. He's customized handlebars to cope. Yet another has moved his throttle to the left side because he's missing his right hand.

My Moto Knee gets looks, too, and a couple inquiries. We mingle in the race pits. It's like a camp trip, everyone hanging out and telling stories, excited to learn about our individual adaptations. In snocross everyone was out to win first place. Here, someone is more likely to ask, *How can I help you? How can I learn from you?* Or invite you to their campsite dinner. These stubborn, persistent racers, who push past barriers and refuse to make excuses, are my kind of people. For the first time since my accident, I've found a place where I feel like I belong.

AT EXTREMITY GAMES, the track is long, with elevation changes and a few humongous jumps. Once practice gets underway, the track proves difficult to ride, too. It's sandy and filled with sets of moguls known as whoops and a terrifying 80-foot double jump called "Kong," featuring a blind landing, in which you cannot see the landing from the approach. I stick close to Wazny, pacing him during a practice lap. Before arriving, I had only spoken to him a few times on the phone. Now, I see that with hair tips frosted in the latest style, Wazny projects a youthful image, not one of a married father pushing 40. He is loud, enthusiastic, and always moving, like an excited squirrel. I see his extraordinary energy, too, while serving as both a competitor and event organizer. Wazny works as an auto mechanic, and he's attending school to learn to be a prosthetist. This week he's brought along his wife, Stacy, and their two children. I marvel at how he manages it all.

As we approach Kong, I ease off the throttle and stop the engine at the top of the launch so that I can size up the challenge. Wazny roars from behind, throttle on and flying up the face of the jump with a whoosh and sailing away over my shoulder.

"Holy shit!" I blurt out loud. "That's frickin' huge!"

This jump will be how I measure my performance here. Now that I've seen Wazny do it, I'll need to match him if I want a chance to place come race time.

Following practice, everyone catches on that the prosthesis I've built is working. A lot of the amputees have said they think it's cool, but it's big and bulky, and I know a few must be thinking it's a hunk of junk. I show Wazny my prototype. I value his opinion since he's experienced in this amputee and prosthetic world. He eyes the slab of metal, noting its bulk and weight. He's grudgingly intrigued, all while no doubt wondering what kind of competitor I will be.

While everyone else sizes up my prototype, Chris Ridgway sizes me up. He's of medium height and build, perfect for motocross. His shaggy brown hair sticks out from beneath a floppy baseball cap, and his round face is covered in a black beard that he's shaved down the middle of his chin, giving him a unique look. He gives me a wide smile, but I sense an intense competitor behind his mischievous hazel eyes. He's driven from Southern California in a van with a military trailer. There's a precision to his program. A former professional racer during the 1990s, Ridgway is a below-the-knee amputee, meaning he has better function than I do. He will be the fast guy riding a Suzuki 450, and he wants everyone to know it. In the pits, he spins stories of his pro days, name-dropping racers we all know from the mid- to late '90s. He's the most serious competitor out here. This is his race. He wants us to know he's going to win, and everyone else can just fuck off. Ridgway maintains his distance, content to eye me on the practice track. He knows I was a professional snocross racer and I may have some skills. In his early forties, he can see I have youth on my side. In a field of amateurs and weekend warriors, he views me as a possible threat to his supremacy.

The truth is, I'm not. By the end of practice, I work up the nerve to go for Kong, throttling it over the gap. *Holy cow, it's huge.* Landing marks a triumph. Still, I accept that I cannot match Ridgway's pace. I vow not to push myself trying to overtake him to the point where I will make a dumb mistake and end up in a pile.

But when it comes to the race, any thought of dialing back my intensity goes out the window. With my race face on, I push hard to keep pace with the guy in front, scanning for a chance to pass. I'm having a blast, banging handlebars, competing for position again. I vacillate between telling myself to take it easy because I don't want to be busted up again and pushing 100 percent of my ability. When I get to Kong, I grab another gear and pin it, soaring clear over the big 80-foot double.

In the end, I finish second to Ridgway and ahead of Jason Woods, the rider missing all his fingers and toes, who takes third place. Between races Woods needed a flat tire changed. With no fingers, he couldn't do it himself. He gave Sara and Luke instructions, and they changed his tire. This spirit of cooperation and competition prevails here. Another wheelchair-using rider has traveled from South Africa by himself in order to compete, crashing at the houses of other competitors.

Although not thrilled with my new, slower pace, I've still done better than expected, considering I've only resumed riding my dirt bike two months ago. Less than six months earlier, I thought I was finished.

I was preparing to sell my motorcycles. Now I'm racing again, this time in the company of inspiring riders who've overcome their own pain and obstacles. My passion and hope reignited, I wonder what I might be capable of someday, with more experience, with a chance to refine my leg. I'm about to find out. Second place qualifies me for the 2009 Summer X Games in Los Angeles, the biggest stage—and challenge—of my career.

SECTION TWO: ASSEMBLY

The only disability in life is a bad attitude.
—Scott Hamilton

7

X Games

TWO MONTHS AFTER EXTREMITY GAMES, I'M INSIDE THE HOME
Depot Center, a 27,000-seat soccer stadium in Carson, California, south
of Compton. ESPN has taken over the open-air arena, and X Games crews
have built a Supercross track that dwarfs anything I've ever ridden. The
course resembles a scene straight out of a video game, featuring mounds
of dirt shaped into gargantuan berms and jumps. This is Los Angeles, the
home of Hollywood. This is the big time, my first trip to the Summer X
Games, an event I've been watching on television for more than 10 years.
Several of my motocross heroes will be here competing in the pro field
for able-bodied racers. I'm so excited to meet them that I feel more like a
crazy fan than a professional athlete who's actually here to race.

Walking onto the stadium floor for the first time, my palms
instantly start sweating. I'm nervous, excited, scared. I've ridden my
share of challenging tracks on snow and dirt, but the size and scale
here is intimidating. Some of the leading motocross riders are tearing
up the track during practice, flying around the course at a pace I can
only dream of, engines whining as their tires kick up clouds of brown

dust. Launching from mammoth jumps, their bikes arc through the California sunshine.

In the weeks following Extremity Games, ESPN filmed a segment at my house in Brainerd about the Moto Knee and my comeback. Now the footage of my first big media feature plays repeatedly on the scoreboard screen at the Home Depot Center. I haven't had much experience with film interviews other than a quick post-race recap on the podium following a race. I'm not naturally outgoing or sociable. Growing up, I wasn't one to walk into a group and initiate conversation, but I've worked to overcome my reservations. As a professional racer, and a spokesperson for my team and sponsors, I've had to learn to give a good interview. Some of the top snocross teams enroll riders in classes to learn the basics, and I've understood the benefits and tried to take advantage of the opportunities. As a racer, I've always wanted to be on the podium. And if you're on the podium, you're going to be interviewed, so you might as well get used to it.

Still, the attention and spectacle surrounding Summer X Games surpasses the splashiest snocross events. My most high-profile moment had been appearing on the cover of the catalogue for motorcycle, dirt bike, and ATV supplier Parts Unlimited. As a racer, you're geared toward getting on the podium in the hopes of 10 seconds of time on the big screen. So watching myself on repeat on the jumbo display at the Home Depot Center feels like I'm dreaming. "What are we doing here?" Sara asks as we take in the spectacle.

I'm wondering the same thing. My amateur motocross career has mostly taken place on outdoor, flowing tracks along natural terrain. I've competed in the occasional Friday night Supercross, adapting easily to the amateur level courses at fairs back home. Here I am about to race a professional-level Supercross course on steroids, and it scares the hell out of me.

Shoehorned into the confines of a stadium, Supercross tracks are half as wide as a motocross track (with half as many riders in the field) leaving little room to pass and no room for error. The tabletops, triple jumps, and rhythm sections are packed so tightly that riders have a split second to prepare for the next massive feature designed to send them flying through the air, all for maximum audience thrills. Here in L.A., there are two 90-foot jumps that make Kong from Extremity Games look tame—a massive triple and a super-kicker at the finish line. This course would have pushed me to my limit as an able-bodied athlete. As an amputee, I worry whether I'm up to the challenge.

As part of our preparation, we riders walk the track, getting familiar with its features. I'm thinking, *Holy shit! What am I getting into here?* My nerves have risen tenfold. The course is bigger, gnarlier, and more intimidating than any I've seen. The longer I look at the 90-footers, the harder it gets to muster up my courage. Early in my career, I would bomb triples and sometimes overshoot the landing. "There's Monster Mike, airing it out," the announcers would say. My nickname came from a willingness to test my physical limits, including the strength to hang on during a hard landing. At 27 years old, I've become more conservative, especially following my amputation. I'll need to be calculated in my approach just to stay on my bike. Sizing up the challenge, I'll be happy if I can simply flow around the track and not look like a goon.

I remind myself that I haven't come here intending to win, only to compete and challenge myself on this massive course, on this larger stage with bigger crowds and TV cameras. On the other hand, I want everyone to see this one-legged guy hitting these humongous racecourse jumps. I want them to say, *Wow!* But I've got to be smart, and control what I can to prevent another crash. I'll need to take it slow, be patient, and not tackle the bigger course features before I'm ready. Of course, I worry that once I get my race face on, my competitive instincts will push me to keep pace with the riders in front of me, and possibly pass. That's when things can go wrong.

I'D BEEN PRACTICING INTENSELY since Extremity Games. In the week before X Games, I loaded my bike and gear in the back of my pickup and drove to Des Moines, Iowa, where I met up with Jim Wazny. He was driving a big motorhome with a trailer from his home in Michigan to L.A., on his way to X Games. Stashing my truck with a family acquaintance, I loaded my bike and equipment in Wazny's trailer and we headed west together to California. Along the way, we stopped to meet up with Chris Ridgway. He lives in Apple Valley, California, about 30 miles south of Barstow, on the edge of the Mojave Desert. It was hot, 100 degrees or more, and we spent a day practicing at Competitive Edge Motocross Park just southwest of Chris' home. Coming from Minnesota, I'm not accustomed to such intense heat, and my leg sweated so badly that I was afraid my socket and Moto Knee would slide off. Every three laps, I pulled off the track to remove my socket and pour out the sweat that had pooled in the bottom of my silicone leg liner. I worried that I wouldn't be able to complete an entire race in the Southern California heat, but luckily it's been milder near the coast since we've arrived in L.A.

Sara has flown out to meet me. So has her brother, Luke, along with my brother, Chris; his girlfriend; and my nephew, Tucker. A couple old friends from school have come out, too. I'm thrilled for the support but a little uneasy about Chris and Tucker being on hand. My family has seen me busted up in the hospital at my worst, and I want to spare them further anguish. Here I am putting myself in a high-risk situation again. Chris must be thinking, *What the heck is he doing?* I know he's scared to see me tackle the big jumps at X Games, aware that the dirt on a Supercross track is much harder and hurts more than a crash on snow. Chris quit motocross due to a series of injuries, and he seldom comes out to watch anymore. He's salty about the whole scene, so it means a lot to me for him to give a thumbs-up as I resume my career.

IT'S TAKEN SO MUCH EFFORT to learn to how to ride again and create equipment to make it possible as an amputee. I've had to develop a shifter, and a modified foot peg, and a prosthetic leg. Extremity Games gave me a taste of racing again and showed me what dedicated amputees can achieve. There are probably easier sports than motocross for an amputee to pursue and still have loads of fun. But motocrossers possess a stubbornness to develop whatever we need and to ride injured or in pain. The excitement of riding dirt bikes outweighs everything else. In addition to Wazny and Ridgway, I've met a group of awesome guys who are willing to do anything to adapt and get back on their dirt bikes. Their example has inspired me and given me hope to continue moving forward. I want to see how far I can take racing. So far, it's taken me to X Games, a point I'd never thought possible.

It's been a happy reunion seeing friendly faces from Extremity Games again out in L.A. One of the riders, Sampie Erasmus, uses a wheelchair, and he has traveled alone from South Africa. He lined up a bike in the States through fellow adaptive rider Jesse Gildea and wound up staying at Jesse's house for more than a month so that he could compete in Extremity Games and at X Games. To see such passion lights a flame in me and reminds me why we return to the racetrack following injuries and inevitable long recoveries. We do it for the positive, "never give up" energy we cannot find anywhere else.

On the shuttle from our hotel to athlete registration at the venue, I encounter Dan Gale and Kep Koeppe, who helped organize adaptive sports disciplines at Extremity Games. Sara and I met them two months ago in Michigan, and they made us feel welcome from the start. Compactly built, with dark hair and a permanent five-o'clock shadow, Dan is a chill, smooth personality, passionate about adaptive sports. He projects a West Coast surfer and skater vibe, never getting too wound up or excited about things. In the summers, he's an enthusiastic skateboarder. In wintertime, he snowboards with the same passion. Kep is one of Dan's snowboarding buddies from Colorado. Burly, with a mountain man beard and standing well over 6'0", he serves as a workhorse, doing whatever's necessary to assist adaptive athletes. Dan and Kep are both good people and seeing them again instantly bolsters my mood.

Dan introduces Sara and me to his girlfriend, Amy Purdy. Together they founded Adaptive Action Sports (AAS), a Colorado-based program that introduces disabled athletes to competition in snowboarding and skateboarding. Tall and fit, Amy wears her striking reddish-blonde hair long. What really stands out, though, are her long, beautiful legs. I'm attracted to them because Amy is a bilateral below-knee amputee. She contracted a blood infection when she was only 19 and lost both of her legs, her kidneys, and her spleen. Doctors gave her a 2 percent chance of survival. Now, Amy wears skinny jeans rolled mid-calf to reveal shiny carbon and titanium lower legs. She and I instantly strike up a conversation about prosthetics.

I've recently designed and built a new upgraded, stronger Moto Knee—two of them, in fact. I hand-fabricated half of the components but left the precision parts to a professional machine shop in Brainerd. I had blueprints made of all the parts. The results are much improved over my prototype, which I wore out from use. As Amy and I talk, I can't hide how excited I am to test my new equipment on the Supercross track.

WE GET THREE PRACTICE RUNS ON THE COURSE, and I'm determined to make them count. Heath Voss is a pro rider from Minnesota who will be competing in the main event, and he's offered to pace the adaptive riders during practice. We chase him around, getting acquainted with the pace needed to negotiate the super-sized features. It's a highlight to be on a challenging course with a pro racer from my home state whom I've admired. Voss' example helps me approach the big jumps as I work up the nerve to hit them on our final practice. When I finally go for the 90-foot triple, I come up short, casing the top of the landing—the front wheel lands over the knuckle, the rear tire comes up short, and the bulk of the impact is made with the frame of the bike. The force causes my face to bounce off the handlebars, stunning me and leaving me seeing stars. The chin guard of my helmet bears the brunt of the violence. Still, it hurts like hell, bringing my practice session to an abrupt end and leaving me with two enormous black eyes. With one day till the actual race, I'm now timid about hitting the big jump.

On race day, I show up to the Home Depot Center with black eyes and a stomach full of butterflies. *What the hell are we doing here? Look at this place.* It is hot and dusty in the arena, and we are given a short practice session, where I will try to overcome my nerves about the massive jumps. After a few laps, my leg has gotten sweaty and begins to slide around. I want to take the prosthesis off and dry the socket so that I won't have any problems during the race. Since my amputation, I sweat more easily. Simply walking around leaves me dripping. The human body cools through blood flow and skin. I've lost half my leg, so my circulation has been affected, and I have less surface area to cool me. Plus, my stump is sheathed in carbon fiber, which doesn't breathe. I always seem to be running a degree or two hotter than I did before amputation. People see me drenched and assume I'm not in good shape, but I'll start sweating while sitting still. I've heard from other amputees that it's a common condition.

I don't have much time, or any privacy, on the stadium floor. Sara uses an umbrella to shield me from all eyes in the crowd as I drop my pants in order to remove my leg and liner, dry them off, and put them back on again in time to climb on my bike and line up for the race. Because the X Games are broadcast live on ESPN, they run with the precision of a Swiss watch. If I'm not ready on time, officials will not hold the race for me, and I'll be left out. As if I wasn't nervous enough about the race, my heart rate and stress level rise even higher as I think I'm going to miss the start of my race with my pants down.

As I line up, Amy is parading with the start board, meaning there are only moments to go. Suddenly the gate drops, and I twist the throttle, beginning the intense familiarity of racing. Wheels spit dirt and engines scream, emitting puffs of gray smoke. I'm as serious and focused as I've ever been. Ridgway roars out front, grabbing the holeshot, and I'm holding onto the fourth spot as we round the first corner. I make up my mind to go for Ridgway, and try to reel him in. A couple laps into the five-lap race, I've picked my way into second place when I gun it over the 90-foot jump at the finish line, coming up a little short and landing hard. The impact breaks my carbon-fiber foot, a rigid but thin and lightweight design with a rubber foot-shaped covering. Carbon fiber doesn't fail completely. Instead, the foot folds, no longer stiff enough to support me. I had damaged the carbon fiber at practice a day ago and duct-taped it because I didn't have any backup components or prostheses.

Now I've made it worse. I look down and nearly come to a complete stop. There's no resistance when I put my weight on the foot. Standing on the peg, the foot flexes and slides off. I don't have time to think too much. I look up and see Ridgway pulling farther ahead and gun it after him. I've dropped back to third place behind George Hammel. Making awkward in-race adjustments, I carefully pick my way through the features and work my way past George into second place again. But every time I hit a jump, my foot slips from the peg. I can't close the distance to Ridgway while riding like this, and he crosses the finish line first, a full straightaway ahead of me.

Still, I manage to hold on for second place and the silver medal. So much has happened to me in a short time, and I swell with an enormous sense of accomplishment as I stand on the second platform of the podium and Amy slips the silver medal around my neck. Seven months ago, I was in the hospital, fresh from surgery.

In the aftermath, my phone pings with texts from friends and fellow racers who've watched the race on TV and are now offering their congratulations. A few mention that I might have had a chance to win if I kept my foot on the peg the entire race. I'm tempted to tell them: *No shit!*

Racing at X Games has been a thrill, but it's also spurred me to re-evaluate my prosthesis and some of its shortcomings. My latest Moto Knee has worked phenomenally, but my carbon-fiber foot requires the next step in adaptive componentry evolution. I'd turned over ideas for a new foot that would be better suited to riding dirt bikes and snowmobiles before X Games, but I didn't have time to tinker. Now I'm committed to making a foot suited to racing. My return to competition has also taught me that as an adaptive athlete, I not only need parts for my dirt bike, but I also need spare parts for my knee and foot. Chip was right about the limited durability of most prosthetic equipment when tested in the rugged world of racing. After my ordeal in L.A.,

I'm determined to build a better prototype. It's time to return home to the drawing table and the workshop—a decision that will begin my transformation to a full-blown entrepreneur at the head of a real business.

8

Back on Track

IN THE WEEKS AFTER MY X GAMES DEBUT, I'VE RETURNED TO WORK
for my stepfather, Rick, at his construction company. I already have a
couple of sponsors paying me better than what I'd been making before
my injury. Still, my dirt bike earnings don't cover the mountain of
medical bills from my accident, which have Sara worried sick. We're
staring at $1 million in medical bills. The benefit from the racing
community has made a big dent and allowed us to pay the deductible.
Insurance will cover most of what we owe, but there's uncertainty. A
friend of ours through snowmobiling works in the health insurance
industry. Sara has given her power of attorney and she's made all the
calls to providers to help sort out plans for payment. The financial
and emotional support of friends and co-workers has eased Sara's
burden. Meanwhile, she's been easing my burdens, supporting me as
I find my way back into racing. When I leave socks on the floor, she
says nothing. If I ask her for a blanket, she fetches it for me without
complaint. She's a nurse. She takes care of people for a living, but I
know the past nine months have worn Sara thin. I want her to know
how much I appreciate her and, for our second wedding anniversary

on July 20, just before X Games, I'd surprised Sara with a ring. I don't normally buy her jewelry, but it was a gesture of thanks for taking care of me, for loving me. It wasn't an expensive purchase but a very sincere gift that made Sara appreciate the moment and give me a long hug filled with soft tears.

I'm fortunate to be surrounded by a strong network of support. Driving to a job site one day, just the two of us in the cab of a truck, Rick asks, "Now what?" He means with my life. I tell him that I feel like a weight has been lifted from my shoulders and mention that I want to pursue some design and engineering projects.

Rick sees potential in me as a designer and offers to fund me during research and development on what he believes can be lucrative partnerships. I've been the shop guy, a kind of jack-of-all-trades for Rick and my mom's company each summer. I drive the semis, haul equipment. I'm a foreman on job sites where we install telephone communications cable underground with backhoes and directional drills. It's fun working outside with heavy machinery. I'm never bored with the work because my role is always roving within the company. In the shop, I serve as a maintenance guy, fixing equipment and fabricating new pieces. I've built a lot of construction equipment and components over the years. Rick sees me as a bright mind and a problem-solver. With his support, I can build anything I want, really. Rick tells me he thinks I can build something really cool, a prototype piece of construction equipment, and it could turn into a lot of money. He says he'll fund the research and development. The thought of turning the page from being a pro athlete and using my mind instead of my body is tempting, but my heart isn't in building construction equipment. I explain that with the design of my second prosthesis already underway, I'm committed to building something on my own, from the ground up—something that will help others like me who feel they've lost the sport they love. And now that I've seen what I can still do on a dirt bike, the possibility of a competitive career feels real. I tell Rick, "Thank you, I really mean it, but I have some other plans I want to work on for now."

"What the heck?" Rick says. "Why are you wasting time with racing?" Rick has always been considerate of my passion for riding—back when I worked for him after high school, he always made sure to provide the scheduling flexibility that allowed me to compete. But he also sees me as a potential asset to work full-time for his company. Riding in trucks to job sites, we've had long conversations about the downside of being a pro racer. Rick always points to the sport's career ceiling and considerable physical risks. He sees me pushing 30 and injured much of the time.

It's hard for others to understand, but I prefer the passion and company of fellow professional racers over working a typical day job. And without an athletic goal, I've always worried that I will fall apart, physically and mentally. Without a motive to get to the gym, I'm afraid I will become a lazy couch potato. It scares me. When I miss a month or two of competition to injury, new habits form. I easily rationalize that I have too many other responsibilities and tasks that need doing to spend my time on fitness. I require a coming race to actually get me to the gym, to ride my mountain bike, to cross-train. Without a real purpose, I won't work out. I won't load up my dirt bike in the back of my truck and go ride. Spending six hard years training for snocross has helped me build a routine that lends structure to my life. I love the routine.

I also think back to my conversation with Sara, when we talked about looking out for ourselves, forming our own two-person team. For all my career, I've been on someone else's program, biding my time for funding, waiting my turn for a slot to open on one of the premier outfits. But my accident has forced me to start over and reassess, to begin thinking that maybe it's time to live and race on my own terms.

Of course, I still worry about making it on my own—it feels much less stable without the considerable backing of a major team like Warnert Racing. So far, though, I've gotten good results on the track and chased down sponsors by being my own best advocate—cold-calling, working the phones, and networking. I have spent my entire racing career pursuing a position on a team that had the money to pay me the best wage. My destiny has always been tied to the way I fit into a team dynamic. I've always worked for someone else, waiting for owners to tap me on the shoulder and point me in the proper direction. My injury has forced me to re-examine my place in racing, changing my outlook. I've become more self-reliant because there's less of an existing framework for amputees. If I can run my own race program, I start to think maybe I can run my own business, too. Otherwise, I'll continue showing up for the day-to-day grind, punching in and punching out. That's never been what I've wanted for my life.

Sara and I attended the same high school, where she followed a more conventional path. She took classes that would allow her to attend college in order to get a degree in nursing so she could start her career. But by 16, once I got my driver's license, I began to build my life around racing. I attended school till 1 PM and worked nights at dirty, heavy metal-welding shops— building EZ Crusher machines, and fixing railroad cars for R.M. Johnson Rail Car repair—so that I could earn the money to support my passion for racing dirt bikes. By my senior year, I attended school for two hours each day before heading off to work. Sara was already at college and believed that's where I was headed, too. When I told her that I didn't plan on attending, it drove her crazy at first to think how uncertain my future would be without a college degree. We spent weekends together at the races, and I showed her my potential—my willingness to work hard, to pay my own way, to focus, and chase my dream. She could see in my smile the joy I derived from racing. She believed that if my racing career didn't pan out, I could fall back on my aptitude for building things. I'd been building things my entire life.

First, I was determined to make a go of racing. I believed I had the talent, but I had a lot to learn about what else it takes, chiefly the necessary funding. Many of the teams are family-run, with a son who races and receives most of the investment. It's not always the top athletes who wind up in the biggest trailer with the fastest equipment. You have to wait your turn and hope a slot opens up. I love the team structure and the sense of being part of a crew with a shared objective. But I was always with one of the smaller outfits until I finally signed with

Warnert. They have one of the most professional and well-run teams on tour. But even then, because I signed late to the team, I was relegated to one of the smaller fifth-wheel pickup trailers and just enough of a paycheck to make it almost worthwhile. I'd never reached my potential and earned the big deal I'd been chasing. I'd only gotten a taste before my accident and amputation. With adaptive racing, I've got another chance to approach my career differently. I've got an opportunity to do it on my terms.

BEFORE THE END OF SUMMER, I'd bought a mill and lathe for my garage workshop at home so that I no longer need to commute to the Fox shop. I begin cranking out a prototype foot in my garage, welcoming the challenge of striking out on my own and finding out what else I can build. My new foot design will be aluminum, and like the Moto Knee, it will utilize a Fox mountain bike shock, though smaller in size, to create the ankle resistance. With winter approaching and a return to riding snowmobiles, I will be standing on a flat running board, and my prosthetic foot will need more flex than the model I'm currently using for motocross.

In addition to coaching Team Warnert again, I'm hoping to compete in snocross at some point this season. The first race will take place on Thanksgiving weekend in Duluth, just down the road from St. Mary's Hospital, where I had my leg amputated. This race has been the kickoff to the race season since the mid-90s. I won't be competition-ready yet, but I will be there to support my teammates as a trackside performance coach.

Meantime, I've found success pursuing sponsors interested in my story of resilience and innovation. I've engineered my own recovery and returned to racing, and companies want to be associated with me. I've already gotten more media coverage than I had as a pro snocross racer, and my sponsors pay better than I earned before my amputation. A clothing company has agreed to give me racing gear. Amsoil, the oil company and title sponsor of the snocross series, will pay me cash to promote their brand. A new social media site called *doyouknowwhoiam.com* has launched to help famous entertainers share their music and videos. They've agreed to pay me to wear their URL on the sleeves of my racing jersey. It's a lot of letters to fit onto my arms and remain readable. Do YOU KNOW WHO I AM...? It might get awkward. Some will no doubt think I'm really vain. But, hey, they're paying me, and the money frees me to throw myself into racing and developing my prostheses. Most important, I'm having fun. As long as X Games continues to host adaptive events with TV coverage, there's a real opportunity to make a lucrative career of racing.

BY JANUARY, THE PROTOTYPE OF MY FOOT IS READY. It's been easier than developing the Moto Knee; it's a simple design with fewer parts and doesn't require the same precision. Still, it's cost me dozens of hours in my garage shop, and nearly $15,000 in parts, tooling, and equipment. My Moto Knee uses an adjustable 250 psi (pounds per square inch) mountain bike shock. The foot uses a smaller Fox mountain bike shock absorber to simulate the tension of an ankle joint. Compressed air creates resistance and regulates the stiffness in the joint. The assembly is covered in a black, foot-shaped open metal housing with a closed toe and a rubber sole. It looks pretty cool, and it's more streamlined and finished than my first attempt at creating a prosthesis in my prototype Moto Knee nine months ago. I've designed the foot to endure the rigors of racing, plus be customizable depending on which sport I'm doing. I can adjust shock absorption, swap out sole plates, and configure ankle positions. Because it can be tuned up to a variety of settings for use on dirt bikes and snowmobiles, I call it the "Versa Foot." Paired with my Moto Knee, I have a complete leg that's customizable to any race conditions.

I've been testing out my prostheses at Quadna Mountain with Team Warnert, where I've continued as a coach. I've spent increasing time with my teammates on my sled on the courses, readying in hopes of a competitive return. I'm not as fast as I was before my amputation, but the Versa Foot feels more natural than the carbon fiber foot I'd been using. I'd like to make my return to competition at Canterbury Park, in Shakopee, Minnesota, the third stop on the ISOC Tour. Shakopee has the biggest crowds. Located just outside the Twin Cities, on the grounds of a horse racing track, the massive grandstand will be filled with thousands of fans. I won't be able to match my old pace and keep up in the pro class, so I've petitioned to compete in the snowmobile Pro Vet class (typically reserved for riders 30 and older). I'm only 28, so the matter is put up for discussion among the various teams. No one objects, and I'm given special dispensation to compete with the vets, many of them former stars of the pro class who've aged out or transitioned to another phase of life that doesn't allow for the full-time commitment of the pros.

In the run-up, ISOC makes my comeback a pillar of its promotion, and the media covering the races focuses on my return. I'm getting written up in the magazines and online, and at the track I sit for interviews on the broadcast. It feels so good to be welcomed back. Wearing my Moto Knee and Versa Foot, I make my way among the crowds and into the pits, where I run into old friends and rivals. The support and encouragement are genuine. Several people note that I've been dealt lemons and made lemonade. But there are some misunderstandings that lead to awkward encounters. A common misconception concerns the money from my benefit. Most people know I've made a chunk of money, and some assume I've spent it on my dirt bikes and new vehicles. I find myself clarifying matters again and again: *No, man, that's still in the bank,* or *That's been drawn on to build a new prosthetic leg.* One retired racer says that losing my leg has actually helped my career. I nod and agree with him, but the comment rubs me the wrong way. I'm thinking, *Dude, no; just losing a leg doesn't make this all happen.* I hear a variant on this when another pro snocross rider and I catch up. "That accident set you up pretty good, didn't it?" he says. "Look at all the attention you're getting now."

"Yeah," I say, caught off guard. "I'm doing what I can to make the most of it."

I know he doesn't mean anything negative by his remarks; he's just offering the perspective of a professional rider grinding on the tour to make a name for himself. He sees the media attention I'm getting and perhaps thinks it all owes to my injury. Everyone knows that I've lost my leg. But hardly anyone has seen the hard work required to get back to a place where I could even think about racing again. I had to physically recover from an injury that nearly killed me, overcome the mental challenges associated with becoming an amputee and being labeled a handicapped person, and then develop my own leg and learn to ride again. Then, on top of everything else, I've had to build sponsorship relationships just to afford to be here. Some of the comments annoy me and stick with me. Yeah, I'm missing my leg and there's some truth to the suggestion that it's led to increased attention. But I know that being different will get me attention for maybe five minutes. What I do with my opportunity to compete again will determine my staying power. I'm not looking for a handout or for pity. I intend to earn any attention I get with my performance on the track.

SITTING AT THE START GATE ON MY SLED, engine rumbling beneath me, I await the green flag and the start of my return to racing. To my right, the grandstand is packed with spectators. In front of me, thick mounds of snow have been shaped into a tight stadium-style course with big jumps and tight turns winding around the infield of the horse racing track. Around me, seven riders straddle their sleds, poised to crank the throttle and grab the holeshot heading into the first turn. It's time to test myself and my prosthetic leg setup. My heart is beating in my throat just as much or more than it did when I was lined up with the pros. My palms are sweaty, and my nerves are revving faster than my engine.

Once the green flag flies, the nerves disappear and I'm focused on the course ahead of me. We're underway, engines buzzing like a swarm of angry bees. The race starts well. The Versa Foot feels natural and proves more durable than a carbon fiber foot, and the ability to tune the resistance and size makes a difference. I've learned that having a smaller foot length, front to back, is beneficial for finding my stance on the snowmobile's running board. The shorter foot, about 25 centimeters long (equivalent to a size 8 shoe) allows me to rotate my leg as I lean off the side of my snowmobile in the corners to help counterbalance the machine so that the g-forces caused by whipping through the corners don't cause the sled to tip. The new design also allows proper body mechanics during impacts from jumps and rough terrain. As I hit a bump or land off a big jump, the ankle compresses while keeping the sole of the foot flat on the running board. This allows the center of the knee to shift forward over the foot—and allows me to keep my balance.

The race is humming along as smoothly as I could have hoped when, a few laps in, I hit a hole in the track with a jarring thud and the impact snaps my prosthetic leg. One of the adaptors on my Moto Knee has broken clean off, leaving the leg flopping around in my pants leg, freaking out one of the track workers as I roar past. I can't let it bother me too much. I'm in the middle of a race, and I hang on to finish and make the final. Luckily, I've learned from my experience at the Summer X Games. I've brought plenty of parts in my trailer to repair my prostheses and get ready for the next race. I don't land on the podium this time, but I've shown to myself that I belong among the top riders in my class. I know that with more experience using my prostheses I can charge to the front of the pack.

FORTUNATELY, I WON'T HAVE TO WAIT LONG for another opportunity to prove myself. Later in the month I travel to Aspen to compete in adaptive snocross at Winter X Games. Being at Winter X Games this time provides an entirely new experience compared to the previous seven I've competed in on my snowmobile. This is my chance at snocross redemption. I've never had great results at Winter X. My best finish was ninth. I could never get all the pieces of the puzzle to line up at the same time. I either had poor performance from my machine, poor performance from myself, or just straight up bad luck. This time is different.

I know I have the skills and experience to outrace any other adaptive snocross rider. I was one of the top pro riders in the world when my accident happened, and nobody else in the adaptive field has near the experience I do. This race isn't about me beating my competitors. This race is about me getting on the course at X Games after I thought I would never be there again. ESPN has filmed another feature with me leading into the competition, which airs several times before our race, announcing my return.

The racecourse is incredible this year, too, amplifying my excitement. In true X Games fashion, the course features are on steroids compared to all those on the Amsoil Tour. In Aspen this year there's a 120-foot double jump and a 180-degree vertical wall berm, which they've coined the "Talladega Turn" after a similar setup at the famous Talladega Superspeedway NASCAR track in Alabama. The course crew used the "Pipe Dragon" machine that cuts and shapes the ski and snowboard halfpipe on the slopes of Buttermilk Mountain. The result: a berm 18 feet tall, including a 4-foot vertical section. Riders must carry a ton of speed to get up on the top rail. The turn is fun to ride, and I smile from ear to ear with every lap. The g-forces from the speed keep the machine, and me, pressed to the vertical wall. I feel my body being smashed down into the seat and handlebars. *This is frickin' awesome! I love the X Games!* I cheer out loud as I rip through another lap.

During our riders meeting, the snowmobile sport organizer at X Games, Joe Duncan, whom I've known pretty much from the start of my race career, mentions that adaptive riders will not be permitted to hit the two big double jumps on the track, for safety reasons. Although bummed, I understand his reasoning.

Still, I can't quite let it go. Following our first practice, when I kept looking at the big double jumps, longing to test myself on them, I talk with Joe to see if I can take a lap and huck them once, just for fun. Joe looks at me and chuckles. "I suppose, Schultzy, you can go out right after your practice and before the pro group."

I am so pumped with excitement that I ask my good friend and previous competitive rival in the pro ranks T.J. Gulla, one of the top riders at X Games, if he wants to take a lap with me so I can pace him over the big kickers, to get his timing and speed right. He says, yes, of course. In the moments before we go out for the lap, I'm so overwhelmed by nervous excitement that my leg starts twitching and bouncing. *Let's go!*

We cruise halfway around the course together and exit the corner before the biggest jump on the course. Pinching the throttle flat to the handlebar, I accelerate up the 10-foot-tall face of the jump, and soar 30-plus feet above the ground, touching down on the snow again with a whoosh after traveling 120 feet from where I started. I've still got the skills I had before my injury needed to tackle the gnarliest terrain. Sharing such an awesome moment with one of my previous pro competitors has been so gratifying. T.J. feels it, too, and stops after the lap and gives me the biggest high-five.

The good vibes continue into competition. I pull a great holeshot and then just charge forward with the goal of showing the crowd and other riders what I'm still capable of on my snowmobile. By the end of the six-lap race, I have a commanding lead to finish on top. Standing at the base of Buttermilk Mountain, atop of the podium on my self-made prostheses, a gold medal around my neck, I gaze up at snow-covered trails snaking down the mountain that have been completely transformed into a playground for this world-class competition.

One year earlier, I was watching Winter X Games on TV from St. Cloud, learning to walk on my new prosthesis, depressed to think I'd never return here, or to racing. Now I'm back, and on my own terms—and it feels better than I could have ever dreamed it would.

MY SUCCESS ON SNOW INSPIRES ME to dream a little more. If I can build a leg out of necessity, what else can I create? What are my limits? And who gets to decide what they are? An idea has been bubbling in my brain. So many prostheses are geared for everyday use. Few are suited to sports. There's a model made for skiing, and another for riding bikes, but nothing specific to motorsports, and none that I think offer the versatility of the Moto Knee and Versa Foot. While at Extremity Games and X Games, I noted that many of the amputees competing in wakeboarding, mountain biking, motocross, and snocross were wearing everyday mechanical knee systems. Jim Wazny's was a little more rugged and versatile for hard use. Built by Ossur, a company based in Iceland and one of the largest manufacturers of prosthetics, his Mauch model knee features adjustable hydraulics for dampening shock. It absorbs impact well, but there's no spring pressure to help the joint extend. I think I've built something better suited to riding a dirt bike or snowmobile. Now I wonder if I can build a company to sell my creations. I wouldn't have to work for anyone else. I would have 100 percent control over my time and labor. I would have a career, and it would complement racing. I'll need to come up with a plan, but I'm not constrained by any boxes that an employer wants to place me and my ambitions in. My only constraints will be time, money, and my willingness to work. A little research and consultation with Chip reveals that Otto Bock, out of Germany, and Ossur dominate the prosthetics marketplace. In the U.S., one of the largest manufacturers is Freedom Innovations, based in Utah. Maybe there's room for me, too.

9

In Business

Sara and I roll into Millington, Michigan, over Memorial Day weekend in 2010 for our return to Extremity Games. Loaded into the trailer behind my truck is a new dirt bike, a lighter 250cc Honda that's easier for an amputee to handle. I've equipped the bike with a modified foot peg system to accommodate my Versa Foot. I've been training on the bike all spring at my home track outside Brainerd while spending weeks refining the foot peg in my shop at home. Bolting it on the bike, I would drive out to the track, climb on for a ride to test it, and realize it wouldn't work, or worse, break it. Unable to ride, I'd return to the shop to fabricate a new modified peg. I just wanted to ride, but doing so as an adaptive competitor has meant making unfamiliar, time-consuming adjustments.

Another aspect of my new reality as a rider: I regularly begin sweating before I'm completely dressed. My liner on my stump fills with sweat and slides around, forcing me to undress to drain it and start over. I'm trapped in a constant cycle of getting my equipment on, beginning to ride, then stopping either to fix something or take off my leg and dump the sweat. Riding requires so much work at times that I feel like I'm beating my head against a wall in my determination to continue. The upside is that even with all the struggles of testing, I've been improving.

Last year at Extremity Games, I was just happy to be back riding. This year I expect to be the best. Chris Ridgway expects to be the best, too. He has a chip on his shoulder. When we're talking face-to-face, everything is cordial. I've had fun riding with him in his hometown of Apple Valley, California, in the hot high desert east of Los Angeles. But underneath that placid exterior wheels are turning, like with two old gunfighters eyeing each other. We are headed for an epic showdown.

Ridgway has years of pro experience, and I can tell his bikes are all dialed in and in top performance. But he's on the tail end of his riding career, and it appears he doesn't have a whole lot of sponsor support to allow him to pursue competing at the level I'm going for. The more I talk to him, the more I'm convinced his lack of sponsors probably results from his salty attitude.

I'm treating motocross as if I'm a professional athlete, only now I run my own program, create my own sponsor partnerships, and only compete in select races. I'm the owner of my one-rider team and the crew chief working together with Sara to continue chasing my dream as a professional competitor. Through hustle, cold-calling, and telling my story, I've landed a stable of sponsors—Loctite, makers of industrial adhesives, which I use with my prostheses; Amsoil, manufacturer of synthetic motor oil and the title sponsor of the snocross tour; Fox, which provides the shocks used in my prostheses; and Fly Racing, an apparel and riding gear company.

Another sponsor: Chip's clinic, Prosthetic Laboratories. Chip facilitates my racing, which will raise the profile of his practice. He says that if I can fly 40 feet through the air wearing one of his sockets, then other patients will reason that they can use one of Chip's creations to safely walk across the street. Chip is not an amputee, and therefore cannot test the sockets and prostheses himself. We have an arrangement: when a new product hits the market, he'll often have me demo, say, a new foot, or a socket, so that I can provide valuable feedback before he recommends the product to other clients.

Chip and I talk every few weeks, having developed a relationship founded on more than just our shared interest in prosthetics. Chip is an outdoorsman, and often we talk about the latest elk he's shot or a new rifle he's bought and recently sighted in. Meeting other amputees through the adaptive racing world, I'm learning not everyone has been as lucky as I've been to find a prosthetist who supports their ambitions and can create a perfectly fitting socket. Our rapport will inform the way I deal with patients once I begin to get my company up and running.

Until I do, I earn from all my sponsors as much as I did during my pro snocross days. Still, Sara and I continue to live paycheck to paycheck, and she picks up extra nursing shifts when possible to help us pay our bills.

IN THE FIRST HEAT AT EXTREMITY GAMES, I'm prepared to put all my practice into play. I roar out of the gate, seizing the holeshot. Ridgway isn't about to cede his status so easily. Not even half a lap in, he rides right over a berm on the inside line of a tight left-hand corner and T-bones me, punting me completely off the course. I scramble back on my bike and roar back in the race, but I'm too far behind and cannot catch the leaders. I was prepared to establish myself as the man to beat, and instead I've finished out of the top three. After the heat, I hear from others that Ridgway slammed me on purpose. I thought he'd simply gotten squirrely coming over one of the features into the corner. "Nope," another rider who witnessed the collision tells me. "He straight-up cleaned you out."

What an asshole! I act as though I don't take it personally, knowing that I'll have another chance to beat him in X Games qualifying. When I do, I expect this will grind on him. Wazny and all the other adaptive racers see how I've come in with a professional manner and how I threaten Ridgway's supremacy. I'm convinced Ridgway sees it, too. Ridgway is in his early forties, and I have youth on my side, with good support and fresh, well-tuned bikes. To me, it's obvious a changing of the guard is imminent.

OTHER CHANGES ARE IMMINENT, TOO. With the Moto Knee and my prototype for a new foot, I officially and unceremoniously found BioDapt, a portmanteau of *biology* and *adaption*, in order to sell production prostheses to other adaptive athletes. For more than a year, my mind has been turning over the idea of founding my own business, being my own boss, and retaining complete control over my career. I realize that I can do anything I want; it's only a matter of time, money, and effort. I'm ecstatic about the possibilities. For now, though, they are just that—possibilities. I have no customers, but by July 2010 I file my articles of incorporation to federal and state tax authorities. I now officially have a corporation and a tax ID number as a way to separate the accounting for all the money I'm spending on development. I haven't begun advertising my equipment other than by telling my story in the media and to sponsors. I'm looking forward to the attention and exposure that will come with competing in Supercross again at Summer X Games later in the month.

IN JULY 2010, two months after our run-in at Extremity Games, Ridgway and I are bound to settle the score at X Games, this time on another mammoth track inside the historic Los Angeles Memorial Coliseum, the city skyline looming to the north. The first ever motocross race inside a stadium was held at the L.A. Coliseum in 1972. It was called the Super Bowl of Motocross, and its success ultimately led to the development of Supercross, the most popular form of dirt bike racing. Since then, the Coliseum has hosted some of the most iconic races in the history of the sport, along with the biggest crowds. I'm thrilled to be part of the tradition.

X Games organizers have built a track for the ages. The gate starts at the concourse level, and immediately the track descends 120 feet to the stadium floor, where there's a massive set of double jumps. I'm the only adaptive rider able to dial them in, which gives me at least a half-second per lap advantage. Then it's back up to the concourse level, where dirt wends through 13-foot-wide arches at one end of the stadium. Maybe it's the venue, or the moment, but I feel better mentally and physically than I have on my dirt bike since my accident. I've sat for video interviews all summer in the lead-up to X Games, and I do more once in L.A. I sense my professional racing career ramping up and envision great things happening with BioDapt.

My showdown with Ridgway fizzles when he pulls out of the race, citing a knee injury from coming up short on a jump in the second practice. On one hand, I'm bummed I don't get to line up and do battle on the race track, but on the other hand, without Ridgway in the field, my pace will be a notch above the other competitors, putting me much closer to the possibility of winning gold.

ON RACE DAY, the pit board goes sideways and about three to four seconds later the gate drops. I release my clutch and accelerate forward but this time I get buried in the pack as we leave the gate, and I'm in about fourth or fifth place as we make it to the bottom of the downhill start section. I put my head down and work my way past one rider, two riders, and then another just as we finish the first lap. This is my moment to take the lead while launching over the biggest set of jumps on the course. After practice I was fairly confident with sending it big over the back-to-back super-kicker tabletops, but my heart rate slams into overdrive as I grab a handful of throttle and accelerate up the 12-foot-tall, nearly vertical jump face. As I leave the ground and begin to float through the air, I pass over the lead rider, Dave Turner, who's below. My heart suddenly stops as I think about the possibility of actually landing on him. "Oh shit!" I yell into my helmet, more to myself because there's no way he will hear me above the track noise. "Hold your line, Dave!"

As I descend and impact the ground, I've made the pass, landing a few feet in front and just to the side of Dave's bike. I am now in the lead on my way to my first Summer X Games gold medal, basking in the setting as I buzz through the Coliseum's stately arches and columns, soaring above the field where USC football plays its home games, where Super Bowls have been contested, past stands where fans from around the world packed to cheer athletes during the Summer Olympics in 1932 and 1984. In 1973, Evel Knievel launched his Harley-Davidson successfully over 50 cars at the Coliseum. Now it's my turn for a moment of glory. But with the white flag signaling one lap to go in the race, I launch off the dirt from one of the massive jumps, the same 80-footer I'd used to make the pass for the lead. This time, my acceleration is slightly low and I come up just shy of the landing transition. I hear a smacking sound as my Moto Knee joint compresses from the impact, bending a component. The result: I cannot straighten my leg.

With the knee damaged, I cannot stand on the foot peg. Every time I try, my knee remains bent and my foot slides off the peg. To the crowd, it looks like I'm fatigued and fading at the end of the race. Glancing down, it's actually that the push rod controlling my knee mechanism is bent 90 degrees, putting me in a permanent crouch. I don't know what my competitors think. I glance over my shoulder and I have a straightaway lead, roughly six seconds over Todd Thompson, which is an eternity in Supercross under normal circumstances. But being unable to stand is not normal, and sitting the entire final lap is no way to ride my fastest. I've got a lot of features to negotiate before the finish, including the technical rhythm sections and the big kickers that have helped me gain time over the field.

The final lap feels excruciatingly long and intense. As I approach the checkers at the finish, I finally dart a look over my shoulder. *Oh, shit!* Todd Thompson is on me, a mere bike length behind. I can hear him, feel him, and finally see him—there he is! But we've run out of track, roaring past the checkered flag. I've managed to hang on for the win—my first gold medal in motocross at X Games. I am ecstatic, out of breath, and *so* pumped with my performance. With my knee bent, I cannot get off my bike, instead sitting in the saddle for post-race interviews. I hope no one notices. The win is sweet, but the scenario is not ideal as an advertisement for my new prosthetics business.

10

Two Good Legs

ELK RIVER IS JUST A 45-MINUTE DRIVE NORTH OF MINNEAPOLIS. AT the end of December 2010, I host an adaptive snowmobile clinic here, at a new venue called ERX (Elk River Extreme) Motor Park, a hotbed for powersports, featuring a winding dirt track for motocross and off-road trucks in the summer months. In the winter season, ERX focuses on snocross racing on Thursday nights and opens to practice a few days a week, making the venue a great destination for teaching other amputees. I'm no longer coaching with Team Warnert. I cannot afford the time and focus required now that I'm trying to launch a prosthetics business and training more on my dirt bike and snowmobile in hopes of competing in increasing events as a professional racer.

There aren't many adaptive riders competing with me at a high level. I want to help others learn to ride, and share some of my racing knowledge, in hopes of elevating the entire class. Hopefully some of these riders will be inspired to believe they can do it, too.

A big part of my success owes to my Moto Knee and Versa Foot, and I'm hopeful that showcasing my prosthetics to other amputees will demonstrate how well my equipment works and help BioDapt take off as a business. At Extremity Games and X Games, I've been around amputees in a situation like mine, but there are crucial differences in our equipment. My Moto Knee allows me to stand on my running board or the pegs on my dirt bike, giving me an advantage over conventional walking prosthetic designs.

Jim Wazny is on hand at ERX Motorpark, too, helping teach aspiring adaptive racers. He's become a good friend, and Sara and I have grown close with him, his wife, and his kids. He's watched as I've developed new iterations of the Moto Knee but remained cool to giving it a try. As an amputee, competitor, and future prosthetic technician, Wazny can provide valuable feedback. Others in adaptive racing have seen how well my design works, but Wazny acts skeptical. My early prototypes didn't look very impressive. Some can't look past how the Moto Knee is bulkier than other models and heavier when walking around. But standing or sitting on a snowmobile or motorcycle, you don't feel the extra weight. And watching me ride shows how much better my design functions for racing.

I've been working up the nerve to ask Wazny to test the Moto Knee. Here at the clinic, I finally do.

"My system works really good," he says, dismissively. "I've been using it a long time." He wears one of the more advanced adjustable hydraulic walking knees called a Mauch. Made by Ossur, the Mauch is an everyday model meant for active users. But Wazny is more than just an active user; he's a professional athlete. I'm confident my Moto Knee will be much better for him than what he's been using. "We're here just riding, practicing," I counter. "Just give it a try."

"Okay" he says, finally relenting. "I'm tired of you talking about it."

He straps on my knee for a couple of practice laps. "This thing is funky," he says when he returns. "It's bucking me all over the place. It's really uncomfortable."

I persuade him to ride for another 10 minutes to give it a fair shot. From across the track, I can see him stand up and balance, riding smoothly over rough terrain. When he returns, I tell him to take the

Moto Knee off. "Take a couple laps on your other leg you've been riding and let me know."

With his old leg on, Wazny roars off and makes it three-quarters of a lap before slowing to look over at me, shaking his head. He rides back over to where I'm standing trackside. "This thing sucks," he says. "I want your leg back."

This is a cool moment of validation. Wazny is the first to test my equipment. And he's about to become the first customer. I end up building Wazny a knee and sell it to him for $1,500, my bare-bones cost in parts and labor. It's a sponsorship opportunity for BioDapt, and he'll give me valuable exposure and feedback. Wazny is a born talker, and I know he will spread the word at X Games and elsewhere. My knee is serial No. 1. Wazny's is No. 2. I have a client now. I've always believed in my ability to build a better prosthesis for dirt bikes and snowmobiles. I'm thrilled someone else finally believes, too. BioDapt is officially in business.

ONE MONTH LATER, IN JANUARY 2011, I'm back at Winter X Games. Every year I get goosebumps when rolling into Aspen after dark and gazing up at the sprawling competition venue under the lights on Buttermilk Mountain—the enormous halfpipe, big air jump, and slopestyle course for skiers and snowboarders, along with the snocross track. In the athlete lounge, I mingle with Olympians and the best of the best in these winter sports. Outside, everywhere you go there are TV cameras, interviews underway, a buzz from the crowds, and massive LED screens on the mountainside showing the action. It never gets old.

One afternoon I'm signing autographs at the base of the mountain at a table set up by Loctite, one of my sponsors, when I run into Dan Gale and Amy Purdy. Sara and I have become close friends with Dan and Amy, and we all look forward to seeing each other several times a year at events. Dan tells me about an adaptive snowboarder, a wounded veteran, who rides for his and Amy's team at World Cup and national events. "I've got this snowboarder, Keith," Dan says. "He's been riding for years on an XT-9, a sport knee developed for skiing, but I think you should talk to him about your knee for snowboarding."

"Send him over," I say.

This is how I meet Keith Deutsch, an animated little guy with a goatee and shaggy black hair standing straight up in a tangled mess.

"Hey, what up?" he says when we meet at the autograph table, launching into a fast-talking monologue that calls to mind a California surfer. "So, I've heard you've got this knee. Think it will work for snowboarding?"

I ask what prosthesis he's using to snowboard now. "How does that work?" I ask, as we chat for about 15 minutes.

I'm optimistic the Moto Knee will be suited to snowboarding, but I want to test it myself first. The only problem: I've ridden a snowboard maybe once or twice in my entire life. My wintertime focus was snocross and nothing else.

I've been wakeboarding and skiing, but not seriously in years. I skied up until sixth grade and was later a liftie at Powder Ridge, but I've only put on a pair of skis a handful of times since. I've already tried skiing with my Moto Knee and Versa Foot setup and know that it will work. Sara is a dedicated skier and has urged me to get back on the mountain. I've always worried about getting hurt and wrecking my snowmobile season. I tell Keith that I'll try the knee out on a board and call him if it works well.

At home, I acquire a snowboard from my brother-in-law Luke and head out to Powder Ridge to start a new sport from scratch. Can I ride a board with my Moto Knee and Versa Foot? I'm excited to find out what my equipment and I are capable of. At first, the answer appears to be no. Every time I try to engage the toe edge of the board, the foot isn't stiff enough and I slide out, or I can't seem to keep the board pointed in the right direction. I'm all twisted and counter-rotated; I look like a beginner who only has one leg. Seriously, it's frustrating.

I make a few tweaks and calibrations and return to Powder Ridge four times before the Moto Knee, Versa Foot, and my skills begin to click. I'm no longer sliding out on every turn on my toe edge, and I can actually go in the direction I intend. Sara and Luke rip around on skis while I teach myself to slide down the hill sideways and occasionally link turns together. I'm no good at snowboarding, but at least I know the equipment will work. It's just a matter of learning to ride and calibrating the foot correctly, as I've learned to do for a range of sports. All that's left to do now is call Keith Deutsch and ask when a good time would be to try the Moto Knee.

A FEW MONTHS LATER, in April, Sara and I drive to Copper Mountain in Colorado, 75 miles west of Denver and 9,000 feet up in the Rocky Mountains. Keith is in town with the Adaptive Action Sports team for nationals. The resort village is thick with condominiums, and we show up late in the evening at Keith's, where he's staying with a group of other riders.

A smiling Keith ushers us inside, where maybe a dozen adaptive snowboarders have crashed in a space meant for half as many. I'm not sure how many people are staying there, but it's a big group based on the dripping jackets and snow pants hanging from every available surface. The floor is wet from boots and boards stacked haphazardly by the door. Gear bags and outerwear are strewn everywhere. A faint odor of Colorado herb mixes with the stink of gear, socks, and boots soggy from a long day of riding. Confronted with every stereotype of the snowboarding lifestyle, Sara and I look at each other, wondering what we've gotten ourselves into. We're both outsiders in this world of snowboarding, and neither of us is into the herbal party scene.

The plan is to get Keith set up with my equipment so that we can catch one of the first chairs up the mountain early tomorrow morning. I'm eager to get down to business and ask Keith to see his current configuration.

He retrieves a socket with the knee still wrapped in snow pants and the boot attached to the foot. The whole system is soaking wet from riding earlier in the day, and unlike anything I've ever seen. I grab hold and start to take it apart, first trying to remove the boot.

I unlace the strings and tug to separate the boot from the prosthetic foot. When the boot doesn't budge, I use all the force I can muster. Finally wrenching the boot free, debris flies loose and showers the floor with wooden wedges, steel fragments and dirt, releasing a rotten stench of rusted metal and whatever else had dropped in there over the last few months of riding.

My hands and the carpet are stained orange from rusty water. "Oh, my God!" I say, looking up at Keith. "When was the last time you had this off?"

"I don't know," he says, shrugging. "Last season sometime."

All the melted snow has festered inside the boot for an entire season. The foot appears solid, but wood and metal shims wedged underneath to prop the foot into proper alignment have scattered on the floor. It's clear Keith and I have different standards of care and maintenance when it comes to our prosthetic equipment. He seems to be sort of winging it. Okay, maybe totally winging it, while I'm more obsessed with order and precision, an attitude honed during my career as a professional athlete. I inspect all my equipment daily, and I'm meticulous with all my components. Keith hasn't had his boot off his prosthetic leg in months. Bolts are loose. He and his roommates will compete in nationals in a few days. They are part of an adaptive snowboarding World Cup series, and I know Dan and Amy to be serious about snowboarding, too. So far, though, I've only glimpsed a loose operating side of the sport.

I swap out my leg for Keith's, and we agree to hit first chair in the morning to test it all out. If he can ride on the prosthesis he's been using, rusty setup and all, I know he'll be able to ride on my meticulously tuned equipment. Still, as I step out of the cluttered and stifling atmosphere of the condo into the Colorado mountain night, I take a deep breath of bracing air. I'm not a snowboarder, and I'm apprehensive about Keith's feedback.

IN THE MORNING, I step outside into the first rays of Colorado sunshine rising over the mountains and remind myself to breathe.

I'm still nervous about how the Moto Knee and I will perform on the soaring steeps of the Rockies. I've never ridden anything bigger than the hills of Minnesota, and now I'm practically straddling the Continental Divide. I start on skis so I can keep up. We ride a chair up the mountain, excitement building as we climb higher above the base area, higher than anything I've experienced at Powder Ridge. Like me, Keith is what snowboarders call "regular-footed;" in other words, he rides with his left foot in the forward binding. The difference is that Keith's prosthesis is on his right leg, or his back foot when it comes to snowboarding. Like me, he's an above-knee amputee. I'm excited but uncertain how Keith will take to the Moto Knee.

His skills are obvious instantly. Off the lift, he carves right and left, slides, spinning 180 degrees, just flowing, blowing my mind with how well he's riding on something I've built.

Keith leans into turns and flexes the knee. When we meet at the bottom of the run, he smiles and gives me a high-five, excitable as ever. I'm smiling, too. Sara snaps a photo of Keith on her phone. He looks delighted.

"I haven't snowboarded this good since I had two good legs," he boasts.

This is the feedback I've been dreaming about. My hunch about my equipment has been correct: it's not just for me; it will help others achieve their goals, too.

We ride together for two days, getting to know one another. Keith was a staff sergeant in the Army, his squad's automatic weapon (SAW) gunner. In August 2003, three months after arriving in Iraq, he was riding in the rear of a truck on patrol, a big machine gun with 40 pounds of ammo in his grip, when his convoy came under fire. Keith returned fire, and in the ensuing battle, he lost his right leg above the knee in a rocket-propelled grenade attack on the truck.

He had been stationed in Colorado with the 244th Engineer Battalion of the U.S. Army before he was deployed. He was an avid and accomplished snowboarder and had earned a certification as an instructor. I find out that his family is from Minnesota, too, where they own a construction company. Keith grew up in New Prague, just over an hour away from me, south of Minneapolis. He's a country boy and a hunter. We're not that different after all. He's a free spirit, a little on the wild side and never hesitant to take a chance. Behind it all, he has a kind and thoughtful personality. He and I hit it off, and I feel as grateful to have met him as he is to have a new prosthesis.

Keith's first attempts to ride his board as a recent amputee were heart-breaking. He hadn't only lost his leg but an activity he loved, too. His first job outside of his military service, before he'd been deployed to Iraq, had been as a snowboarding instructor, and much of his identity was wrapped up in the sport. Maybe he would never shred the same way as an amputee, but he was stubborn, and he stuck with snowboarding. Just like with my peg leg, his walking prosthesis wouldn't straighten once bent, making riding nearly impossible. So he cut the shovel end off of a spade and stuffed the sawed-off portion of the handle into his boot. He would reach down with his right hand while riding and use the protruding shovel handle like a lever to straighten his knee when needed. It wasn't pretty, and Keith got a lot of looks and questions about the shovel handle, but with that kind of ingenuity and some duct tape, he'd gotten back on his board and was ripping around the mountain the next winter after his amputation. Hearing this story, I'm beginning to understand Keith and the puzzling low-tech modifications I'd discovered when first taking apart his leg in the condo.

After one day on skis, I pull out my board with a custom binding system for my Versa Foot. I want to hone my riding under more challenging conditions while I'm in Colorado. By the time Sara and I leave Copper Mountain, I'm competent at snowboarding and Keith has committed to ordering a knee through his prosthetist at Walter Reed Army Medical Hospital in Bethesda, Maryland.

WEEKS LATER, WHEN THE ORDER COMES IN from Walter Reed, it's actually for two Moto Knees—one for Keith, and one for another veteran and snowboarder with Adaptive Action Sports named Wayne.

I hadn't even met Wayne, but Keith must have talked him into it. These are BioDapt's first actual sales for profit: two $6,157.00 orders. Keith's knee is serial No. 55003. The sale feels like a triumph, and Sara and I hope that with a snowboarder or two as a customer, BioDapt will make more sales to practitioners of the sport.

Anticipating further sales, I manufacture parts for 10 knees during 2011, and sell eight: four to the military and four to others who've seen me competing at X Games. I quickly learn that there's more to being an entrepreneur than I initially considered. In addition to designing and manufacturing new prostheses, I must learn to run a business. My mother, who does the books for her and my stepfather's construction company, gives me a tutorial on Quickbooks accounting software. I muddle through hours of learning graphic design programs so that I can design brochures, fliers, and user manuals for the knee. I've always enjoyed drawing, but it never really had a purpose. Now, drawing blueprints for my equipment and creating detailed images for manuals and marketing material, I'm having fun with the challenge.

Money from sponsors funds my racing. Income from BioDapt helps, but Sara and I have little savings. We're in our late twenties and want to start paying off debts. Sara has some substantial student loans. We have a mortgage and car payments. The year before I was injured, I had just bought my first-ever brand-new vehicle. It was a 2008 metallic-silver extended-cab Chevy Silverado. I was proud of this purchase, but my fancy new truck also comes with a fancy monthly payment.

Sara continues to work full-time as a labor and delivery nurse at the local hospital, picking up double shifts when available because we remain unsure where my business is headed. We are about to find out that my budding relationship with the military will soon mean a flood of orders.

11

War Zone

THE PLANE LANDS AT A COMMERCIAL AIRPORT IN SOUTHWEST
Germany with a thud, turbines roaring in reverse to slow us down.
It's July 8, 2011, and I'm headed overseas with Robi Powers, a veteran
who's an emcee at snocross events. Powers has begun a program called
American300 Warriors Tour, escorting Olympians and professional
athletes to military bases around the world on goodwill and mentoring
missions. This time, he's asked snowmobile freestyle rider Levi
LaVallee—one of my old Minnesota buddies from the snocross tour—
Levi's crew chief, Glen Kafka, and me to accompany him to Europe and
the Middle East on what he's called the XHeavy Metal Tour. We will
spend 12 days in the Middle East, visiting troops.

We've all known each other for several years on tour. Levi is a year
younger than I am. He stands about five-and-a-half-feet tall, but he's
one tough little dude. Both he and I started our careers around the
same time, in the late '90s. We've become close friends even though
we were direct competitors while working up through the semi-pro
and pro ranks. Levi is a wild man on the race track, unafraid of testing
the limits, and he's always the first rider to send it big. He's recently

made the transition from snocross racer to professional freestyle rider, showcasing his jumping skills while doing crazy inverted tricks.

We won't be going to any forward operating bases (FOBs), but combat continues to flare in the region. Before agreeing to go, Sara and I had a talk. *Is it safe to go over there?* We were a little uneasy about it. Especially when I was recently refused a life insurance policy after I had to answer "yes" to this question from the insurance agent: "Will you be visiting or staying in an active war zone in the next year?"

On the ground in Germany, we disembark and catch a short ride to Landstuhl Regional Medical Center, a hospital perched on a hill above a forest near Ramstein Air Base, a U.S. Air Force station in the German state of Rhineland-Palatinate. The busiest trauma hospital in the world, Landstuhl is a destination for every injured American soldier coming from combat overseas. They're staged and spend a maximum of three or four days in Germany before they're sent back to the U.S. for further treatment and recovery at Walter Reed Military Medical Center in Bethesda, Maryland, or Brooke Army Medical Center at Fort Sam Houston, outside San Antonio. The freshly wounded arrive daily at Landstuhl, on the enormous C-17 transport planes from the theater of war in Iraq and Afghanistan. They are mostly young men whose flesh and limbs have been ripped apart by bomb blasts.

Wars in Iraq and Afghanistan are now fought by insurgents using improvised explosive devices (IEDs). Unable to face the military might of coalition and U.S. forces, enemies have resorted to planting roadside bombs and ambush attacks, the kind that result in legs and arms getting blown off when they detonate. Where once these types of injuries would lead to death, advances in medicine now mean that soldiers can survive such catastrophic wounds. According to a report by the Congressional Research Service published in 2015, amputations resulting from battlefield injuries to U.S. personnel in conflicts worldwide surged from 91 in 2009 to 209 in 2010. This year, in 2011, amputations increase further still to 260.

We arrive at Landstuhl during the peak of combat casualties. We are about to meet kids who are 19 or 20 years old, fresh off the battlefield.

Some saw buddies get killed in the same attacks that injured them. For most, the war is over. They are headed home, changed forever.

I've always respected our veterans. Rick's dad served in Korea. Sara's dad and her mom's current partner, Clayton, were in Vietnam. I have a cousin who's in the Air Force. I'd dreamed of becoming an Air Force pilot someday before my racing career took off. Meeting injured vets in this way is about to broaden my perspective. The majority are my age or younger. Seeing them in the hospital is a reality check and gives me a deeper appreciation for all the military forces are asked to do. The sacrifices they make are real. There's nothing more real than a soldier getting injured in battle, fighting for not only their own life, but the lives of their brothers and sisters in arms.

We are led into individual rooms occupied by recuperating soldiers. Shock registers in their young faces and hits my heart hard. I've been injured, sure, but this is much heavier. In a bed on the left side of the room lies one young soldier with bandaged limbs, his face covered in scratches and burns from a bomb blast. Not everyone we meet is ready to engage, and I can tell by his expression that he's not interested in talking, especially not with civilians. We keep moving toward a room occupied by another soldier with a leg swaddled in bandages and covered by blankets. Upon closer inspection, I can see he's a fresh amputee. When we approach, he's not much for talking, but then he sees I'm an amputee, too, and grows curious. I'm not sure how to interact. Yes, I've been through a terrible time with my amputation, but this soldier was just blown up in combat a day ago while fighting for his and his fellow soldiers' lives. *How can I start talking to him about being positive, having fun, and getting back to the activities he enjoyed before his amputation?* I start by telling my story and transitioning to a discussion of prosthetic equipment. I show him my Moto Knee, which I've been lugging with me. He brightens up, brimming with questions, realizing maybe he hasn't reached the end of his road. I'm beginning to understand why we are here, meeting these injured vets who've just been whisked from the battlefield, but aren't yet home. Suspended in a limbo between war and civilian life, they remain uncertain of adjusting to a new reality. We're here to offer distraction and show that maybe there can be fun ahead. Our conversation may be just the ray of light that will help them get through the next hour, day, or week of a hellish unknown.

I show off my four X Games medals, three golds and a silver, a glimmer from home that elicits a smile. "What do you like to do for fun?" I ask.

This soldier rides ATVs and horses. I share how I've returned to both activities since my amputation. It's an ice-breaker, and we chit-chat about riding horses, getting in the gym again, and snowboarding.

I'd never wanted to ride horses or snowboard or ski for fear of an injury that would jeopardize my racing career. Skiing and horseback riding are two of Sara's favorite activities. Getting bucked off was risk enough to avoid horseback riding altogether, and I was never truly interested. Plus, Sara and I only had one reliable horse; the other one was pretty sketchy. Sara and I had always wanted to do an activity together, especially after my amputation. She'd dutifully chased me around while racing. It was time for me to slow down and appreciate some of the things we hadn't been able to pursue together. In the months before leaving for Germany on the troop tour, we'd agreed to find me a horse. Sara knows horses and she began the search online. We found a stable with several to choose from. I was interested in one in particular. He was a brute, tall and wide. His body was like a 55-gallon drum through the midsection. He was so big I needed to use a step to climb into the saddle. As a man, I wanted a big horse. Bigger is better. The problem: he was not comfortable. The way my socket fit around his side forced me into an uncomfortable position, creating a constant pressure that pried my hip apart. Also, when I gave him a sharp kick with my right leg to get him going, he responded with a mopey walk. He didn't have any go. Ken, the trainer helping us, suggested I try another horse.

The other horse was smaller, allowing me to climb on his back more easily. He was a little peppier, too. I gave him a little kick and he started trotting. With little prodding, he wanted to go. He had some giddyup in his step, too. I fell in love with his attitude. His personality was a good match for me. He was animated, responding to different cues. His ears were always alert, trying to figure out what I wanted him to do. Whenever Sara or I stood next to him, he put his nose in our arms or hands. I said, "I think you're the one."

The stable had owned him for just over a month to tune him up and train him. They'd given him a name—Ranger. I wanted to give him a name that reflected that he would allow me to hit trails that were off-limits with my prosthetic leg and experience the outdoors again. I decided to call him Walker because he would be my legs—my off-road legs. His full name would incorporate his stable name, too—Walker, Texas Ranger, after the popular TV show from the 1990s starring Chuck Norris.

We had been boarding a pony for Sara's friends at our house so that her horse, Ivan, would have company. Her friends no longer wanted the pony, so we bought it, but he was too small for me. He was too small for anyone but a child to ride. So we traded the pony for Walker and moved him in with Ivan. The horses meshed, and Sara and I could finally go riding together. I'm a cowboy now, sort of. Well…not really at all. I have nothing to do with cows. At least I can talk like one when discussion turns to riding horses.

I MEET THREE AMPUTEES IN GERMANY, some in worse condition than others. I'm uneasy trying to feel them out to determine whether it's the right time to talk. Once we get a conversation going and pull out our medals (I've won four at X Games so far, and Levi has a bunch, too) the soldiers brighten up and begin to ask questions. The conversations revolve around racing snowmobiles and dirt bikes mainly. Also, Levi set a record by launching his snowmobile more than 300 feet through the air during a training session. He was preparing for a telecast on last New Year's Eve of a jump over a section of San Diego Bay. Before he could pull off the New Year's stunt, Levi was injured in a wreck in practice, but he's planning to go for it again next New Year's Eve. Talking about our careers, stuff we've done that seems so far away from this hospital, and seeing these injured vets go from being torn up to smiling makes a powerful impression on me.

Later, Levi and I are led outside and shuttled to a tarmac on the air base and onto a C-17 airplane, a colossal military transport jet being loaded with troops for a return trip to the States. In the belly of the plane, a half-dozen wounded vets occupy beds lined up in rows. Some are ambivalent about returning home, leaving behind brothers and unfinished business. One of the soldiers is strapped to a stretcher and I take his hand as we pose for a photo, each giving a thumbs-up. I wish him good luck on his return trip home to family and friends. I know he and the other wounded will need more than luck and good wishes. I think back to my own recovery, and the importance of my prosthesis in regaining the confidence to resume activities that have given my life meaning. Once the fat plane lumbers into the sky, the wounded vets aboard will be on the first tentative leg of that very same journey.

FROM GERMANY, WE'RE OFF ON A 12-DAY whirlwind trip through Kuwait, Qatar, and Oman, where the temperature can reach 120 degrees Fahrenheit. We land first in Kuwait, and when we step from the airport terminal, we are met with a wave of heat that feels like a kick to the face, stunning me for a moment. We are also met by three big SUVs. We climb into one, and just like in the movies, the convoy roars off through traffic, bumper-to-bumper, 90 miles per hour down the highway. The vehicles in front and behind us are a mere six feet away. Levi and I look at each other. *This is nuts!* The drivers are civilian contractors whose job is to get us safely from the airport to the first stop of three military bases in Kuwait. Maybe driving at high speeds doesn't seem like the safest way to get us to the base, but they want to ensure that we are not targeted for an attack or ambush. The drivers explain to us that it will be easier to spot someone trailing us when driving significantly faster than the surrounding vehicles. We are in a theater of war, after all.

Ali al Salem Air Base is home to 15,000 Kuwaiti and U.S. servicemen and contractors, making it like a small city. Officers on the base greet us, give us a briefing, and take us to two more bases, Camp Arifjan, a U.S. Army operating base, and Camp Buehring, an Army staging point in the sparsely populated remote desert of northwest Kuwait. Driving through the desert, where sand drifts across the road, we see camels and settlements of nomadic people. We're a long way from Minnesota. I've never experienced heat like this. The amputation has affected my circulation, causing me to sweat easily. In the Middle East, rivers run from my body, soaking my clothes, evaporating just as quickly in the dry, desert air.

An officer provides a tour of the bases and introduces us to soldiers during their daily duty. None of the soldiers are expecting us. We simply drop in and surprise them. We roll up in our air-conditioned SUV onto the tarmac at Camp Buehring and approach a hangar surrounded by several airplanes. We open the door and are immediately hit by a shock of 125-degree-Fahrenheit desert air, which feels as though we've stepped in front of a blast furnace. The B-1B bomber catches my eye right away. I grew up playing with model airplanes and dreamed about serving as an Air Force pilot. Sara says that if not for racing, she's convinced I would have wound up in the military.

I've memorized all the specs of the B-1B Lancer. Nicknamed "The Bone" from "B-One," it is a long-range supersonic bomber with a 137-foot variable wingspan and four turbofan afterburner engines that propel it to Mach 1.2 (900 mph). With its wings swept back, the B-1B resembles a giant fighter plane. The plane is a beast at 146 feet long, with a max payload of 75,000 pounds, and can carry 265,000 pounds of fuel. The Bone was developed in the 1980s to carry nuclear weapons, but it was reconfigured and first used in combat in 1998 during Operation Desert Fox in Iraq.

The sun explodes off the gray body of the plane and a crew works up on one of the wings. "Let's go see what they're working on," says the officer escorting our group. Seeing these enormous planes up close—and having a chance to talk to the men who fly them—is the experience of a lifetime. As the five of us walk to the plane, circling it on the tarmac, I'm in awe of the machine's size. The officer approaches the wing and begins climbing a ladder, motioning for us to follow. I'm first in line, and when I reach the top, I see that three maintenance crew members are at work, one of them inside the wing. The plane sits baking in the Kuwait sun atop blacktop, and the crewman is wrenching on a component. *Holy shit!* I think. *It must be hot in there.* We all scramble onto the scalding wing and the crew looks up. Levi and I are wearing baseball caps and button-down shirts. We look out of place, like a couple tourists in a war zone. The crewmen give us quizzical looks. *Who are you? Why are you standing on my airplane?*

The officer introduces us as X Games athletes. "We have a few special guests I'd like you to meet," he says. The soldiers brighten and begin to explain the work we've interrupted. I'm far more interested to learn about their jobs and this plane than they are to know about our careers as athletes. We begin to ask questions about their work and the aircraft. We're having a casual chit-chat. We learn that the friendly crewmen put in dozens of hours of maintenance for every hour of flight for the B-1B. They explain the intensity of their jobs, the 24-hour nature of keeping planes fit to fly missions. I pepper them with questions, and it's eye-opening to learn the commitment required to keep these planes in the air.

Fifteen minutes into our discussion, I work up the nerve to ask if I can check out the cockpit. The soldiers chuckle and explain that the interior of the plane will be stiflingly hot, nearly unbearable. If I really want to, I'm welcome to climb into the cockpit. They warn me not to touch any of the metal surfaces; not because I'll break it, but because it's so hot. The plane has been sitting in the mid-afternoon sun baking in 125-degree heat on the tarmac. "You won't be in there too long," one of the soldiers says.

Levi and I look at each other with a smile. "Let's do it," I say. We excitedly weasel our way inside, where it's cramped and 152 degrees, according to a temperature gauge—hot enough for metal components to singe our skin on contact. Crawling inside, we take turns sitting in the pilot's and co-pilot's seats, snapping a few photos. There's only space to accommodate a crew of four. The rest of the aircraft is devoted to the bomb and fuel tanks.

Crawling from the cockpit back into the confined bomb bay feels like entering the belly of the beast, and all my giddy excitement drains away as I'm reminded of the seriousness of our environment, the conditions these men and women work in so far from home. A dozen bombs hang in the bay, bombs that will soon have targets. This is a reality check. This is no airplane sitting at an air show or a museum. This plane sits on an active airfield, ready for another mission. When these bombs are released, people will be killed.

Levi and I can no longer stand the stifling heat inside. We're dripping with sweat as we crawl out of the bomber. The 125-degree heat outside delivers a relief that feels like air conditioning. We blink as our eyes adjust to the blinding desert sun. It feels good to be out in the air again.

Later in the day the officer arranges something special for us. We assemble on a hillside adjacent to the runway to witness one of the B-1Bs during takeoff. The pilot pours on the afterburners and the boom from the engines rattles our chests and ears as the sleek bomber, in an awesome display of power, tears off into the blinding desert sky. It's a moment I won't ever forget.

We spend the next 12 days on a grueling schedule touring bases across the Middle East, in Kuwait, Qatar, and Amman, Jordan. We're put up in barracks or platform tents, dozing off to the rumble of generators pumping air-conditioning. We seldom get more than five hours of sleep because we're bouncing around to different briefings, changings of the guard, and groups of soldiers. It's an intense timetable. I've never put so many consecutive days into any project on such little rest. By the end I'm stupid from heat and sleep deprivation, operating on autopilot. Still, being in a theater of war has served as an eye-opener, leaving me with a heavy feeling. I've met 19- and 20-year-old soldiers who may not make it home alive. Others may make it home in pieces, like the guys we met in Landstuhl Medical Center. Driven by a strong sense of patriotism and the call to serve, these young men and women have seen and endured more in a matter of years than most do in a lifetime. Those who are grievously injured make an incredible sacrifice for their country, and though they may receive medals and medical care upon their arrival home, it must be hard for them not to feel abandoned—and completely cut off from the active, thrill-seeking lives they once lived and always pictured themselves living.

I board my flight home from the war zone endowed with a sense of mission: building prostheses to make me, or others, a better performing athlete will be only a small part of my business. A greater purpose can come from using my prostheses to help reconstruct the lives of wounded servicepeople. Seeing these overseas bases firsthand has a great impact on my respect level for my military friends and customers down the road. Above all, I want to help them regain a part of their lives they feared was lost.

12

A New Mountain to Climb

Months after I've returned from my trip overseas, I learn that for 2012, Winter X Games has dropped adaptive snocross racing from its lineup but will add adaptive snowboardcross, a downhill snowboarding discipline similar to motocross in which six competitors boom through a twisting course of gap jumps, tabletops, and high berms. When the start gate drops in snowboardcross, riders jockey for position into the first corner, elbow-to-elbow. It's close-quarters racing, with riders trying to draft behind one another for speed. Crashes are common. Unlike motocross, a single mistake usually means you're out of a race, which lasts about two minutes.

I can get down the mountain decently on a snowboard, but I'd be lucky if I could survive just sliding through a boardercross course, much less hucking the big jumps and features. Still, Dan Gale, who runs Adaptive Action Sports and acts as an event organizer for X Games, talks me into giving the sport a try. He explains that it's only an exhibition this year. He says he's willing to set me up with training. Though I lack experience on the snowboard, I still want to compete at X Games, to maintain a presence in order to satisfy sponsors and raise the profile of BioDapt. To help me prepare, Dan and the Adaptive Action Sports crew hook me up with a coach: Kep Koeppe, Dan's burly snowboarding buddy from Colorado.

IN NOVEMBER I DRIVE TO COLORADO, pulling into Crested Butte, an old mining town in the remote western part of the state, hours from Denver and Copper Mountain. It's a pure ski town, with the Crested Butte Mountain Resort the biggest draw. It's early in the season and though there isn't much snow yet, it's one of the few places to ride. This is Kep's home base, and he's invited me to spend three days with him on the slopes. He's been steeped in the snowboarding industry for years, acting as a coach, and he enjoys assisting adaptive athletes with the sport. Though I've known him casually for a couple years, I'm grateful that he's willing to help me out in my quest to cram for Winter X Games.

Kep reminds me of a mountain man. He's a legit backcountry dude with a beard and long hair. He resembles a snowboard bum, big, burly, and forbidding, but he's on point with his instruction and he has a big heart. Kep will help anybody, and he badly wants to transform me into a snowboarder. He sees me as his project; Kep wants me to shift into competitive snowboarding and to travel the world with him and the rest of the adaptive crew. To do that, he's going to push me outside my comfort zone on the mountain. Pressing a race board into my hands, we hop a lift up the mountain so that I can get acquainted with the equipment and with going fast. Off the lift, I strap in and Kep remains at my side, calling out instruction as I try to keep up. High on the mountain, I'm thinking, *Wow, this is scary shit!* Kep keeps pushing me to go faster than I want to go, flirting with 60 miles an hour down the mountain. I'm not a very good snowboarder and I'm afraid I'm going to lose control and catch an edge, and it's going to hurt. This is just the beginning, though.

"Alright," Kep tells me while we're stopped on the side of a run. "From this point here, I want you to point it. No speed check at all and just let her fly."

"Noooo," I say.

Kep won't hear of it. As we get underway, he sticks by my side. "Alright, Schultzy," he shouts, "here we go! Just let her fly! Point it down the hill!"

As I gain speed, the material on my jacket makes a buzzing sound and I feel like I'm flying downhill, out of control. The race board starts to get a little greasy underneath me, slipping and sliding, but stays straight and it turns out well when I don't crash. After more dramatic speed sessions each day, I'm growing comfortable controlling my board and learning a new sport with a prosthetic leg. Off the slopes, I calibrate the Versa Foot for best performance, adjusting air pressure, hydraulics, and alignment.

One of the biggest challenges concerns my stance on the board. Am I "regular"—standing with my left foot forward—or "goofy," with my right foot forward? Neither feels natural. Once riding at a faster pace, I seem to enjoy better control in a regular stance, with my prosthesis in front. The problem: I struggle to initiate turns, which ideally are done with the leading foot. To compensate, I slide the tail of the board with my back foot, left or right depending which direction I want to go. As a result, my turns are not as smooth or controlled as they are when I'm riding goofy-footed. The benefit of standing regular, though—with my prosthesis on the front of the board—comes in steeper terrain. With my real leg in the back, I can flex better and maintain balance. Flipped around into a goofy stance, with my prosthesis in back, turns initiate smoothly, but steeper terrain kicks me forward so that I feel like I'll go head-first over the front of the board because my Moto Knee wants to extend into a straight position. If I plan to ride goofy, with the prosthesis in the back, the alignment of the knee must be flexed farther, which makes it uncomfortable when it comes to walking. I keep second-guessing and going back and forth. *Am I goofy or regular?* I'm going to need to make a decision before X Games and stick with it.

After helping me work on speed for three days, Kep tells Dan and Amy that I'm doing well but still need more time on snow. At Crested Butte, there hasn't been much snowfall this early in the season, so we haven't been able to hit jumps. I'll need to tackle them in training if I'm going to have any hope of competing in boardercross. Kep instructs me to go home and hit the biggest jumps I can handle. "Put in as much time as possible on the board," he says. "Hopefully you'll learn a lot, pick up your pace, and get comfortable with flying."

I'll have to learn how to ride at a high level in a short amount of time. Winter X Games arrives in two months.

WEEKS LATER, I'M BACK IN COLORADO about to deepen my relationship with snowboarding and the military. I've flown out to Breckenridge for Ski Spectacular, an event hosted by Disabled Sports USA, an organization founded in the 1960s and devoted to increasing participation in sports among people with disabilities. Many of the adaptive athletes here to learn to ski and snowboard are veterans.

Breckenridge sits two miles up in the Rockies, along the Continental Divide an hour west of Denver and only a few miles from Copper Mountain. It's an old gold-mining town from the late 1800s that's been transformed to serve a tourist economy with a historic business district full of art galleries, breweries, and restaurants. The Breckenridge Ski Resort sprawls across five peaks of the Tenmile Range.

Ski Spec, as everyone calls it, is a ginormous event, attended by hundreds of veterans and paraplegics, along with equipment manufacturers eager for them to demo their gear. Everyone is set up in the Beaver Run resort area, not far from the lifts. There are mono ski manufacturers and a few prosthetic companies offering knees and lower legs. I'm not prepared for the scale of the event, but I've brought a few Moto Knees along to demo.

I've been invited by Harvey Naranjo, who runs the adaptive activity program at Walter Reed. Harvey works with veterans, mainly amputees, coordinating with their prosthetist to find the best equipment to pursue their favorite activities. Some of the vets in Breckenridge this week want to learn to snowboard on my Moto Knee. This is a chance for me to develop a personal connection with one of the guys at Walter Reed. This is a chance for him to size up my Moto Knee—and me.

I've connected with Harvey through Keith Deutsch. When Keith tested my knee, he told Harvey and his prosthetist that he needed a Moto Knee in order to snowboard. Harvey got the ball rolling for Keith's purchase and several others. Harvey and I have had ongoing conversations about Walter Reed's prosthetics program. As part of his duties, he helps create programs that allow veterans to engage in winter sports. He works with the amputee and the prosthetist to find the best equipment for their activity. Although not a high-level snowboarder himself, Harvey can strap in and navigate a run decently. He enjoys riding, though he only gets on the slopes a few times each season. Every year, he invites a select group of veterans who've worked hard in their recovery to Ski Spec, and he wants me to help fit Moto Knees so that these amputees can get on the slopes.

In Breckenridge, I'm scheduled to meet with Harvey and Wayne Waldon, a veteran and Keith's buddy on the Adaptive Action Sports team, to help calibrate his new Moto Knee and Versa Foot.

WHEN I MEET HARVEY for the first time in person, he gives me a good solid handshake and we dive into conversation right away about BioDapt and our equipment and the story behind why I created it. Short in stature, with dark hair, Harvey is one of the sincerest people I've met. He enjoys helping veterans move forward in their lives. Wayne accompanies Harvey for our initial meeting, and I learn that he enjoys snowboarding and has been occasionally competing with the crew that I have recently met through Adaptive Action Sports. Wayne's second passion is riding sport bikes (road racing motorcycles). He has a designated bike for riding on the racetrack during open practice days. We all chat about competition and motorsports for a long time, and we all learn a lot about one another. I realize that this crew from Walter Reed are great people and I feel like this is the start of something really good. Their program revolves around the goal of getting injured soldiers back into a high level of mobility and performance, the kind they were accustomed to before their injury. They use recreational sports for the mental motivation needed to push through the challenges of rehabilitation.

This is only my second season on a snowboard. I know enough to get down the mountain, but I'm worried they'll respect me less because I can't teach these vets any high-level skills. In fact, they end up instructing me when I set them up on my equipment, not in terms of riding, but in more meaningful ways. They're incredibly grateful, and they want to wring every second out of their time on the mountain. At mealtime, there's deep camaraderie and an excitement to spend time with their brothers and sisters of the armed forces.

Coming off the troop tour, I feel a strong connection to the veterans Harvey has introduced me to on this trip. I envision how my equipment will have a positive impact on the recovery of those who embrace this opportunity to get on the slopes and ride. Harvey sees the potential in my equipment, too, and we bond while talking about my prosthesis and his plans for using it to help motivated vets with their recovery. Harvey would give the shirt off his back to help any of these vets with moving forward in their lives, but he's not about to dole freebies to those trying to take advantage of the system. He distinguishes between those working hard and those looking for a handout. "Nope," he says, "I'm not interested in helping those guys. I want to help those who want to help themselves." Not everyone gets to go on the junkets to Ski Spec or another one held at Vail later in the season—only those veterans who've been committed to working the hardest.

He sees in BioDapt a small business that is sincere about trying to help others, too. He and I have a similar mentality. We want to assist people in achieving their capabilities. He's enthusiastic about how I'm building a small company and assisting veterans. Harvey will take a lot of the information he's learned about the Moto Knee back to Walter Reed to the prosthetists to clear the way for ordering more for their guys. To become an official vendor, I've had to register with a couple government agencies, and they require testing. This trip will satisfy some of those requirements.

It's a busy and exciting trip that leaves me stoked to have met so many inspiring people. If they can learn a new sport after all they've endured, I decide, then so can I. If I'm going to be serious about helping vets with recovery through snowboarding, then I'd better learn to really ride. I'm about to make a commitment that will launch me on a new, exciting trajectory in the sport in the months to come.

BACK HOME AT POWDER RIDGE, the weather in Central Minnesota in mid-December has turned cold enough that the resort can make snow and begin shaping jumps. It's an awkward feeling to fly through the air without handlebars to grab onto or the weight of a machine beneath me. On a dirt bike or snowmobile, the machine provides stability in the air. If I'm pitched one way or another, I can pull myself around with my hands or legs to get my body back in the saddle. With a snowboard, once you leave the ground, your body is mostly airborne. It's a whole new feeling to try to hang on and center my balance. My arms flail. I look and feel awkward as hell. I'm trying to ease into launching myself into jumps, but I slam a couple times hard to the snow. If I get my body too far forward over the front of the board, my weight comes down on my prosthetic leg, causing my knee to compress. Once it does, the toe edge of the board catches and I loop out onto my back in a millisecond. This happens again and again, and I compensate by landing more on my rear foot. I'm learning to make adjustments. One constant: I've committed to riding regular-foot, with my prosthesis in front.

I spend the next several weeks flailing through the air, looking like a goon. I'm definitely improving and learning to calibrate the Moto Knee and Versa Foot for snowboarding. I've been tinkering with the linkage system on my Versa Foot to better adapt it to snowboarding.

Luke has been helping me at Powder Ridge. He's experienced on snow, and I need someone to shoot video of me hitting some big jumps. I'll need to send the footage to organizers at Winter X Games to prove that I'm capable of competing on their course. I'm practicing on a 35-foot booter jump that Powder Ridge has built in its terrain park. Although I'm accustomed to sending it on a dirt bike or snowmobile, flying with a snowboard scares the heck out of me. I have no muscle memory. It's all brand-new. I'm going from being a novice to training for competition against the best adaptive snowboardcross racers in the world. I've seen boardercross at X Games live while on hand for snocross. It's nuts! The courses are big, and the speeds are extremely fast. The jumps and features are massive. I have no business dropping out of the gate at X Games.

In late December, after seeing footage of me riding, organizers accept me into the competitive field and send a preview of the course setup. The start gate features an eight-foot drop. Pulling out of the start will lead immediately to nearly a one-story vertical drop to the snow. It's going to be a crap show if I pull out and promptly crash. Wrecking at the start is my worst fear. For one thing, falling on snow from that height hurts. For another, I don't want to be that guy who crashes right out of the start gate.

With weeks to go till my debut in snowboardcross competition at Winter X Games, I still don't feel ready. It's my first real snowboard race, and I enter with no idea how much it will change the course of my life.

13
Transitions

In Aspen again, the scene at the base of Buttermilk Mountain looks as familiar as the half-dozen other times I've been here for Winter X Games. There are the athlete lounges, temporary structures built from scaffolding and covered in white nylon. There are portable trailers and toilets set up for workers and athletes in the spaces between the resort's wooden lodges. Thick electrical wires protected by plastic conduits run in every direction along the snow, connected to generators rattling somewhere out of sight. Sponsors' flags and banners for energy drinks, beef jerky, and the military compete for attention. Jumbo screens erected on towering poles flicker with images of live feeds from cameras stationed along the mountain, where some of the ski and snowboard courses snake into the trees out of sight. Yet everything feels different, like it's my first time. There's no snocross competition this year, and I'm here as a snowboarder. I've been on my board 17 times at Powder Ridge, a little mole hill back in Minnesota compared to the soaring peaks of the Rockies. *Will it be enough? Am I ready?*

I meet up with Kep, who's acting as my personal coach. On the lift and the mountain, he prepares me for course tactics, telling me where to check my speed, where to let loose, and where to point my board. "You want to scrub speed here," he says. "You want to initiate your turn here. You want to keep your board flat through this section. From this point here, in order to clear this jump, you'll need to keep your board flat-based and no speed checks."

The jumps and features on the course are massive, and I've never been so nervous for competition. I keep thinking that I have no business dropping out of the gate at Winter X Games on a snowboard. I'm a snowmobile racer, accustomed to wrangling snarling machinery, not cutting sharp turns on a snowboard. Kep keeps it real with me. He boosts my confidence, telling me, *You are able to do this.* But he also refuses to sugarcoat it when I encounter a course feature that's beyond my ability. I try to soak in as much of his guidance as possible, but it's all new to me. I contemplate line choices on the bumpy, twisting terrain. I'm familiar with rhythm and roller sections from motocross and snocross, and I know how to traverse them in theory, but I don't know what my feet are supposed to do to make it happen. If there was a throttle and brake, I'd be "sending it" over this course, but it's just my feet on a 12-mm-thick board made of a few layers of wood, fiberglass, and wax. I haven't had enough time on a board, and I'm up against the elites of snowboardcross. There is Keith Gabel, an animated dude from Utah with a strong personality and a sense of fun. There's Evan Strong, tight-lipped, who shuts everyone else out as he prepares for a race. There's Carl Murphy, from New Zealand, who's built a foot in his garage similar to my Versa Foot design, employing a Fox shock, too. When he spots my foot, it gets awkward. He doesn't hide his annoyance that I've come up with something similar and have already pursued a U.S. Patent.

Then there's me, the new guy. I don't even look like a snowboarder. I'm wearing my snowmobile gear up top, my moto pants, and a full-face mountain bike helmet. I'm also the least experienced and most physically impaired racer in the field. All the others are below-the-knee amputees, giving them more strength, knee flexion, and shock absorption needed to control a board through jumps, rollers, and sharp turns. As well as my Moto Knee works, it's no replacement for the real thing. Below-knee amputees still have their knees—and in some cases, most of their lower legs intact—giving them greater function and a decided advantage in performance over an above-knee amputee like me.

My competitors have also been racing in World Cup events in hopes of qualifying for the Paralympics in two years, in Sochi, Russia, where para snowboarding will make its debut at the Games. They're here trying to win a gold medal. For them, it's a high-stress environment. Some of them don't have two seconds for me, walking past without any acknowledgment. My nerves kick in; maybe it's only in my head, but I can't help but wonder if they're thinking, *This newbie will only get in our way and likely injure himself.*

For Sara, the biggest adjustment will be not having our usual setup with a race trailer in the paddock, where we have food and some control over our environment. As a snowboarder at X Games, we're set up in the lobby of the lodge at Buttermilk Mountain, a space strewn with bags, sopping wet gear, and seven competitors huddled around a big fireplace, trying to get warm and dry. Sara and I prefer a tidy space. I try to contain all my gear in a bag. If I need something, I unpack the bag, find the item, and then repack. Others have their shit strewn everywhere. We're amid a chaotic disaster compared to our typical program, and it wears on my nerves. Sara looks panicked by the mess, the unfamiliarity, and the fact we were supposed to be racing snowmobiles, and we're not.

I miss snocross, too, and the snowmobile scene. Other than Dan, Kep, and Amy, we know few people in the snowboarding world. Sara and I make our way over to the pits, where the freestyle snowmobile crews have set up their rigs and trailers. We spot Levi LaVallee, my longtime friend from the military tour in the Middle East. When he asks how snowboarding is going, I admit that we're winging it. We don't have much of a plan, and though I've put time on the mountain and worked with Kep, we're not prepared. The start gate will be a challenge, as will the final 55-foot kicker before the finish. I don't know that I can clear it. And if I try to go around the jump, I'll be disqualified.

Near the finish, the course comes over a roller and drops into a jump section with three options. There's a 55-foot, 75-foot, and 95-foot booter to choose from. Kep has told me to approach the jumps with the base of my board flat and pointed straight downhill. "Do not speed check!" he says. "Or you'll come up short."

In practice, I've been able to traverse all the features at speed, except for the gap jump at the finish. I've wanted to huck it, but I've been focused mainly on maintaining momentum through the berms. When it comes to the last 200 feet of the course, I've let fly the way Kep has suggested so I can get familiar with the speed needed to clear the gap. With the board flat, I accelerate fast, wind whipping my jacket, making me nervous. Hauling fast at the jump, I veer away at the last second. *Holy shit, that's going to be big!*

On the final practice run before the race, I set up, get stacked over my board, and point it toward the final jump again. It's now or never if I'm going to dial in the feature before competition. Every ounce of muscle in my body tells me to put on the brakes. *No, no, no!* I ride off the eight-foot tall jump face and soar over the 55-footer, arms whirling and flailing for balance, what snowboarders call "rolling down the windows" because your hands are making fast elliptical motions and it looks like you're furiously trying to roll down the car windows using the old manual crank method—a concept probably not understood by the younger generation. My board lands with a thud and I skid on my seat briefly before riding away. "Woooooh!" I scream like a little kid, having made it. I'm giddy. Mission accomplished.

WHEN IT COMES TO THE ACTUAL RACE, the start gate still gives me trouble. Standing in the gate with the five other competitors, we are suspended eight feet above the course. We must pull off the gate and drop straight to a landing transition packed with snow. I've done it successfully twice in practice. Still, the start has gotten into my head pretty good. The rest of the course consists of rollers that I can pump through easily. I'm not fast enough to double or triple any of the rollers like some of the other guys in the field. I'm honest with myself: I cannot compete with the top guys, or any of them for that matter. My plan is to wait a half second once the race begins before pulling out of the gate. I'm planning to get down the course the best I can and try not to tangle with the others pushing the pace.

Once the gate drops, events don't unfold quite so cleanly. Last out of the gate, I'm given a gift when two riders crash in a pileup on the second feature, and I scoot into fourth place. Three guys have gotten through the crash cleanly. The others are on their asses. I make my way down several more features and a series of banked turns. The pack has pretty much disappeared from view. Then I launch over a high-speed gap and notice another rider down. *Oh, man! I'm now in third place!* All I need to do is maintain control and not wipe out, and I'll land on the podium. I begin to push the pace, but my priority is to stay upright. Features fly by quickly, and two-thirds of the way down, there are some rollers followed by a flat section. I exit one of the rollers and come into the flat section. I try to keep my board flat to reduce drag, but the bottom feels greasy and I lose my balance, catching the heel edge of my board, causing me to slam to the snow. It's nothing dramatic. I pop up instantly. Unfortunately, I've fallen on the flattest part of the course, and I can't get any forward momentum. I have to hop for what feels like an eternity to a steep enough section of slope so that I can get moving again, allowing two riders to pass.

This is how I finish the race, in fifth place, sticking the landing as I send it over the massive 55-foot gap. It's not pretty, but I've hucked it.

I'm bummed that I was in a podium position but made a mistake and crashed. Still, not too bad for my first snowboard race, against the best one-leggers in the world. It's been fun, and eye-opening, to compete in a new sport, but I'm not sure I have any real future on a snowboard, not against lower-limb amputees who have much greater function than I ever will. I doubt I will ever be able to beat them, much less compete at a similar pace.

SNOWBOARDING IS ABOUT TO BECOME A BIGGER PART of my life. My brother-in-law Luke teaches machine shop classes to high school students, and he's introduced me to a filmmaker who's working on a documentary about sports and the science of manufacturing. Jeremy Bout runs an educational production company called Edge Factor that uses documentary storytelling to teach students about modern manufacturing. I've told Jeremy about my company and explained the mechanics and manufacturing process of my prosthetic. He'd asked if I have any connection to snowboarding. This was before my trip to Crested Butte to train with Kep. "I'm not much of a snowboarder," I'd explained, "but I sell my equipment to snowboarders." I've tried to steer him toward motocross and snowmobile racing because that's what I know best, but Jeremy prefers snowboarding. He's a snowboarder himself. He's outlined a plan for a heliboarding trip in the mountains of British Columbia. He needs to capture action on camera and wants me and my prosthetic involved.

I told him, in that case, I'd already planned to spend time snowboarding this winter in preparation for X Games, and I'd be thrilled to join him for what sounds like an epic adventure.

During the next six weeks, while I was training in Crested Butte, Breckenridge, and Powder Ridge, we'd talked again several times to outline what's needed for the story. Jeremy will need another rider, a client who uses my equipment. I'd phoned Keith Deutsch. "Hell, yeah," Keith shouted when I proposed the heliboarding trip. "This sounds awesome!"

THE DOCUMENTARY FORCES ME TO RECALIBRATE BIODAPT for improved performance. Jeremy Bout wants digital models of my knee and foot to show in his film. He's especially interested in the Versa Foot, which I have in prototype form. I'm using the foot, but I haven't sold any yet. When he asks for CAD files, I explain that all I have are blueprints from my pencil drawings.

To show how I develop my equipment, Jeremy says we'll need digital files.

I know just who to ask for help. Chris Carlson is a snocross race team owner out of Elk River. He's part owner of the ERX Motor Park, where I've been riding and teaching clinics for adaptive snocross racers. He also owns a company, Sport Tech, which manufactures and supplies parts and components for the powersports industry. He's offered help with design for BioDapt if I ever need it.

I phone him for a favor, explaining that I have a cool opportunity to feature my company in a documentary. He hooks me up with two of his experienced designers, Marc and Jesse, and they transfer my pencil drawings to CAD files. I sit in their offices for hours, looking over their shoulder, as these top-notch engineers donate their time to help develop and build my Versa Foot on screen in digital form. Over these last several weeks we've become great friends as we talk about prosthetic design, riding motocross and snowmobiles, and the latest hints of top-secret components they are developing for some of the biggest powersports manufactures in the world. I can't help but feel kind of guilty as they are racking up hours and hours of design time on my Versa Foot and Moto Knee. I don't know what their hourly rate is for custom design, but for how talented they are I can only imagine the price it would cost me if I had to pay out of my pocket. I'm incredibly grateful for this opportunity Chris has given me. They've helped me get the designs ready to send to Andrew Tool, the company I've hired for machining. All of which not only streamlines my manufacturing and assembly process, but will look great in the Edge Factor show.

In a short time, I've learned some high-order truths associated with being an owner-operator of a small business. Working in isolation has forced me to become an expert in every aspect of the business. And being hands-on in every phase of design and manufacturing has allowed for quality control. Working by myself has made me nimbler in terms of decision-making, too. On the other hand, my lack of formal training has meant that I lacked some institutional skills common in a modern manufacturing operation. There's been no one else to tell me that there's a better way to design and build prosthetic limbs. In some cases, I've had to learn the hard way.

IN FEBRUARY 2012 I PREPARE TO TRAVEL to British Columbia to spend five days riding out of a helicopter to a mountain summit with Keith Deutsch and Jeremy Bout for the Edge Factor film. The trip will be pure pleasure—performing laps with the chopper, riding fresh powder runs. I'm firing on all cylinders in life, learning a new sport, building a business, and having fun. And things are about to get better.

I've resumed the snocross tour during the winter of 2011–12 to satisfy sponsors and continue to pursue what I love. I'd competed at the first tour event of the season in Duluth and did well. Then, on a Friday night in December, on the third anniversary of my accident, I was at home watching the livestream of the current pro race in Ironwood, Michigan. Sara and I had said we would never race in Ironwood again because it lacks a trauma center to treat serious injuries. We have driven through Ironwood a few times on our way to the Extremity Games and it always haunted us, especially Sara.

This time the race was not at the ski resort where I was injured, but another one about a mile down the road. The track looked rad, though, well-built with great jump lines and a downhill rhythm section.

Sitting together on the couch, around 8 PM, watching the pro class, I started to get butterflies. I looked at Sara. "This track looks fun. I want to race it. Should we go?"

She laughed. "Tomorrow?"

"Yeah! That's when the Pro Vets will be running."

Sara hesitated. Ironwood conjured negative feelings for her, but she knew how badly I wanted it. And she's always looked forward to seeing friends at the races as much as I do. "Uhhh," Sara said as I tingled with anticipation. "Yeah...let's do it."

We scrambled to get ready, packing that night to leave in the morning, my heart pumping with excitement. I knew my normal mechanic wouldn't be available on such short notice, so we asked Luke to join us as a wrench. Most of my trailer had already been loaded from practice days earlier. It was just a matter of throwing in my gear and some food and hooking up the trailer to my truck.

The next morning, we were on the road long before sunrise for the five-hour drive. We rolled into Ironwood with scarcely enough time to set up and ready for the race with a few practice laps. On the way through town, we drove past the resort where I'd been injured, and Sara confessed to some uneasy feelings. I knew she was nervous. The weather was good this time, though, and so was my morale. I was ready to check this race off my list of unfinished business.

The weekend was a blur, but I conquered the course without incident, finishing in third place in the Pro Vets class. Standing on the podium with a leg of my own construction felt like redemption. I'd conquered Ironwood and reached another way station on my road to recovery. I was ready for the next challenge, and there would be plenty coming in the next months.

FOLLOWING MY SUCCESS IN SNOCROSS AT IRONWOOD, I'd raced at Canterbury Park in Shakopee and again landed on the podium, pushing high into the points standings, which encourages me to show up at ERX, in Elk River, Minnesota, in early March after my heliboarding trip to British Columbia with Jeremy and Keith. Another reason for showing up to the Elk River event: Jeremy wants to shoot footage re-enacting my injury on course for his documentary.

In the morning, during a two-hour window after practice but before race time, Sara and I make our way onto the course with Jeremy and a camera crew. I play myself, lying on the snow, with fake blood spread around. I wonder how all of this looks to other competitors about to line up for a race. Not everyone has been informed about what we're doing, and some curious racers and crew are attracted by the cameras. They see us re-enacting a scene in which one of their own is badly injured, with massive blood loss. I'm somewhat enjoying acting out my parts but feeling guilty because I know the effect such a scene can have on the mind of a rider as they're preparing to compete. No one wants to think about such a gruesome possibility. Following filming, course maintenance vehicles cover the fake blood with snow, but as the day wears on, a red mess begins to emerge with each wave of sleds passing over the spot, giving me an uneasy feeling.

At Elk River, I again place in the top five. I haven't won a race the entire season. Still, tabulating the points, heading into the final event of the season in Lake Geneva, I have accumulated enough in the vet class through six stops to possibly win a tour championship, my first ever national-level championship.

ALL SEASON, I'VE PURSUED RACING ONLY FOR FUN, but now that a tour championship is within my grasp, the pressure gets to me. Arriving in Lake Geneva, Wisconsin, in mid-March for the final event of the season, I hold a nine-point lead, and maintaining it should not be any great challenge, but then I never seem to be able to coast to victory. It's always a dramatic struggle. Maybe these thoughts become self-fulfilling because once the Lake Geneva race begins, my riding quickly falls apart.

When the green flag flies, I hammer the throttle and promptly tangle up with another rider in a multi-sled pileup at the first turn on top of the long uphill start. By the time I right the sled and roar off, I'm one of the last guys to reach the first corner.

I put the hammer down and charge back toward the pack, picking my way up in the field. Feeling good, riding hard, I'm flowing when suddenly my sled bounces sideways in a rhythm section, causing me to slide down the side of the machine and veer off course, wedging between a pole and a hay bale, peeling my side panel off in the process. Riders pass me as I struggle to reattach the plastic piece. "Nooooo!" I scream, sensing the championship slipping through my fingers.

I hop back on the sled after freeing the machine and take off, chasing down and passing two riders before reaching the checkered flag to finish the race far from the podium. Knowing I've thrown away the title, I slowly ride my sled to our trailer in the pits, hanging my head, elbows on my knees. All bummed out, and by myself, I think about what might have been if I'd ridden a better race, and not a roller coaster of emotions. I am so bummed to have crumbled under the pressure and made too many mistakes.

That's when Sara comes running through the pits, out of breath, shaking. She's yelling. I can't make out what she's saying. "Three points!" she gasps.

What? Have we lost by three points? She's emotional and I can't tell if it's a good crazy face or a bad one.

"We got it!" she yells, catching her breath. She's just come from where the final points standings are posted. "We won! We won!" Sara trembles with excitement. These are the moments I know she enjoys the emotional roller coaster of racing as much as I do.

Throwing my hands in the air, I let out a *whoop!* of celebration.

At the end-of-season banquet later that weekend, with an enormous feeling of accomplishment, I announce my retirement from the national tour. I stand up and deliver a short, emotional speech, promising to continue racing at Winter X Games. "I'll stop by and see you guys from time to time," I say, my voice cracking with emotion. The other racers, mechanics, crew, owners, and officials have been my family for a decade. It will be bittersweet, good to go out a champion, to complete a circle by coming back from injuries, with doubts about my ability to continue. They had all thought I was done. I had, too. Three years later, even though it wasn't at the elite pro level, I've won that national-level championship I was chasing at last.

14

Momentum

ONCE THE SNOWMOBILE SEASON CONCLUDES, WARMER SPRING weather melts the remaining snow. I'm back at home in Brainerd playing catch-up with BioDapt. We've expanded the garage to create a bigger workshop. I have an office, too, where I work on marketing materials and brochures, in addition to the day-to-day paperwork required to run a business. The designers at SportTech have improved my manufacturing process as I pursue research and development with the Versa Foot. Jesse and Marc are using a fairly new 3-D printing technology to prototype full-scale models of all the parts out of durable materials similar to plastic. They cannot bear my weight, but I can assemble all the parts to make sure the components fit together before I start machining metal versions. Once the prototype models have been tested to fit, I can now send digital files of my parts to Andrew Tool & Machining, a company based in Plymouth, outside Minneapolis, to make components.

Sales for BioDapt have begun to take off. I made eight sales in 2011, and the momentum continues. I enlist Luke to help me keep up with business. So far sales have come through word of mouth among the military, a rudimentary website, and social media videos that Luke and I shoot together of me riding motocross, mountain biking, and wakeboarding. I always see a spike in interest following competition at X Games, too. The Moto Knee continues to drive sales, with more than 30 units moved in 2012. Still, we receive a half-dozen orders for the new Versa Foot units this year, which I expect to rise in coming years.

In December 2012, Sara and I travel to Ski Spec in Breckenridge, where, at an end-of-week party, Amy Purdy introduces me to Miah Wheeler, the coach of the U.S. Paralympic Snowboard Team. Paralympics organizers have added snowboarding to the coming 2014 Sochi Games, and Wheeler is on a mission to get the program ready to dominate. Amy has Paralympic ambitions of her own. "This is my coach, Miah," she says by way of introduction. "He's interested in seeing what kind of foot you're working on."

Amy has been interested in possibly using the Versa Foot as she trains to qualify for the Games, but she hasn't committed yet.

I run to my room at the resort, fetch my Versa Foot prototype, and return. Miah looks it over as I explain how the foot can be adjusted, and how it works. He seems intrigued by the design.

"What do you think about not releasing it until after the Games?"

Miah doesn't want me selling the foot to any snowboarders from rival countries. He's concerned that with my equipment they could gain a competitive advantage.

"If you want to buy a couple hundred of them, I'll hold it," I say. "Otherwise, I've got a business to run."

IN MARCH 2013, following my third gold medal in snocross at Winter X Games, Luke and I travel to Colorado for Vail Veterans, an event for injured military personnel who've worked hard in their rehabilitation. It's a small group of badasses (most are from special ops units) compared to hundreds who attend Ski Spec.

The patients invited to Vail have the best attitudes from the three military hospitals. Harvey Naranjo from Walter Reed selects them, and he has asked me to assist with equipment and help fit Moto Knees so that these amputees can get on the slopes. Harvey puts Luke and me up in an epic hotel, one of the nicest places in Vail. Vail is a sprawling 5,300-acre resort that is difficult to traverse on foot, even without a disability. With a prosthesis, navigating can be daunting. If the vets can manage the challenges of being here and get themselves to where they need to be, they are prepared to go home.

My relationship with the military has continued to grow. Last June I'd gone on domestic troop tours with Chris Ridgway and Paul Thomas, a recreational off-road rider from Southern California. Ridgway and I have become friendly, and we look forward to riding together. We've developed a mutual respect—me for his career as a pro motocross rider, and he for the professional athlete and adaptive rider I've become. We'd cemented our bond while visiting global strike command bases at Malmstrom Air Force Base, in Montana, where intercontinental ballistic missiles launch. We went 60 feet underground to visit the launch pad for live intercontinental nuclear missiles and learn about the global network of firepower. We toured Minot Air Force Base in North Dakota, a place with one of the highest suicide rates among soldiers of any in the U.S. They drill 24 hours a day, seven days a week since the Cold War era of the 1960s, always on alert. They never see any real action. They are mainly on site for security, biding time in the middle of nowhere, with little to do.

In Vail, my respect for military service personnel only grows as I get to know some of them personally while setting them up on the Moto Knee. One day, I'm sitting with a charismatic, talkative Army veteran and a double below-knee amputee. He's appraising the Moto Knee, describing it as "a strange leg with all these shock absorbers in it." I listen without saying anything. "I don't know how I feel about this new knee everyone is wearing," he says. "It's kind of bulky and complicated."

I give him a look. "Oh, yeah? I think it's pretty good."

He fixes me with a stare. "Well, how would you know?"

"Well," I say, "I invented it."

An awkward pause follows. That's how I meet Matt Melancon.

Although Matt had put his foot in his mouth, he and I soon hit it off while snowboarding. A retired Army infantry sergeant, Matt's feet have been amputated as the result of a bomb blast in 2011 while riding in a truck in Afghanistan. The explosion shattered both his feet, leaving them damaged, oversized, and extremely painful. Afterward, Matt struggled with physical and mental challenges. He suffered from depression and overeating. His weight swelled to 300 pounds, and he endured 28 surgeries in an attempt to salvage his limbs. He finally persuaded doctors to amputate. Once introduced to snowboarding through veteran camps, Matt witnessed wounded military on the slopes who were in much worse shape than he was. The experience shocked him into shedding weight and his glum outlook. He's since embraced snowboarding and moved to Park City, Utah, to take advantage of opportunities to ride. Maybe it's because he's endured an emotional roller coaster and was so down before, but Matt is always pepping himself up in a way that can come across as excessively positive. I sometimes wonder: *Are you really that happy? Or are you talking yourself into being happy?*

Matt is one of these guys whose jaw moves and words come out. He's not shy about sharing his unfiltered thoughts and opinions, which sometimes cracks me up. He sees me as a like-minded soul. I'm not an engineer in a lab coat. I'm a dude, like him, who got knocked down but refused to stay down. He will buy a couple sets of Versa Feet, and one of the foundations of our ongoing relationship will be his regular feedback for how I can improve the design. "I like your stuff, Mike," he says routinely, "but here's how we can make it better."

IN VAIL, LUKE AND I SPEND A LOT OF TIME with one particular wounded veteran named Andrew, who's originally from Wisconsin. Fit, with a small build, dark hair, and a bushy beard, Andrew was a Navy Explosive Ordinance Disposal (EOD) technician. He was deployed to Afghanistan in 2011 with Seal Team 10 to defuse bombs and clear improvised explosive devices (IEDs) placed by insurgents. Caught in an explosion while on patrol, Andrew sustained extreme injuries, leading to amputations above his left knee and below his right knee. His left arm above the elbow was also amputated, leaving him with only one fully functioning limb. Still, he wants to snowboard.

The first thing that catches my eye when we meet are Andrew's three black carbon-fiber limbs, which look pretty rad in my eyes. He wears the latest and most advanced carbon-fiber sockets, feet, knee system, and the coolest-looking robotic hand. I'm geeking out over his equipment.

Andrew shows interest in my gear, too. Set up on a snowboard, with a Moto Knee and two Versa Feet, he wants to understand every adjustment and alignment detail to make the equipment work most efficiently. I suspect his approach to problem-solving likely served him well as an EOD tech, where he was forced to solve life-threatening problems in dangerous and hostile environments. The work he'd done was badass, and kind of nuts, too.

Once on snow, Andrew faces some unanticipated difficulties. Simply strapping into his board presents challenges. Standing up and riding down the mountain on prosthetic feet will prove a colossal struggle and require some creative configurations. Andrew tries mightily to snowboard on leg sockets that don't quite fit right. We work together, adjusting the alignments of my prostheses in order to dial in Andrew's stance on the board and allow him to carve effectively. He falls again and again, slamming so hard to the snow that Luke and I wince.

I'm feeling pissed off for Andrew. His sockets don't fit right. Simply putting on his boot and strapping his binding tight is challenging. I can see the pain in his face. He's trying so hard and continues to slam to the snow with force.

Pausing a second to problem-solve, Andrew maintains his poise and never surrenders. Sitting on the snow staring off into the mountains, I know his wheels are turning. *What do I need to do?*

"Let's take a break," I say, suggesting it's more for my benefit. It pains me to watch him because I understand his struggle so well. Your mind still knows exactly what it needs to do to perform at the highest level, but your body can't quite catch up.

"Yeah, let's sit for a second," Luke adds.

Andrew refuses to give up, or express frustration or anger. He simply pauses a few seconds to plot how he will solve the next problem, whether it's standing, sliding, or turning. He's kind, respectful, and a lot of fun to be around. His attitude inspires me, as he learns, *Which way do I have to lean? Should I stiffen my foot or soften to get more knee movement?*

We want to give him a breather, but Andrew simply wants to conquer the mountain. He and other veterans here have been through some crazy things in life that I can't fathom. They possess a bond, a brotherhood borne of their shared military and combat experience, setting them apart from civilians like me. But our personalities line up in at least one way: they don't give up, and neither do I. Give these veterans a task or a goal and they will achieve it. It takes three days of riding and slamming, but when he's able to negotiate "blue runs," the medium level of difficulty, from top to bottom, Andrew is at last ready to call it quits. It's been a tough, bruising process, and we finally coax him into the lodge, riding high on the feeling of triumph.

It's been fun to hang out with 15 or so badass veterans in Vail. The majority are my age or younger, and I've had a chance to interact with everybody. Four of them have been using my equipment, and I see it as an opportunity to help them out after all they've sacrificed. Their experiences make for interesting conversations about problem-solving or simply an appreciation for life. They've been through the shit and come out with a unique perspective on society. Obviously not everyone has a great attitude. Some suffer from post-traumatic stress disorder from their combat experiences. They're trying to conquer their demons. Sometimes they have a short fuse, flipping out over seemingly simple things. But I understand, especially from my own head injuries, how situations can cause intense, irrational anger. Mainly, I try to give them respect and a little extra patience. Most of the vets I've met are motivated to make the best of their lives, and I admire them for it. In turn, they admire me for the professional athlete I am and seem grateful for the chance to learn.

The fact is, I don't try to pass myself off as one of them. They've been through some things I can't fathom. I walk softly around veterans until we've had a chance to get acquainted. I'm upfront with them that I'm not a veteran and acknowledge my respect for them. I tell my story, which doesn't take place on a battlefield. Once they've heard what I've been through, dialogue opens. Sometimes there are uncomfortable moments, where they're just eyeballing me. *Who's this guy!?* The Marines can be a little rougher around the edges and standoffish. But they're also some of the best clients because they never give up. Bottom line: I must earn their respect.

Volunteering with Vail Veterans has allowed me to complete a circuit that began on my first troop tours overseas. Given how members of the military sacrifice their time, and their lives, it's put a knot in my throat to aid in their recovery.

When I return from Vail, I tell Sara how much I enjoyed the clinic because I was connecting with clients in a personal, profound way. I can see how the prostheses, and sport, truly help with healing, motivating veterans in their recovery. These clinics have been a boon to business, and I've been having a blast riding with clients. *Let's do more of these,* I tell her.

Soon Sara has something to tell me, too—on March 25, 2013, she learns that she's pregnant.

15

A Growing Team

In 2013, Jeremy Bout finishes his Edge Factory documentary, *Metal and Flesh*. Last summer, we finished up filming scenes with me riding my dirt bike in Southern California. I teamed with Ridgway to ride in the desert filming by helicopter. In the fall, I returned out west, and we filmed at Fox headquarters, in Scotts Valley, California, and continued down to Baja, Mexico, riding with Ridgway and Paul Thomas.

We hold a premiere April 10 at a converted schoolhouse in Brainerd. The visuals and story are incredible. I'm in awe of how this project turned out, after the hours and hours of film we shot in a total of seven different locations around North America. The filming took place over the course of a year and a half. I have to admit, it's pretty rad to see myself on the big screen in front of a couple hundred viewers.

We attend with friends and family. With a baby on the way, we want to be closer to them in Kimball, near St. Cloud, a city of 68,000 along the Mississippi River in Central Minnesota known for its granite quarries and St. Cloud State University. We look for a house outside of town with some land, more space for a growing home business, and only one floor so that I can avoid stairs.

Complications with Sara's pregnancy have led her obstetrician to put her on bed rest. She becomes the patient and I'm the caretaker, roles neither one of us is good at playing. I'm a better patient. As a nurse, Sara is a natural caretaker. I struggle with showing the patience she needs. "Dude, I'm too far pregnant," Sara tells me. "I can't be moving into a new home."

Sara and I are about to enter the busiest phase of our life together. In mid-June, X Games announces that adaptive motocross will be returning to the lineup on August 3 after a two-year absence. With six weeks to get ready, I immediately pause everything else and begin riding and training just as seriously as I did when I raced in the pro snocross class. I know there will be some major competition on the dirt track this time around. I use earth-moving machines to convert some features on my personal moto track to mimic some of the Supercross features I'll encounter on the racecourse in L.A. I also learn that there will be a 55-foot ramp in the racecourse, creating an unusual jump setup. I have little experience with hitting ramps on my bike. The feel is different than a jump made of dirt, so I hit up my buddy Levi for some help to prepare the best I can. Levi has an outdoor compound in northern Minnesota with a few freestyle ramps, which he mainly uses for snowmobile training. I'm grateful when I show up to ride and his crew drops everything to set up a ramp for me so that I can train. ESPN's fickleness when selecting which events to include at X Games and which to drop makes it difficult to plan long-term. Still, once snow starts flying in late fall, I'm on my sled till the spring thaw in April. Then it's back to my dirt bike for spring and summer. My life has been ruled by the rhythm of these riding seasons for almost 20 years.

TWO WEEKS OUT FROM X GAMES, on July 4, we look at a house for sale in St. Cloud, just miles down the highway from where Sara and I grew up and where our parents still live. Sara's mom, Deb, who's a rock of reliability for us, works as a realtor. With her help, we find a very nice bi-level house with an attached garage on 10 acres with a massive 60-

foot by 40-foot shed out back that I envision as BioDapt headquarters. There's no barn or fence for our horses, and no motocross track, but we can build those and create our dream compound. Caught up in the excitement, we don't think through the fact that we will actually have to haul all of our stuff an hour south in the midst of one of the busiest times of our lives. We buy the house a week after taking a tour. It's mid-July.

I'm feeling the pressure. In the days before departing for Los Angeles and Summer X Games, while in the middle of packing for our move, I'm driving to see my mom at her house in Kimball. I'm on the phone with her and suddenly I'm gripped by a splitting headache. I'm dizzy, and I cannot talk. I know what I'm trying to say, but my mouth is unable to get the words out. I veer off the road and throw the truck in park to gather myself. I can't move. I've had my first migraine. I've been juggling so many responsibilities that my stress levels have pushed into unhealthy territory. I'm unsure what to make of it other than to try and take some time to mentally regroup. Sara has suffered from hemiplegic migraines for years and I've had to support her through similar situations. Honestly, it scares the hell out of me.

I will need to pull myself together quickly. The competition at X Games will be harder than ever. In addition to Ridgway, Wazny, Todd Thompson, and Steve Howe, there's a teenager named Max Gomez who will be a major threat. A new client of BioDapt, Max is a below-knee amputee who was injured while racing moto. His dad called me in November 2012, following his son's amputation, and I sent a Versa Foot. Not long after, his father called back to tell me how once Max bolted on the foot, he ran through their house, up and down the stairs, with excitement that he would be able to ride dirt bikes again. His dad saw him with his fire back and grew emotional while trying to explain the significance. His voice cracked as he described his son getting back to what he loved most, and he wanted to give me credit for making it possible.

In our first duel at Extremity Games, Max beat me in the first moto before I stepped up my speed and shut him down. He's fast and young, with loads of potential. He will be another contender, along with my old rivals Todd Thompson and Ridgway.

ON RACE NIGHT AT THE STAPLES CENTER in Los Angeles—home of the Lakers and Clippers of the NBA, and the Kings of the NHL—the stands are packed and bouncing with energy under the arena lights. We adaptive riders will be competing directly before the pro class, and the venue crackles with anticipation. We're staged alongside many of my pro Supercross heroes, guys like multi-champion Chad Reed and veterans Justin Brayton and Josh Hill. I have to pinch myself to see if this is real or if I'm dreaming.

ESPN and GoPro have teamed up, attaching a camera to my prosthesis during practice, giving a close-up of the Moto Knee while I'm riding. The footage will air in heavy rotation on ESPN during the broadcast, giving me and the company valuable publicity.

True to my prediction, the race is tight from start to finish. I'm neck and neck with Thompson and Ridgway. Max is there, too, but I can only assume that the gravity of the moment, the stakes, unnerve him and he makes a mistake, falling back in the pack. Ridgway has taken the lead right away. I've kept close for the first few laps and shown him a wheel a few times as we enter the berm before the ramp jump. When he takes the inside line and I try and rail the outside, he stands me up and I have to let off. With a couple laps to go, I need to make my move. I grab another gear going into the whoop section and blitz by Ridgway for the lead and hang on for the win.

On the dirt track, Sara totters out, fully pregnant, to give me a huge hug as I sit beaming and sweaty on my bike. From the race, to the venue and fans, to the amount of work to physically prepare, this becomes my most satisfying X Games performance. Given all that's happening away from the track, with Sara now seven months pregnant, the past several months have been grueling. I'm definitely enjoying the moment and riding a high as we celebrate in L.A. later that night with Sara, Luke, and a couple great friends and supporters from my title sponsor company, Loctite.

AT THE END OF AUGUST, Sara and I close on the house in St. Cloud, a few miles outside the city and 20 minutes from the farm where I grew up. We're back among the familiar, surrounded by flat seas of corn and soybeans. Tractors crawl along the roads. The sound of corn dryers carries for miles, and the wind brings a whiff of manure. All of which is starkly different than the thick woods crisscrossed by recreational trails that characterize Brainerd. For a month, we own two houses, until our place in Brainerd sells—adding further financial strain and stress. To keep our health insurance while pregnant, Sara has been commuting from St. Cloud to her nursing job in Brainerd, more than an hour each way. I'm working my tail off, too. My priorities are about to shift— fatherhood is looming, and business is rocking.

I'm sending knees and feet out to customers all over the country and overseas. The word is out among the veteran community that our products are good. Patients at Walter Reed in Maryland, Brook Army Medical Center in San Antonio, and Balboa Naval Hospital in San Diego are getting fitted for BioDapt equipment. I work night and day out of a makeshift office in the lower level of our new house—so much for avoiding stairs. We have a workshop in the garage, too, and I've enlisted my brother, Chris, and my dad as contractors to finish the inside of the 40-foot by 60-foot shed. I design the layout and they build an office, fitness center, and multiple workshop rooms within it. Our property buzzes with activity, like Grand Central Station, making it difficult to get any production work done.

In 2013 I sell more than 30 Moto Knees and about 80 Versa Feet. Approximately 60 percent of those go through the three main veteran rehab facilities. We get orders from cancer patients and those who've lost limbs to injury, like me. Word has gotten out among the amputee community, and media coverage of my appearances at X Games has raised the profile of the company. But the bulk of BioDapt's business at the time comes from veterans who've lost limbs in combat. Due mainly to the military, BioDapt is having a banner year in 2013.

ON NOVEMBER 20 AT 11 PM, Lauren is born at Lakewood Health Systems, where Sara works, in Staples, Minnesota. She's a healthy 7 pounds, 8 ounces and measures 19 inches long. She's beautiful and I get choked up at the sight of our baby girl as I physically help deliver her. Her nose appears smooshed and crooked, and being a first-time dad and naïve, my heart sinks for her. The doctor assures me her nose will straighten out within several hours.

Once we're all home from the hospital, I confront my limitations as an amputee dad. At night, once I've removed my prosthesis for bed, I cannot go to Lauren and pick her up when she cries for milk or a fresh diaper. I'm afraid I will lose my balance and drop her. Even with my prosthesis on, I remain cautious. We have a close call: cradling Lauren in my arms, my knee gives out and I feel myself going down. Acting quickly, I toss Lauren as gently as possible on the bed before collapsing to the floor with a thud. Thankfully, she's uninjured, but the episode leaves Sara and me shaken.

Lauren is a game-changer for our household. Although Sara serves as her primary caregiver, I can no longer take off at a moment's notice to head into town to mess around or ride my bike or snowmobile. Not that I have the spare time anyway. With my brother-in-law Luke returning to his career teaching technology at a high school just over an hour away, I'm shorthanded amid growing demand for our equipment. I can't keep up without help.

With business surging, Sara elects not to return to nursing following maternity leave and instead goes to work with me, managing the administrative, financial, and social media marketing side of the business. We quickly find that working together every day tests our relationship in fresh ways. Sara has given up her nursing career and friendships in Brainerd. She misses her co-workers and the daily interactions outside our home. If Sara needs to vent about me, how

I'm getting on her nerves, where can she turn? In addition to her office duties with BioDapt, she's caring for a newborn. All of which requires an adjustment for everyone.

In January 2014, I return to compete in snocross at Winter X Games (ESPN has returned snowmobile racing to its lineup, too), and the crew traveling with me grows by one. Sara bundles an eight-week-old Lauren in a backpack carrier and hauls her around Buttermilk Mountain in Aspen. With my family trackside, I win easily for a change, my fourth Winter X Games gold. Returning home from Colorado, Sara officially starts on the BioDapt payroll, beginning February 2014. I badly need her help.

16

Down and Out

IN MARCH, ADAPTIVE SNOWBOARDING MAKES ITS PARALYMPICS debut at the 2014 Sochi Games. I don't attend, instead watching from our new house, where we receive a constant stream of family and friends wanting to visit us and see Lauren. We've come from Brainerd, where we lived in the woods in comparative isolation, to a community where we have deep roots and a large social circle. It's great to be back among family and friends, but I quickly find it's difficult to get work done with so much activity buzzing around the house.

No members of the U.S. team use my equipment at the Games. Some of them have tried it but second-guess its effectiveness. Others are concerned about changing up their gear in the months leading to the Games when what they had was working for them.

Still, two BioDapt clients compete in snowboarding at the Games. Michelle Salt of Canada and Andre Cintra of Brazil both use a Moto Knee and a Versa Foot. Michelle lost a leg in a motorcycle accident. Her background in motorsports led her to me and BioDapt once she committed to making a run at the Paralympics in snowboarding. Andre was referred to me through Kep, who coached him on the World Cup circuit. Neither one of them medals at the Games. Amy Purdy wins bronze, although not on my equipment. Still, for me, and BioDapt, the months afterward will be pivotal, deflecting my life on a new and exciting course.

Immediately after the Games, I receive a phone call from Evan Strong, who won gold in snowboardcross for the U.S. Evan and I met while competing together at the Winter X Games. I know him to be an intense and determined rider who's always looking for an edge. "I've been hearing about your foot and thinking about it," he says. "I'd love to give it a try."

I've been fortunate that the reputation of my equipment has spread through word of mouth, sparing me from having to aggressively market my prostheses. If Evan, a gold-medal-winning Paralympian, uses my BioDapt equipment, the company will gain even more exposure. I'm excited about the possibilities when Evan invites me to meet him at Copper Mountain, Colorado, in April, where the U.S. team will be competing at nationals.

WHEN I ARRIVE AT COPPER, nearly two miles up in the Rockies, I meet Evan so that he can demo a Versa Foot. It's like déjà vu. Three years earlier, I'd met Keith here, an experience that kickstarted BioDapt. I'm hoping for another positive outcome, but I'm nervous. A below-knee amputee, Evan can apply more force than an above-knee amputee can. I'm uncertain how the foot will react under extreme stress and speeds, but I needn't be. As Evan rides on a Versa Foot, I watch him test it for feel in different terrain and riding positions. "Yeah, this is pretty good," Evan says at the end of a day of riding together.

The next day, Evan lines up for his first snowboardcross race of the weekend, flies through preliminaries to the finals, and wins a national championship on a foot he's worn for one day. Sold on the Versa Foot, he turns the tables and tries to sell me on an idea. "Schultzy, why don't you race? It's no big deal."

Evan and a group of other competitors team with Dan Gale and Kep to talk me into racing in a time trial run right there, right then, at nationals. I had ridden at Vail Veterans Program weeks earlier and during Wednesday night ski league racing at Powder Ridge back home. But I hadn't spent much time on a board that winter. Plus, I'm an above-knee amputee and the rest of the field is composed of below-knee amputees.

Caught up in the moment, the next morning I complete the necessary paperwork and entry forms, line up on the gate, and let it fly. I finish with a time that places me fifth out of 10 in a field that has just competed at the Paralympic Games. Afterward, Sara and I are in the Adaptive Action Sports office with Kep, who encourages me to make a run at the next Paralympic Games in 2018 in PyeongChang, South Korea.

"You can have Mike for the next two years," Kep tells Sara, "but after that he's ours. He's going to become a full-time snowboarder."

We all laugh, and I explain to Kep that I'm not interested. I don't believe that as an above-knee (AK) I can even come close, much less beat below-knees (BKs). With only one class in men's and women's competition, regardless of the level of amputation, AKs are at a distinct disadvantage. If I can't win, or at least have a realistic chance to earn a medal, I doubt I can find the motivation for all the dedicated training and hard work required to compete at the Paralympics.

I PUT TO REST ANY THOUGHTS of competing seriously at the Paralympics throughout the summer, focusing instead on keeping up with increasing orders for BioDapt. On October 22, 2014, new circumstances cause me to reconsider. U.S. coach Miah Wheeler sends me an email inviting me to compete at a World Cup event in November.

Looks like IPC is going to create two lower limb categories, Miah writes about the International Paralympic Committee. *Having said that, I wanted to see if you're interested in going to the first World Cup with us. You'd need to cover your own plane ticket. Team will cover entry and lodging. Please respond ASAP as we leave November 16.*

The International Paralympic Committee has created three classifications: above-knee amputees, like me, will compete in their own class, apart from below-knee amputees, who will now have two classes. My chances of contending have suddenly improved.

I tell Sara the news and explain how I feel I've accomplished everything I set out to with adaptive motocross and snowmobiles. "How cool would that be, to be part of Team USA and wear the red, white, and blue jersey?" I'm really only fantasizing, knowing that this would be a total change after dedicating my whole adult life to motorsports.

I recall a conversation with my dad after the Sochi Games. We were sitting in his fishing boat. I mentioned that I had been asked whether I was interested in attempting to pursue a spot on the U.S. team. I told him I'd said no, explaining that with only one classification I'd never be able to compete with the BKs.

"Yeah," he'd said, surprising me, "but it's the Paralympics! Wouldn't you want to go for that?" My dad has always been more of a motorsports fan, but he'd seen how big the moment was, and how important a Paralympics opportunity could be.

Sara sees it, too. "What if you could get on the podium," she says, "or win at the Paralympics?"

My entire competitive career, beginning when I was a teenage BMX racer, has been motivated by getting on the podium, standing on the top riser, secure in the knowledge that I was the fastest. Competing for a sponsored team in snocross or on a dirt bike at X Games is one thing. But wearing the USA jersey would be the ultimate honor, especially after all the work that I've done with our veterans. I recall athletes at medal ceremonies, the look in their eyes as the anthem plays, flag rising. No feeling would top that release of emotion.

After a long discussion and psyching myself up, I'm excited about finding a way forward. "Let's give it a try."

I call Miah and tell him I'm willing to try snowboarding at the World Cup. I'll have three weeks to get ready, and I haven't touched snow since last April. I cram in two days of riding with Kep and the Adaptive Action Sports team on a quick trip to Copper Mountain. Then I board a flight for the Netherlands, where, in November, there isn't any snow either. The flight to Europe feels surreal and incredibly spontaneous compared to anything I've ever done before. I'm flying by the seat of my pants with no idea how things are about to unfold.

I ARRIVE IN LANDGRAAF, in the southeast of the Netherlands, near the borders with Germany and Belgium, where an indoor ski hill called SnowWorld will host the season-opening World Cup races. The largest indoor ski facility in Europe, SnowWorld is essentially a giant warehouse built on the side of a hill containing a resort, with a gym and spa, and several restaurants with glass windows to look out on the ski areas. The entire setup appears industrial, with one lift running down the center and five slopes for riding. And it's frickin' cold inside, like a giant freezer.

I'm competing here under the Adaptive Action Sports umbrella. The competition has been organized into a Continental Cup (an amateur level) on the first day and ends with a World Cup—both in banked slalom, a downhill discipline in which riders run a winding course, navigating a series of berms that flow around gates on a timed run. In order to be eligible for the U.S. team, I will need to accrue points at World Cup events like this one.

When I line up, I'm nervous as hell and feel pretty sketchy sliding down the course but make a few respectable runs, especially for a rookie. I wind up winning a silver and a gold medal in banked slalom, with my main competition being a young Dutchman named Chris Vos, a fast racer who's competing on his home turf. This earns me enough points to be added as a full-fledged member of the U.S. team. I've done far better than expected, and I commit to three more competitions this season.

In addition to wearing the team colors, the greatest benefits of being on the national team consist of coaching and travel assistance.

The team organizes all travel to training camps and competition and covers all costs. I show up at the airport at the appointed time, and all my airfare has been comped. When I arrive at our destination, I check in at the team hotel or rented house, and it doesn't cost me a cent. Although there's no salary, team members get paid a small stipend during competition season, too. Wax, equipment service, and training are all provided for the A-Team members. I've run my own program now for six years. I've loved it, but I also can't deny that it's a welcome change to have most of my needs met as part of a team again.

IN DECEMBER 2014, I train for the first time as an official member of the U.S. team. The training camp is held at Breckenridge at the same time as Ski Spec, the annual adaptive sports extravaganza for amputees. Balancing my duties as an athlete and as an entrepreneur has only become more challenging now that several Team USA athletes are onboard with BioDapt. My new commitment to snowboard racing comes at the expense of my business duties. The camp demands most of my time, leaving little to assist any of the amputees attending the convention with equipment. Harvey Naranjo, adaptive activities coordinator at Walter Reed, has brought a handful of vets. I slip away from training for a few hours here and there to assist Harvey and his crew, but my priority now will be riding, and our team schedule for the weekend is full. This is my first training camp on snow. I'm hoping that all the time on the mountain with Kep and my new teammates will pay off. Back at home, I continue to hit the slopes at Powder Ridge as frequently as possible in preparation for a World Cup event in Aspen in mid-January.

Once in Aspen, I pull the red, white, and blue U.S. jersey over my head for the first time, and it's a proud and emotional feeling when I take a moment to understand the significance of representing Team USA. To make it sweeter, I take gold at my first World Cup boardercross event, my budding snowboarding career off to a better start than I could have imagined. To observers, maybe it looks like I just show up and win, but the fact is, this has been an incredibly challenging and scary sport to learn in a short amount of time. Every time I'm on course for training or in a competition, my nerves are hitting their rev limiter, and it honestly scares the hell out of me. I have no throttle or brake levers to control myself, and that's all I've known. Snowboarding is all still new for me. Every time I drop into a course, I'm trying to figure out how my legs and body need to operate to get my ass down the course as fast and safe as possible.

A FEW WEEKS LATER I return to Aspen, this time on a snowboard *and* a snowmobile at Winter X Games. I will be the first X Games athlete to compete in adaptive snowboard and snowmobile events—two entirely separate sports—and I'm expecting a swarm of media coverage. I've hired a publicist, Katie Moses-Swope, to help manage interview and related media requests.

Competing against a field of the world's best BKs, I expect my winning streak on a snowboard to end at X Games. With a field of 12, I'll be thrilled just to make the six-man final. Then I can concentrate on winning my record sixth gold medal in adaptive snocross.

First, I must get through a nerve-wracking boardercross practice. The X Games course on Buttermilk Mountain is fast, with big features— far larger and more technical than any of the World Cup runs I've raced so far. The most challenging section appears at the top. A straightaway leads to a set of rollers followed by a daunting 50-foot jump, which I know I will struggle to clear. I must pump through the rollers to maintain sufficient speed. Ideally, I should accelerate through the rollers during the approach to the jump.

I watch the other riders work hard pumping with their entire body in order to hit the sweet spot in the transition of the jump landing. I know they have better function than I do. One of my weaknesses is the ability to pump through rollers. Being an above-knee, riding regular foot—with my left leg in front—makes it difficult to absorb the face of rollers and then generate force down the backside. By the end of the first day of practice, I manage to clear the 50-foot jump, but it's a hard and sketchy landing.

When we show up to practice on the morning of race day, the course has been altered. Overnight, designers cut a two-foot drop just beneath the start gate so they can place a banner for the Navy, one of X Games' sponsors. Two feet might not sound like a big deal, but it's a new wrinkle that we haven't practiced. Considering that I don't have control over my left foot, my leading foot, the drop makes for a challenge. I take two training runs on the morning of the race to get the start dialed, and then it's time to compete.

As I line up for the first qualifier with five other riders in my heat at the start gate, Sara waits at the bottom of the course, near the Jumbotron, with Lauren in a baby backpack, along with her mom and our new publicist, Katie. Luke stands midway along the side of the course to watch as I fly past. My biggest X Games weekend is about to get underway.

The gate is electronic and drops on the official start. Some riders push the board right up to it. I slide mine back as far as possible in order to give myself a little momentum heading over the drop-off. When the gate drops, I pull out using my arms to catapult me onto the course. Clipping the edge of my board on the ledge, I'm immediately off-balance, hitting the snow while skidding to my right and toppling over. *Ugh. I'm already behind the rest of the field.* Popping up quickly, I look down course and see a messy start has left a pileup of riders on the front stretch. Three guys have crashed on the first feature. If I can get up and going before they do, I'll scoot into third place and in a transfer position to the final. I pop up and try to accelerate the best I can down the 50-yard stretch with the three rollers between the start gate and first gap jump that had given me such difficulty in practice. I pass the downed bodies of my competitors, who are struggling to get on their feet and sliding again. I only need to finish without falling or veering outside the course markers in order to qualify through to the final.

I pump through the rollers but don't generate as much speed as I would like. Approaching the daunting 50-foot jump, I must make a

January 2006: WPSA
National Snocross races
at Canterbury Park in
Shakopee, Minnesota.
This weekend I earned
my first-ever pro podium
(third place). Pictured
left to right: Me, nephew,
Tucker; my dad, Scott;
and my brother, Chris.
(Credit: Sara Schultz)

January 2007: ESPN
Winter X Games Snocross
in Aspen, Colorado. The
X Games racecourses were
always built to showcase
high-flying action. This
jump was 120 feet from
takeoff to landing. Nothing
like flying a snowmobile
through the air at X Games.
(Credit: Sara Schultz)

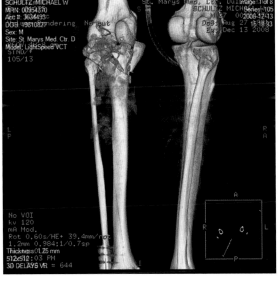

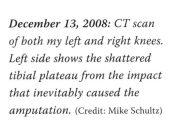

December 13, 2008: CT scan
of both my left and right knees.
Left side shows the shattered
tibial plateau from the impact
that inevitably caused the
amputation. (Credit: Mike Schultz)

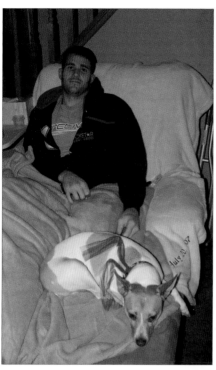

December 24, 2008: The day I came home from the hospital, with our dog, Zeus. He would always lie down in the open space of my left leg. (Credit: Sara Schultz)

February 2009: Warnert's Quadna Mountain Park practice track. Five weeks post-amputation, one of my first rides back on the snowmobile before wearing a prosthesis. I was riding Darrin's practice sled. (Credit: Mike Schultz)

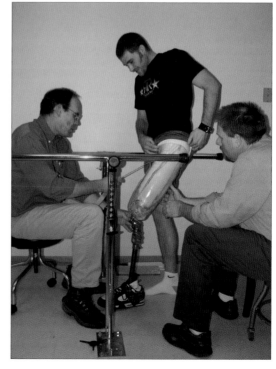

February 2009: My first prosthesis fitting at Prosthetic Labs in Baxter, Minnesota. This is a temporary test socket that I wore for a few weeks. Pictured left to right: Chip Taylor, me, and Ron Staples. (Credit: Sara Schultz)

February 2009: ISOC National Snocross in Brainerd, Minnesota. This is the entire Warnert Race team on the finish line jump right after my parade lap, when ISOC retired my No. 5 race number. The Snocross community and race fans rallied behind me.
(Credit: Gary Walton)

Photo By: Wayne Davis Photography

January 2010: ESPN Winter X Games Adaptive Sno-X. Racing around the vertical wall in the "Talladega" turn. One of my favorite features ever to race on. The turn was shaped with a half-pipe groomer/auger that is used for the ski/ snowboard halfpipes.
(Credit: Wayne Davis)

July 2011: Heavy Medal Tour visit at an air base in the Middle East standing in front of a B-1 Lancer Bomber aircraft. Pictured left to right: Byron Turk, Levi LaVallee, AF pilot, me, AF pilot, and Glen Kafka.
(Credit : Rob Powers)

January 2012: ESPN Winter X Games in Aspen, Colorado. My coach Kep and I preparing for the boardercross race. My first time on a snowboard at X Games. (Credit: Sara Schultz)

February 2012: Atop a mountain in British Columbia, Canada, with Keith Deutsch while filming the action scenes for Edge Factor's Metal & Flesh documentary. (Credit: Mike Schultz)

March 2012: ERX Motorpark in Elk River, Minnesota. Filming my crash reenactment scene for Edge Factor's Metal & Flesh documentary. I raced in the Pro Vet class later that afternoon. (Credit: Sara Schultz)

July 2013: ESPN Summer X Games in Los Angeles, California. Opening lap of the Moto-X Adaptive Final in the Staples Center. I would end up winning my second Moto-X gold. Pictured front to back: Chris Ridgway, me, and Todd Thompson. (Credit: Joe Wiegele)

2014 in Washington, D.C. Family picture before receiving the Jaycees TOYA national award ("Ten Outstanding Young Americans"). Pictured left to right: Stepdad, Rick; Mom, Carrie; baby Lauren and Sara; me; and nephew, Tucker.

January 2016: IPC World Cup Snowboardcross race in Snowmass, Colorado. Chris Vos and I racing in the Final. I took the win. (Credit: Natasha Vos)

2017 Dew Tour Banked Slalom competition in Breckenridge, Colorado. My teammates and BioDapt sponsored athletes showcasing medals and legs. Pictured left to right: Noah Elliott, Brenna Huckaby, me, and Keith Gabel.
(Credit: Mike Schultz)

Spring 2017: Copper Mountain, Colorado, nationals snowboardcross competition. Standing with my biggest cheerleaders: my wife, Sara, and daughter, Lauren.
(Credit: Mike Schultz)

August 2017: New Zealand snowboard training and competition trip. Sitting on the mountain with my teammates (Mike Shea, Keith Gabel, and Brittani Coury) in awe of the surrounding landscape and views.
(Credit: Mike Schultz)

March 2018: Paralympic Games in Pyeongchang, South Korea. Just before the opening ceremony where I'm about to lead Team USA into the stadium as flagbearer. A few of my snowboard teammates standing to my far right: Keith Gabel, Mike Shea, and Amy Purdy.
(Credit: Brianna Tammar/ U.S. Paralympic Snowboarding)

March 2018: Paralympic Games in Pyeongchang, South Korea. Our first view of our competition venue at Jeongseon Alpine Center. The finish line of the snowboardcross course is in the far left of the image.
(Credit: Mike Schultz)

March 2018: Paralympic Games in Pyeongchang, South Korea. Bottom of the snowboardcross course after I won gold, the best feeling in the world! Standing next to silver medalist Chris Vos.
(Credit: Joe Kusumoto)

March 2018: Paralympic Games in Pyeongchang, South Korea. The first time Sara and I saw each other after I won gold in the boardercross competition (in the finish line corral). (Credit: Brianna Tammar/U.S. Paralympic Snowboarding)

March 2018: Paralympic Games. Taken after receiving my gold medal at the medal ceremony. One of the most amazing feelings I've ever experienced. I couldn't help myself; I had to throw a heel clicker on the stage! (Credit: Mike Reis)

March 2018: Winter Paralympic Games, PyeongChang, South Korea. Showcasing my gold and silver medals with Sara at the closing ceremony. (Credit: Mike Schultz)

difficult decision: if I try to go around, I will be disqualified. If I go for it, I might not make it. A fall could take me out of the race, but I have to try! On the approach, it's clear I won't have the necessary speed, but I focus forward anyway. I'm going for it, planning to absorb the landing the best I can.

Launching from the lip of the ramp, I spot the landing and know immediately that I'm coming up short and I won't make it past the knuckle (the transition of where the highest point of the landing meets the downslope). Coming down about eight feet short, on a flat section, the full force impacts my back leg, my good leg, causing me to slam hard on my board and skid out. Popping up to continue, my heel squashes beneath my weight and a surge of pain shoots from my foot, crumpling me to the snow. Pressure building in my foot and ankle, I scream out in agony. Every second brings increasingly unbearable pressure in my foot. It hurts so damn bad, as bad as my knee injury had before amputation. *What have I done! Why the hell did I try and go for it!?*

Lying on my back in agony, I watch Chris Vos, the teenage phenom from the Netherlands, approach on the course. He checks his speed and hops to the top of the jump and lowers himself down the vertical backside of the jump face. It's eight feet to the snow and he lands flat. It looks like it hurts like hell, but he's still on his feet and he skates by on his way toward the finish. That's what I should have done. I should have checked up and jumped down. Instead I'm in overwhelming pain.

Drawn by my screams, Luke slips past the course marshals and arrives at my side soon after medical personnel. The other competitors eventually whizz by. On the Jumbotron at the base of the mountain, looking for a glimpse of me racing down the course, Sara spots my Moto Knee sticking out of a clutch of medical personnel working on one of the racers. She phones Luke, who delivers the news that I'm down and out.

AT THE SMALL HOSPITAL IN ASPEN, I receive intravenous pain medicine, but my foot throbs as if slammed by a hammer every time my heart beats. I'm pissed at myself for choosing to go over the jump. Everything was rolling perfectly and I made a stupid mistake—a rookie mistake that I will pay for, far more than I know. The realization eats me up.

Scans show my heel is shattered into a dozen pieces. The break is so bad that doctors here cannot fix it. They provide Sara with the names of specialists, one of whom is in Seattle.

"We live in Minnesota," she tells them.

We can't do anything for you, they say. *We'll just bandage you up and give you another dose of pain medication.*

"We're staying in a condo up two flights of stairs to the front door," Sara explains. "We don't have a wheelchair. How is he going to get around? Am I supposed to carry him?"

The hospital staff offers no answers.

Doctors write a prescription for pain meds. I've already been getting fentanyl every 30 minutes via IV. I'm also getting oral pain medicine. Yet I'm in agony. As I'm discharged, I ask my nurse, "Should we be going? Why can't I stay here at least until we get my pain under control?" She replies that the prescription should take care of it. But neither Sara nor I am convinced. I'm frustratingly helpless, at the mercy of the hospital staff.

Kep has come to the hospital to check on me. He lifts me into our rental car and helps me out once we're at our condo. I lean on his big frame to reach the top of the stairs. Sara's mom, Deb, has brought Lauren back to the condo, and she's cleaned up the place in preparation for my return.

Inside, lying on a couch shortly after I arrive, my pain quickly grows more intense, causing my heart rate to rise. I start to hyperventilate, my difficulty breathing exacerbated by altitude. In shock, my chest heavy, my body cramps, and my hands close into claws. I can't control them. I've never felt anything like this, and it frightens me. I'm in more pain than when I lost my leg. I begin convulsing and I'm unable to breathe. *What is happening to me?* I'm helpless, and afraid that I'm going to die right here on the couch in this condo in front of my terrified family.

Luke has taken our car to the pharmacy to fetch my meds. Kep has left, too. It's Sara; her mom, Deb; Lauren; and me. Deb phones 9-1-1, but none of us knows the address of the condo. With Lauren on her hip, Deb runs downstairs with the phone to flag down the ambulance. She's good in a crisis; she doesn't get emotional. In her hand, she holds a commemorative lightsaber handed out at X Games as part of a promotion for the latest movie in the *Star Wars* franchise. Battery-operated, the lightsaber glows blue and makes a humming and slashing sound as Deb waves it in the air as a beacon for the first responders to find us. It's a ridiculous sight, and if I didn't fear for my life, maybe I could laugh.

Once the EMTs get to me, they place an oxygen mask over my mouth and immediately administer a shot of fentanyl, which relaxes me instantly, allowing me to take a much-needed deep breath again. Loaded into an ambulance, I'm back at the hospital 45 minutes after being discharged. Wheeling through the ER, Sara glares at the nurse who had refused to admit me earlier. This time the hospital will allow me to stay overnight.

The cramping in my calf muscle had been pulling on my bone structure. The excruciating pain I was feeling? That was my ankle being pulled apart by contractions, into 15 pieces.

IN THE MORNING, I'm discharged and return to the condo, where I watch the X Games adaptive snocross race on television, the one where I was supposed to win my sixth snocross gold medal.

When my phone rings, Sara answers. It's U.S. coach Miah Wheeler, who tells her that because I'm on the national team, I have access to team surgeons. Some of the best are nearby in Vail. "Okay," Sara says. "Tell me what I need to do."

First, we must get home, though. I need to wait for the swelling to subside, and our animals and business responsibilities await us in Minnesota. My mechanic, Kyle Youchman, was en route to Aspen with my truck and snowmobile when I was injured. He arrives and spends one night in Aspen before it's time to head home. Kyle drives my truck while I sprawl in the back to elevate my leg, sedated by medication. Sara's in our car with Deb and Lauren. It will be a long-ass drive to Minnesota—17 hours.

ONE WEEK LATER, Sara and I fly to Colorado to meet Dr. Clanton, a renowned orthopedic foot surgeon in Vail. He's worked with athletes on the U.S. team before and many elite-level professional athletes from many other sports. Sara and I are thinking there must be a specialist closer to home in Minnesota who can help me. We have a baby. We can't be in Colorado for surgery and recovery, but we resolve to at least meet with Dr. Clanton to hear what he has to say.

"That's bad," he says, examining my right foot, my good foot, the one I will need for the rest of my life. But he's seen worse. He's reassembled athletes in more dire conditions. His bedside manner gives me comfort that I'm in good hands. Through all the injuries, I've seen a lot of doctors, but never felt as at ease around a surgeon as with Dr. Clanton. I expect him to say, "Dude, why do this to yourself?" I expect him to advocate fusing my ankle, a process that will restrict my ability to flex it again, making walking more difficult, never mind competing on snowmobiles and snowboards. The ankle joint is so badly broken that fusing makes sense, but I would lose my ability to flex my ankle and balance. I'd be even more disabled.

Instead, Dr. Clanton surprises us. Sara overcomes her skepticism and comes to see Dr. Clanton as our guardian angel. He wants to get me back into shape for competition. Maybe I'm not interested in continuing—snowboarding is not my favorite activity at the moment— but Dr. Clanton wants to fix me so that I can carry on or not, on my own terms. "I'm going to do everything I can to get you to that point," he promises.

I undergo surgery on February 4 and Dr. Clanton uses 11 screws to put my heel back together. I spend 10 days recovering in a Vail hotel room. Sara had sat in the waiting room alone during surgery. This latest injury has put our situation in stark relief now that we have Lauren. All the worrying has given Sara a chronic migraine, which makes caring for me more challenging. I've got to think about the future. Racing and doing what I love is one thing. But how am I supposed to provide for my family if I'm unable to walk? Sara's and my mutual reliance is about to be put to its toughest test yet. It will be two months before I can graduate from a wheelchair and knee scooter to using crutches and three months before I can walk again and start training. It will be more than a year before I'm no longer in constant debilitating pain.

In some ways, this injury is worse than my amputation, which required only eight weeks of recovery. I cannot ride a snowboard. I cannot race snocross, or my dirt bike. I'm 34, a father and husband, with a successful business that depends on me staying healthy. My athletic performance and the subsequent media coverage provides the most visible marketing for BioDapt. Yet I question whether it will be worth the risk to resume competing.

Snowboarding? It was a nice dream while it lasted. But who needs it? Not me. I need my health. I need a change. Just like when I lost my leg, I'm thinking that I'm done. The injuries, the constant sacrifice—are they worth it? Maybe it's time to settle down, run my business, and tend to my family. *What would that kind of a life look like? And could I commit to it?* Just when I thought I'd found my groove, all of a sudden, my future looks scarily uncertain.

SECTION THREE: OPERATION

Great things are done when men and mountains meet.
—William Blake

17

Range of Motion

MY LATEST INJURY HAS FORCED ME TO SLOW DOWN AND CONTEMPLATE how caught up I've been in racing. Stuck in a chair in our living room at home and in constant pain, I'm often angry, giving me a glimpse of what life would be like if I were permanently disabled. As I recline in our living room, looking out the window, snow blankets our property and beckons me, but I cannot ride my snowmobile through the remainder of winter. Once spring arrives, I'll be unable to ride my dirt bikes or our horses, either.

A toddler now, Lauren wants to crawl all over her dad. I remind her to be careful around my right leg. "Ouchie!" I say.

"Ouchie," she repeats.

The upside of being out of commission is that I'm spending all my time at home, giving Lauren rides around the house in my wheelchair and lying on the floor with her while playing with Legos and puzzles. I gaze at my beautiful little girl, her big blue eyes and curly blonde hair. Is it worthwhile to miss these moments with my daughter while I'm traveling, training, and competing?

My family, not only Sara but my parents, can see the pain I'm enduring. I know they wish I would hang up my racing bib permanently. They had thought, *It's snowboarding. You can't get seriously hurt while snowboarding.* Well, actually, you can. I've learned, too. I'd pushed beyond my abilities, and now I'm paying a heavy price.

I remain in a wheelchair until March 30, when I graduate to a knee scooter. A week later, I begin to use crutches and a walking boot. By the end of April, I begin a hardcore rehab regimen to get me walking again. I'm making progress, but the pain never subsides entirely. Every time I take a step and push off from my toes it causes tremendous pain in my ankle joint. For my prosthetic to swing through properly, I must make an exaggerated movement, rising slightly on the toes of my right foot. If not, my left foot kicks the ground and fails to swing through to full extension, and I stumble back on my right foot, which is incredibly painful. "Goddamn it, I can't take it anymore!" I yell as I stumble again. I take a moment to calm down.

IN MAY, I MISS OUT on racing motocross at the Extremity Games. No matter how many times I get injured, once the initial pain is gone, I always want to return to my two wheels. I'm not ready to ride yet. Eager to get back to my dirt bike, though, Sara and I find a partner to create a motorsport adaptive racing series, in part for me to resume racing, but also as a platform to get others on the track. There's talk that Extremity Games will fold, and X Games has discontinued adaptive Supercross. Opportunities for me and other adaptive riders to compete are scarce. Over the last few years, I've become a professional adaptive athlete, and the reason that's possible is because there's been a few high-profile events for me and others to showcase our stories and talent. I want to see what I can do to keep things moving.

We organize a three-event season. For the first event, we partner with Extremity Games. The next stop will take place on a track just outside Denver, in Lakewood, Colorado, on August 20. The third and final stop will take place in Texas on October 16. I resume riding my dirt bike on July 22, eager for the thrill of competition again. I'm passionate about this venture and put an enormous amount of time and energy into the preparation and marketing of the series. Sara is supportive but isn't the biggest fan. She can see that I'm pulling time away from my other duties with BioDapt and family. Running a motocross series while trying to compete at the same time turns out to be more work than I'd anticipated. I'm carrying a heavy load, and though I'm still fast, some of the younger up-and-comers have closed the gap on the track. Max Gomez, who's using a Versa Foot, battles me in the races. He's been riding more than I have, and he's younger and stronger. Plus, he's only missing his foot, so he's less disabled. He doesn't run away with the races, but he can push the pace harder and longer than I can. I keep him honest the entire way. One slip-up and I can pass. Still, it's inevitable that he's overtaken me, and he wins the championship.

There were so many fun and proud moments during the series, being able to compete at places I normally wouldn't ride and seeing the other riders getting amped up by having a championship to chase after. Despite those good feelings, by the end of the season, I'm burned-out and exhausted. Sara is too, complaining of chronic headaches from stress. I can now appreciate all the work Jim Wazny put in while both racing and running Extremity Games for years. The paperwork and logistics alone are depleting. Liability concerns are real in motocross, especially when dealing with adaptive athletes. Responsibility for the well-being of competitors weighs on us, too. Plus, there's been no financial benefit to all the time and money I've invested in the series. If I could commit more time, or find the right business partner to split duties with me 50-50, I believe I could have made it work. My business partner in the enterprise has really tried, but hasn't been carrying enough of the weight to make it all work out the way I need it to. Before too much resentment builds, and the relationship gets awkward, we need to call it quits.

AS SUMMER TURNS TO FALL, I remain in chronic pain from my injury. And I'm in a catch-22 with our family health insurance, which is provided through Team USA. A stipulation in the team policy mandates that a member must return to compete within one year of an injury to earn points or lose his or her status with the team. With each step, my heel hurts. I don't care to snowboard again, but I must in order to remain on the team and keep our healthcare. The irony is not lost on me: I must risk my health to retain health insurance.

The first race of the season with the national team will be in November, at the giant freezer in Landgraaf, Netherlands. Sara says I shouldn't be snowboarding, but she understands that if I don't compete, and lose my status on the team, then we lose our health insurance. I need to give it a try and see if I can ride.

I fly to Colorado and spend two days at Copper Mountain training with teammates. I'm frustrated by pain in my foot, but a week later I travel to the Netherlands, where I win a pair of bronze medals in the meat locker conditions of the indoor ski hill. I've ridden like crap, barely making it down the course. I leave Landgraaf in excruciating pain and unable to control the toe side of my board under high-g turns. Still, with a competition under my belt, I've bought myself another season on the team—and another 12 months of healthcare.

Sara and I travel to Ski Spec in Breckenridge in December. I ride, but my foot hurts like hell daily. The pain grinds on me, delivering a blow to my morale, fouling my mood. I'm a bear to be around, irritable, snapping easily at Sara, unable to fully enjoy life through the discomfort. Sara has been a steadying influence. Orders for BioDapt have slowed but remain steady, and she helps me keep the company running while simultaneously serving as Lauren's primary caregiver.

In my condition, I won't be able to handle snowboardcross on the monster course at Winter X Games, but riding a snowmobile should be manageable. To get ready, in January 2016 Sara and I load the trailer and hop in the truck to drive the hour and a half to Shakopee to compete in the Pro Vet class at Canterbury Park on the track beneath the big grandstand. I'm dealing with pain daily, and my right foot, my good foot, doesn't work mechanically the way I need. I haven't regained a full range of motion in my ankle. Just being around the track helps my mindset, though. Training and riding still hurts, but racing provides some distraction, and I have a competitive goal again.

I'm back in my comfort zone later in the month when I roll into Aspen and set up at Buttermilk Mountain in the paddock with the other snocross racers. My U.S. snowboarding teammates are on hand, too, and though we catch up a little bit in the lodge, when I gaze up at the mountain at the boardercross course, with its gargantuan features, I'm relieved to have passed on competing. My foot hurts every day, with each excruciating step.

On a snowmobile, the discomfort is tolerable, and on the first day of competition in Aspen, I win my fifth consecutive Winter X Games gold medal in adaptive snocross, beating the second-place finisher by almost a minute. I'm in no mood to celebrate, and neither are my snowboarding teammates. The U.S. has been shut out of the medals in the boardercross final. The future for me, for the U.S.A., looks grim. My mood only worsens during the 17-hour drive back home to Minnesota from Colorado. Chronic pain in my foot dogs me, a reminder that I'm unable to fully participate on my dirt bike, my snowmobile, or a snowboard, leaving me lost and grumpy through the start of spring.

ON APRIL 6, 2016, 14 months after my injury, I fly to Vail again for another surgery. This time, Dr. Clanton plans to remove all the hardware holding my heel together. Once he flays my foot open, he discovers and extracts four bone spurs the size of the tip of my thumb that had grown into my ankle joint, limiting movement and causing extreme pain. With the spurs removed, I regain 40 percent greater mobility in my ankle. Most of my pain and discomfort is alleviated, too, doing wonders for my mood. I recover from this latest surgery in no time.

Working out through the spring, I'm beginning to feel strong again. Since becoming a pro snowmobile racer, I've developed an all-consuming approach to fitness. I'm either in the gym or cross-training on a mountain bike or road bike three to five days per week. I want to feel like a well-oiled machine, not the rusty Tin Man from *The Wizard of Oz*, and working out intensely improves my mood, putting me in a positive state of mind. Once in top shape again, I know I'll be ready to strap on my board and resume making turns on the mountain next winter. Pain-free, I wonder what I can achieve in snowboarding.

But I hesitate. *Is that really what I want?* Snowboarding has brought me nothing but pain and misery for the past year. I'm not making any money on my board. Pursuing competitive snowboarding means my attention has been diverted from other potentially more profitable endeavors. And I want to know I have a legitimate shot at winning before I'm willing to commit the energy to training and sacrifice family time to travel the world chasing results.

Lauren is approaching her third birthday, and there are new changes in her development every time I come back from a training trip or competition abroad. After being gone for two weeks, I returned home to find she's able to carry on a conversation. I don't want to miss these milestones.

Sara has seen the huge difference the most recent surgery has made for my quality of life. The entire year following my heel injury was a struggle. She knows I can do without snowboarding, that I only stayed on the team to have healthcare. None of my U.S. teammates knows what I've gone through, although the coaches have some idea. I'm in a constant mental battle: yes, there are benefits to being on the U.S. team, and there's the opportunity to compete at the Paralympic Games. Of course, I can also get hurt on a snowboard, and that's not a lot of fun. *But can I really just give it up?*

I've been riding snowmobiles and dirt bikes for 20 years, and both have been central to my life with Sara. Every six months brought a new competition for me to focus my ambition and training. Sara may not be in the race, but she gets the same adrenaline rush, the same emotions and frustrations. If I were to retire and Sara and I committed to the daily grind, the implications of a complete lifestyle change, including staying at home together, scare the hell out of me. *Would I be content? Would there be a void in our lives?* When more than several months pass with no real competitive objective, I tend to go out of my mind worrying about what I should be doing. Without competition, I'm lost.

I spend the summer working on BioDapt. Following a banner year in 2013, commissions have slacked off by 2016. Military orders have dwindled due to a fortuitous turn: fewer soldiers getting blown up in the field. Amputations of military personnel injured on the battlefield spiked at 260 in 2011, before beginning a steady decline to fewer than 10 cases four years later. I remain busy, but the workload is manageable. In my spare time, I work out and ride my dirt bike. And think. I've got a lot of thinking to do about my future.

18
Committed

My foot finally healed, I return to familiar routines in the summer of 2016. I've resumed riding my dirt bike, and I'm feeling good. In September, just as I'm feeling healthy and fit again, I injure my shoulder in a minor crash during a big adaptive moto race in Michigan. Once my shoulder heals, I plan to race snocross in Duluth during the first stop on the ISOC Tour. I haven't competed on my snowmobile in awhile, and it will be fun. There's no snow on the ground yet in November, so in order to get into racing shape, I practice riding my dirt bike again at a local private track. Sara and Lauren accompany me for the day, cruising trackside in a golf cart, waving to me as I roar past. I'm feeling good, reaching the end of my training session on a bright autumn afternoon, hitting nearly 60 miles an hour, when bouncing at a funny angle causes me to grab too much gas. Unable to control my speed, I swerve off track to avoid a jump while going far too fast and strike a pile of dirt hidden in the weeds along the side of the course. The rear tire bucks the seat into my ass in a blink of an eye. I'm thrown over my handlebars headfirst, tumbling like a rag doll into the grass at near highway speeds.

Sara peels away in the cart with Lauren so our three-year-old daughter doesn't see the carnage. I'm sitting up, dazed, my helmet split, my right arm hanging awkwardly from my shoulder. There's a sharp feeling inside of broken bones poking at me. I'm a mess. I know there's some major injuries underneath. After my quick head-to-toe self-inspection, I'm fuming that I'm hurt yet again.

Sara bundles me into the car and drives me to the emergency room. I've broken six ribs and torn a ligament in my thumb. My head feels a little woozy, and my shoulder doesn't work right either. Sara is upset. She's exhausted from picking up the pieces every time I get broken. She's always been there for me, but now she has a toddler to care for, too, and the heel injury that left me in a wheelchair has spooked her. She's gotten a glimpse of what it would be like if I were permanently disabled.

"The year has been horrible," she says about the three separate injuries that have sidelined me. "It's breaking me. I have this beautiful little girl that I'm looking at. I can't do this anymore! I can't! It hurts my heart. It's not good for our relationship. We have a horse farm to take care of. Now you can't even lift Lauren for two months because you have six broken ribs. You're so lucky you didn't break your neck!"

My back hurts constantly from the rib injury. It's been a constant battle with major broken bones for two years. All of which has been a drag on my mood. Just when things were beginning to look up, I'm down again. Hit hard, I stop and think about what I'm doing.

Sara says I should be snowboarding, preparing for the winter season. She points out how my foot still hasn't fully healed and now I won't be able to train on my snowboard—the source of our health insurance. "Really!?" she says, pointing out how I won't be able to reunite with teammates on the U.S. Para Snowboard Team in Landgraaf, Netherlands, for another World Cup competition at the indoor ski resort.

Sara has grown exasperated. She's been picking up the extra workload with BioDapt while I'm injured, in chronic pain, and a bear to be around. I have a short fuse. Everything irritates me. Sara and I fight a lot. Straining under the immense load of being a mother and caretaker to me and our household, she wants me to set aside motorsports for snowboarding. I'm not onboard, literally and figuratively, and resent being pushed in any direction. Motorsports satisfy sponsors and make me money. Riding dirt bikes and snowmobiles has been my abiding passion as long as I've known Sara. Snowboarding alone will not pay our bills, but Sara sees the possibility of the Paralympics as a unique opportunity that we shouldn't pass up.

As I'm healing, I debate how to continue my athletic career: *Do I stick with motorsports, or am I going to snowboard?* The decision rends me, and I take out the tension on Sara. Every day, we vacillate on how to move forward and which goals to set for the future.

BY JANUARY, MY BONES HAVE MENDED and I'm back on a snowboard, riding at Powder Ridge. I'm not competition-ready, though, and I skip the Winter X Games snowboardcross event, especially against an intimidating field of the world's leading BKs. Opting instead for snocross, I win a sixth consecutive gold medal on my snowmobile. That makes six in snocross and two in motocross, for a total of eight gold medals in Summer and Winter X Games. I've had a good run in motorsports, and I'm still racking up medals. *Why give it up?*

Still, I have the snowboarding World Championships coming up in Canada in February. I continue riding in preparation and arrive at Big White, a resort in the mountainous interior of British Columbia, outside Kelowna, more than five hours from Vancouver and the coast. I haven't competed on a snowboard in 15 months, and I haven't trained enough to feel good about my coming performance. It shows. I take a disappointing silver in banked slalom and settle for fourth place in boardercross. Maybe I should be satisfied with the results considering my cumulative injuries and all the time I've taken off from riding. I'm not. Second place feels okay, but fourth place is a major bummer. I haven't ridden well, and neither has the competition. They've been training all season, and yet I'm right behind them. The more I think about my riding, the more I fume. *I know I can beat these guys, if I'm in shape and prepared. But am I ready for the commitment required? Is my family?*

There are only 13 months remaining until the Paralympic Games in PyeongChang.

Once at home, Sara and I decide to have a talk.

"What the hell are we doing?" Sara says.

I'm frustrated and angry with my results at the world championships. "Am I going to commit the next year of my life to prepare for the Games?" That's what it will take for me to have a chance at a medal, but I'm not sure whether I want it badly enough. For the last several months it's a daily mental battle that wears on me constantly.

"The reason you're upset is that you want it," she says. "You wouldn't be upset if you didn't care how you finished."

She's right. I do care. I want it. We want it. I cannot give up now with only one year to go. I've got to get off the fence on whether to continue or not. I decide to make snowboarding my priority. No more dirt bikes and snowmobiles.

With Sara's support, I'm fired up to commit to training at home in the gym and at Powder Ridge. I'll have one month to get ready before the U.S. team travels to South Korea for a World Cup test event at the Paralympic facilities in PyeongChang.

THE U.S. TEAM PLANS TO SPEND SEVERAL DAYS in South Korea for a World Cup competition and to test the course. I've never been to Asia. I'm nervous, about my riding and about the unknown. It's half a world away, with unfamiliar foods, language, and customs. We land in Seoul jetlagged after more than 13 hours of flight time, and a charter bus shuttles our team through the enormous city, hilly and dense with high-rises. An hour later, the bus wends into steep, breathtaking mountains, and a growing sense of ease comes over me in the countryside. We roll past villages, tractors, and greenhouses. I can relate to these people and the country livin'—they're farmers.

The venue for downhill snowboarding events is not held directly in PyeongChang, but about an hour away in the Taebek Mountains in Gangwon Province, on the eastern side of the Korean Peninsula, near the Sea of Japan. The racecourses are located at Jeongseon Alpine Centre, a ski resort on Gariwangsan, a 5,000-foot mountain where the setup looks different than those in North America and Europe. Runs consist of narrow ribbons of snow through steep, rocky valleys. Signs for the coming Olympic Games make the atmosphere feel real. Still, the Olympic facilities remain a construction zone 12 months out from the start of the Games. Organizers have one year to ready the venue. I'll have one year to ready myself.

Training on the first day goes smoothly. It's clear right away that the snowboardcross course does not flow properly, though. Designers have built some questionable features into the setup. The speed of the course is too great for the jumps. We all have to throw speed checks into our runs to slow down so we don't overshoot the landings. Several riders misjudge the course and injure themselves before races have even begun. On the second day I become one of them, enduring a nasty crash on my final run of practice. I can't keep the rhythm through a roller section and lose my balance, clipping the heel edge of my board in the belly of a roller, causing me to slam my head on the ground pretty hard. Even though I'm wearing a helmet, my brain feels scrambled, and it's a blow to my morale.

Fuck! I think. *I've hit my head again.*

I endure a roller coaster of emotions. *Why?! Goddamn it!* I'm tired of getting injured, especially my head.

I've got a minor concussion. I sit out the snowboardcross competition, on the doctor's recommendation, resting an additional two days before my next event. I feel off, and my reactions are dulled, but I wind up with a bronze in banked slalom. The winner is Chris Vos, of Holland, who's been training and competing full-time for the past couple years. I'm not too far off his time. There's a glimmer of hope for me, if only I can remain healthy and commit to training. I know in my heart I can be one of the top two racers, and the competitor in me wants to be on top.

THE MEDAL CEREMONY, held on the side of the mountain, is filled with pomp and circumstance. I can already tell the scope of the Games will be bigger than anything I've ever been involved with. The entire mountain has been stripped for one event, and infrastructure and building projects are being purpose-built. One thing that has irked me when it comes to snowboarding has been a lack of coverage of the sport. Other world-class competitors and I have been traveling the globe and no one knows about our achievements and sacrifice. The Paralympics will finally showcase everything we've been working toward for the past three and a half years, in one culminating event, before the eyes of the world. The Paralympics will be the payoff for all of us, though not in a financial way. It's not about money anyway, and I don't expect to make much off the competition. I'm motivated for personal reasons: the chance to set a challenging goal and attempt to achieve it spurs me now. The more difficult the accomplishment, the greater the satisfaction. I'm beginning to understand that all our World Cup competitions so far have merely been training opportunities. My bad performances have fueled me to work harder, and there's a lot more work ahead.

Standing on the podium in South Korea, I begin to imagine what I can achieve if I'm committed for an entire year to preparation. I soak in the scene. Officials wear traditional Korean clothing. There's an Olympics backdrop, and every competitor on the podium receives gifts. I've gotten a taste of what the Games will deliver. My morale soars imagining what it all will be like next year when the venue is packed with spectators and the eyes of the world focus on the performances here.

BACK AT HOME, Sara and I sit down in the office for a heart-to-heart discussion. We talk about my head injury and how she would be okay if

I hung up my racing bib once and for all. "We've had a good life," Sara says. "I could be done."

Head injuries have begun to scare us. I've noticed a pattern in which my temper increases in the months following a head injury. Sara has seen it, too. At first, she attributed my moods to the stress of life and work. In retrospect, she associates them with post-concussion symptoms. I'll get stuck on irritating thoughts, whether trying to solve a problem in my shop, or the sound of the ringing phone, or stressing over a misplaced tool, and simply snap, yelling or grunting and causing an argument with Sara.

"You need to calm down," she urges. "It's not a big deal."

I know I should overcome the negative feelings, but I can't let them go, and they lead to conflicts between us. Sometimes when I'm in my shop working alone, things can get bad over the dumbest thing. I'll be looking for a tool, and I'll swear I know I just set it down, but I can't find it. I'll pace around and start cussing and sometimes get so angry I'll chuck the nearest object across the shop. A moment later, I'll calm down and realize how stupid and unproductive that outburst was.

Hitting my head in South Korea has scrambled my brain again. Bones can heal, but a brain injury can be permanently devastating. Sara wants us to have a good life together, for me to grow old with my wits intact, be a dad to Lauren, and continue to do things together as a family that we enjoy. She doesn't want me in pain for the rest of my life. She has sat me down to tell me she would support me if I decide to call it quits on my racing career.

But I'm not ready for that, not with the Games so close, and my riding nearly at the level of the top competitors.

For more than a year, Sara has been pushing me to pursue snowboarding at the Paralympics, to forget motorsports and commit to this once-in-a-lifetime opportunity as part of a team again. I don't take pressure from others well, and it's been a source of friction between us. By backing off, she's allowing me to own the decision on whether to move forward or not. I know I *must* own it if I'm going to be successful. I've been half-assed all along when it comes to snowboarding, and that's partly what led to my injury in South Korea. If I'm truly tired of getting hurt and hitting my head, I'll have to be better prepared. By making a commitment to ride more, train more, I can reduce the risks.

I know the Paralympics will require a 100 percent commitment if I want to be the best I can, if I want to be standing atop the podium. Sara and I hatch a plan to prepare for qualifying for the Paralympics in 12 months. I will ride as much as possible. I will get stronger and quicker on my feet by training even harder in the gym. Family will have to get on without me while I'm traveling. Dirt bikes will take a back seat. Snowmobiles will be neglected. BioDapt will become secondary behind training and competing.

For the past three years, I've been on the fence, but now that I've committed to making snowboarding a priority, I feel relief and excitement in the simplified program of putting snowboarding first. The grinding pressure and anxiety around competition, the kind that dogged me during my pro snocross days, is gone. I'll probably never have a chance to take athletics this far and travel as widely as I will with the U.S. team. I resolve to enjoy the experience from now on.

19

Enjoy the Ride

INVIGORATED BY MY RENEWED COMMITMENT TO SNOWBOARDING, IN April 2017 I board a flight to Colorado for the national championships at Copper Mountain. The trip means a chance to catch up with Dan, Kep, and Amy, and the crew of Adaptive Action Sports. I will be reunited with teammates, too. I'm expecting a busy week. Any time I travel with the rest of Team USA, I begin the trip with an email to teammates, encouraging them to reach out if they have equipment concerns or issues.

Seven Americans, either teammates or hopefuls, all of them lower-limb amputees, will be using my equipment in the coming season. Mark Mann is a bilateral BK who's missing both feet. He is wearing a set of Versa Feet. A direct competitor in the LL1 classification (athletes with significant impairment of one or both lower limbs), he can push me to my max while on course. In the LL2 classification (impairment of a single lower limb) there's Keith Gabel, Mike Shea, and Evan Strong. All are missing one of their feet and use a Versa Foot. This trio swept the podium by winning gold, bronze, and silver, respectively, at the 2014 Paralympic Games in Sochi, Russia. In the women's class, there is Brenna Huckaby (Moto Knee and Versa Foot) and Amy Purdy, who wears a Versa Foot. Although Amy is missing both feet, she wears only one Versa Foot on her back foot for greater range of motion, preferring a stiffer foot on her lead leg. I don't understand her choice, because there are performance benefits to the Versa Foot, but hey, if she feels comfortable on the other one, then that's all that matters. At least she's wearing one. Finally, there is Brittani Coury in the LL2 class, who is a single-leg below-knee amputee wearing the Versa Foot. This whole crew is incredibly talented, and each one has a shot at Paralympic hardware. I'm so proud they've chosen equipment that I have built, but being responsible for their prostheses carries added stress in multiple ways.

My teammates are thoughtful about not putting me on the spot or taking too much of my time during race day. Usually, I spend a couple hours ahead of competition tweaking, refining, and maintaining their prostheses. Here at nationals I perform multiple roles as mentor, consultant, and competitor. Maintaining their gear in proper functioning order keeps me plenty busy. I don't want them to have any mechanical issues that will prevent them from performing their best. Everything I do for the next year will be aimed at making my equipment look its best through the performance of the other athletes. And, of course, winning a gold medal for myself.

When it comes to competition here at nationals, my main rivals are two double amputees who use my BioDapt equipment. First is my teammate Mark Mann, a 30-year-old double-BK from Minnesota who lost both his legs below the knee in a boating accident while jet-skiing. I've built two Versa Feet for Mann, and he's become a friend and training partner. The other is my old friend and military veteran, Matt Melancon, another double-BK who never hesitates to remind me how I can improve my Versa Foot design. Matt is not at the same level as Mark and me, but it's still cool to be on course with him for this event.

Another fresh competitor on the scene is 19-year-old Noah Elliott, competing in his first nationals. An accomplished skateboarder, Noah lost his left leg to cancer at age 16. Short and wiry, Noah is a chill, friendly dude who wears an earring in each lobe and a hipster mustache, his thick brown hair pulled into a ponytail. He's refused to cut his hair for three years, since it has grown back following radiation treatment. Using a BioDapt Moto Knee and Versa Foot, he has taken up snowboarding and moved to Park City, Utah, where he rides daily, sometimes for seven hours at a stretch. He's only been on snow one season, but he's already proving fast. Noah is so new to racing that he hasn't been classified yet. He does not race in my class here at nationals, but I know we will eventually face off once he's officially designated an LL1. I feel him pursuing me in a coming showdown.

On the courses at nationals, I win both events, ahead of Mann, who places second, and Melancon, who's third. Heading into the final season before the Paralympic Games, I'm a national champion in boardercross and banked slalom. If I want to become a Paralympic gold medalist, I must get faster in the coming months when the U.S. lines up in the gates against international competition. I'll need to catch Chris Vos of Holland, my stiffest competition. The only way I know how to do that: dedicate myself to training and preparation both mentally and physically.

THE NEXT TIME THE U.S. TEAM CONVENES is early June 2017, for a camp at the Olympic Training Center in Colorado Springs. This session is the start of an eight-month sprint to the Games. Later in June, our team training camp convenes on Mount Hood, Oregon, where a glacier allows for riding into summer. The conditions are not ideal. We have limited time on snow when lifts close a couple days due to fog and rain. Temperatures exceed 60 degrees Fahrenheit on other days. If we aren't soaked from the fog and rain, we are soaked from sweating in our winter gear. The snow is in fast retreat from the summer heat, and by the last day of riding, the snow line has receded 75 feet up the mountain from melting, and we must unstrap our boards at the end of each run and walk the rest of the way to the bottom of the chairlift.

Still, I get in some solid start-gate training and have fun making runs alongside top boardercross pros. The highlight of the trip is time spent with teammates off the mountain, soaking in sights in the beautiful Oregon wilderness. We go on a nature hike down the mountain among an alpine forest thick with soaring evergreens. In the parking lot at the trailhead, someone suggests an hour hike to a waterfall. We are all fit athletes, but we're also amputees, and hiking mountain terrain isn't exactly our strong point. "The waterfall is just around the bend," says our self-proclaimed tour guide. "Oh, I think it's just over that next hill."

More than an hour into the hike, the waterfall is nowhere to be seen as we continue charging forward. It doesn't even matter. We are all having fun shooting Sasquatch videos on our smartphones. We laugh our asses off as Mike, Keith, and I act as "Squatch" experts, shooting a mock episode of the History Channel program *MonsterQuest*. The next adventure: watching Brenna nearly fall into a creek as she does a handstand on a couple slippery rocks right in the middle of the water. She's quite talented and obviously has roots in gymnastics.

We finally find the waterfall, which proves well worth the hour-and-a-half walk. The landscape is breathtaking, featuring vertical rock walls with a two- to three-foot-wide trail cut along the edge of the lush green forest with moss growing everywhere. It looks like an environment I've only seen on the Discovery Channel. I take a moment to gather a deep breath and savor the moment. Our return trek proves to be less fun and enjoyable. We all began to get sore spots on our legs where our sockets and liners have been rubbing our skin with each step during the miles-long hike.

To continue training on snow through the summer, we must go farther. We are about to head south of the Equator. August is the middle of the Austral winter, and the team will convene on a flight for New Zealand to ride at the bottom of the world, among the Southern Alps, on the South Island.

Snowboarding has become a year-round commitment, altering how I live my life. I don't question whether it's something I should do. It's my priority. I've continued to ride my dirt bike a few times for cross-training and to keep my skills sharp. I have an open invitation to compete at Summer X Games in the Best Whip competition, which is a judged aerial maneuver performed while soaring from a jump high above the dirt track. I've considered competing—for about a minute. I know it will be very high-risk, and I'll have to push the envelope to come close to the level required for a respectable showing. It would be a bad decision right now. It's not as if I have the time anyway between all the promotions, travel, media summits, and training required by the U.S. team.

THE LANDSCAPE IN NEW ZEALAND is incredible, jagged snowcapped peaks looming over Alpine meadows and valleys thick with vegetation unique to the remote islands. There are fjords and lakes making up varied and otherworldly environments, the kind made famous as the settings in *The Lord of the Rings* movies.

In New Zealand, we intend to compete in a World Cup at Treble Cone, a large ski area on the South Island overlooking Lake Wanaka. It is an off-season training site for many European and North American teams. I'm looking forward to reuniting with Keith Deutsch, who phoned me over the summer seeking advice concerning a dirt bike he was interested in buying. I haven't seen Keith since our final filming session on our boards in British Columbia for Jeremy Bout's *Metal and Flesh* documentary. That was in 2012. Keith hasn't competed on a board in four years, so we haven't connected during my traveling and racing for the U.S. team. Now, he's back on his board and planning to show up in New Zealand to launch his own Paralympics push. He told me he'd been training. "I'm going to take it serious," he'd said.

"Oh, man," I'd said with a mix of excitement and nerves. "This will be good."

I know Keith can let her buck. He's been snowboarding a long time. I didn't say so, but I've been thinking, *Will he be a contender? Is he someone I'll need to worry about on the course?*

Keith is more responsible for my start in snowboarding, and for helping BioDapt make inroads with the military, than anyone. I'm excited when I finally see him and hear what he's been doing the past several years since he stopped racing. Keith has a daughter now. He's been freeriding a lot, too. He's still the squirrely guy I remember, fired up for the coming race, but even more pumped to be on a gorgeous sun-splashed mountain in the Southern Hemisphere. We soak up the atmosphere, 8,000 miles from home and seven months from the Paralympic Games. Keith is grateful to be on the trip, but it's been a long hiatus from racing and it's clear he will be challenged to keep pace with a new crop of competitors who've been eating, sleeping, and breathing competitive snowboarding for the past several seasons.

The trip is a grind, long and exhausting. I'm cooped up with teammates most of the time, on long bus rides from our rented houses, through the mountains, then again in the gym after riding all day. I come to find out that I'm susceptible to getting carsick during all the travel in the backseat of a van. I think to myself, *These places are absolutely incredible and I would never have the chance to see all this without snowboarding, but how many more trips can I handle like this?* Pretty much every day I'm either calling or video chatting Sara and Lauren to give them the latest update on the places I've been, or the latest gossip happening with the team—who's organized, who leaves a mess everywhere, who's quiet, and who's annoying as hell and doesn't stop talking. Life is much simpler and more straightforward at home. When those negative thoughts start creeping in, I do my best to refocus on why I'm here, on the road competing. It's all about the Games in March.

The snow conditions are marginal here, making riding our best a challenge, even for the most talented. In competition I finish third in banked slalom, and BioDapt earns a podium sweep. Noah Elliott, the new kid, has been classified LL1, and he wins gold, confirming my appraisal of his raw talent. Another of my clients, Daichi Oguri, of Japan, claims second place while using a Moto Knee. I know I can ride better. I will have to if I intend to win gold in PyeongChang.

IN NOVEMBER, TEAM USA TRAVELS to Austria for a training camp ahead of the World Cup and Paralympic qualifying season. The team has undergone another internal shakeup, and we have our third head coach in three seasons: former assistant Graham Watanabe takes over with his new assistant, Cody Brown. Both are retired pro snowboardcross racers with loads of experience. Not everyone on the team is thrilled with the new leadership, and they're having a tough time with the transition. For me, it's no problem. I know both Graham and Cody have incredible experience in riding technique and race craft. All coaches run their programs differently, and as a rider/athlete you just have to understand how they work and do what you can to get the most out of your time together.

For me, the coaching is clicking. I'm eager to learn and become a better snowboarder, and the results start stacking up. I go on a winning run, beginning in banked slalom in Landgraaf, Netherlands, and continuing with gold in boardercross and banked slalom in Finland, part of another long haul on the road with more than five straight weeks traveling with the team. The riding is going great. I'm gaining experience on new terrain and courses, which translates into winning in competitions.

In mid-December I compete at an International Paralympic Committee sanctioned event held as part of the Dew Tour action sports festival in Breckenridge. Noah Elliott edges me out for first place. Chris Vos had swept up all the accolades while I was out with injury. For three years, he rode full-time, training year-round for the Games. He was becoming a superstar in the adaptive snowboard world. I thought I could beat him if I could remain healthy. Now I am healthy and beating him consistently.

My main competition now will be Noah, riding on a BioDapt leg. He's improving with each event and will be difficult to hold off. Another rival will be Mark Mann, a friend and client from Minnesota, for whom I've built two feet. Mann has two good knees. With both these natural shock absorbers intact, he has an advantage on rough terrain and roller sections. His ability to absorb and press through these features permits him to charge at a faster pace.

Off the mountain, I am enjoying incredible sights and scenes with teammates while on the road. Throughout my career, I had never been one to take the time to go out and about when traveling for competitions. This year I enjoy a whole new perspective, determined to make the most of it all. It helps that I have some great teammates who are experienced international travelers. Mike Shea and Keith Gabel are my favorites to hang out with, and I look to them for guidance. Both have a great taste for international cuisine, and finally they talk me into trying something different. I have no idea what to order, so I have them take care of the menu. That's how I discover that I love Indian food.

I return home from all the travel excited, comfortable on the racecourse for the first time ever. Now fully healed and with four World Cup snowboardcross races under my belt this year, I feel confident. Until recently, I had been trying to hang on and not crash. Now I don't think about what my feet are doing anymore. I simply focus on racing. When it comes to the Paralympics, I know I've got a legitimate shot.

Still, I'm a 36-year-old father with a toddler and a 10-acre property with four horses to tend. Plus, I have a business to run. Travel for training camps and competition takes me abroad for weeks while work piles up in the office and around the farm. At home I am in the shop for 12 hours at a stretch playing catch-up. In a foul mood, with the phone ringing constantly and emails mounting, I scramble to fulfill orders and keep clients happy. My competitors have no kids to care for, no farm, no business to run. They focus 100 percent on their riding. I resolve not to use these circumstances as excuses. I will use them as fuel to beat these kids. When I get stressed, Sara tells me to approach tasks one at a time. No matter how complex a problem, the solution starts with one step. I know that she's right. After all, those are some of my exact words when I deliver public statements. Reminding me to take my own advice typically calms me.

Sara has remained home while I travel. The time away from family has been difficult. Every time I see Lauren, it seems she has learned how to write new words. Sara keeps track of my progress from home by watching live scoring online. While I'm competing many time zones away, she stays up till 3 AM, monitoring my race times on her phone and imagining how I'm feeling, what my body language looks like based on how I've performed. I hope that my results will make all the time away from home worthwhile as I approach my ultimate goal—the Games.

Sara and I don't want to jinx my run of good fortune, so we maintain a fine balance between confidence and overconfidence. I have momentum, and that's often when I've been hit the hardest by mishaps. "That scares me the worst," Sara says about a run of good luck. For three years, I was repeatedly injured. As soon as I would get healthy, I'd get knocked down. With me upright again, we cannot assume that I will win, so we don't talk about winning the Games. We only talk about preparing for them. We know from 20 years of racing that everything can change in an instant. I draw on my decades of experience in professional athletics, as a trainer, coach, mechanic, and competitor—all in the service of making me ready to react to any race situation. In my head, I constantly visualize a perfect winning run. I know from experience that competition has three main factors that I control: my mental game, my physical preparedness, and the performance of my equipment. I need to make sure all three of these are the best they can possibly be and everything else will come together. I have the speed, but I know in the back of my mind there are factors outside my control.

One aspect outside of my control in the final months of training leading up to the Games? There are no mountains to practice on with challenging terrain in Central Minnesota, only hills with short icy slopes. Still, I have a plan. I apply my mechanical knowledge to fabricate a replica of the start gates we use on tour and set it up on a slight slope in our backyard, out the kitchen window, adjacent to the BioDapt office and race shop. I use my tractor and snow blower to pile up every bit of snow from the yard and Sara, Lauren, and I hand shovel a technical roller section, one of the course challenges for me. I set up cameras to shoot video of my practice starts and analyze the results to learn techniques to make me faster. Through the kitchen window, Sara holds Lauren up and they wave while watching me train, bolting from the start gate, reaching the bottom of the slope, slipping out of my bindings, hoisting my board on my shoulder and hiking to the top of the hill again and again. If I can't be in Colorado, riding the big mountains, at least I can work on my starts, which are the most important part of the race.

Once Powder Ridge opens for the season, I oversee construction of a snowboardcross course with technical roller sections so that I can do laps, dialing in my technique, lines, and strategy. After Christmas, I move my start gate to Powder Ridge so that I can simulate a full run. I'm on snow five days a week through January leading up to Winter X Games in Aspen. There will be no adaptive boardercross race at X Games during the Olympic year. There's no adaptive snocross, either. Instead, I'm paired with a Special Olympian and we compete as a team against other racers in a timed dual downhill. While in Colorado, I get in as many runs as I can on Buttermilk Mountain, fine-tuning my technique.

ALL THE TIME ON SNOW PAYS OFF. In February, one month before the Paralympic Games, I compete at the World Cup in Kelowna, British Columbia. I win gold in snowboardcross and banked slalom and also claim the World Cup season points championship. At the awards banquet, Graham Watanabe, our head coach, pulls all of us aside and announces the majority of the team that will be headed to the Paralympic Games. He turns to me and says, "Mike, you're on the team." I've known it had to be coming, but it feels awesome to finally hear it out loud.

I've been playing catch-up all season, working my tail off. Now, winning all three globes provides a boost of confidence. I'm strong and capable, and my skills improve each time I'm on snow.

Still, the pressure of the Games has begun to affect team dynamics. Coaches arrange a conference call to address dissension within the team. I missed a training camp due to illness where apparently feelings had gotten raw between some teammates. Traveling with the same people for weeks in a pressure cooker environment has begun to grate on some. I know from my experiences racing snocross, especially my fallout with Team Avalanche years earlier, that bad team dynamics create a negative headspace that can ruin performance. This time I'm on the outside, and I'm determined to keep it that way.

Experience has taught me that if you're not in a positive headspace, if there's tension with someone in your circle—someone who's supposed to be part of your support system—that can tear you apart. I can see some of that among my teammates.

When I see them get flustered, I wonder if others are messing with their heads to gain a competitive advantage. I refuse to get involved. We are a unique team compared to most. Yes, we are all part of the U.S. Paralympic Snowboard Team. We train and travel together, but most of us are also competing directly against one another on the racecourse, which is a recipe for disaster, especially when the stakes get higher. When I hear bickering and backhanded comments, I won't be sucked into the nonsense. I always keep my headphones handy so that at the first sign of drama, I can pull them over my ears and crank on some Dierks Bentley, Imagine Dragons, AC/DC, or other pop tunes, whatever makes me happy and puts me in my zone. I'm determined that nothing will distract me from my goals.

I don't want the pressure to ratchet up with expectations. I want to enjoy every second of the experience. This will likely be the only time I'll have this chance. I'll get to travel to South Korea, be a part of Team USA, and race a snowboard, hopefully win. Even if I don't, one of my eight teammates wearing my BioDapt equipment likely will.

Repairing some of the latest round of injured feelings falls to our new coaching staff. Our boardercross coach one year ago was Pat Holland, brother to Nate Holland, one of the all-time leading boardercross athletes. I enjoyed talking to Pat, but his relationship with some other team members was disastrous. They didn't see eye-to-eye. Finally, their differences led to a major fallout, and Pat wasn't rehired heading into the final season leading to the Games. Pat's assistant, Graham Watanabe, replaced him as head coach. Graham, who's known as "Snowboard Ninja" because of his small stature, really low stance on a board, and quick ninja-like moves while flying down the mountain, is a retired boardercross pro with an impressive racing résumé. Still, the turnover in coaching means inconsistency. It doesn't bother me. I'm accustomed to preparing in the off-season. I know from my years as a professional athlete how to train on my own. I try not to lose sleep over matters outside my control anyway. With Graham, I knew him as an assistant, and skill-wise he's an incredible asset. He lacks experience coaching a group like ours, and some of my teammates are unenthusiastic about Graham's coaching style. He's calculated, quiet, not a cheerleader in the way some people need to pep them up. Every athlete needs a tailored approach to push the right buttons to get them in the zone. I have a routine that gets me in the right competitive mindset, but it's been hard-won through experience. For most of my career, I didn't know how to do that on my own, but I've figured it out the last few years. Some of my teammates need more emotional support. I wouldn't say that's Graham's forte. Graham's a professional-level athlete who knows how to snowboard.

My needs are straightforward: I need someone to analyze my riding and tell me how to make it better, and Graham checks those boxes. Our communication is excellent, and I've learned a lot from him and Cody, who both have similar styles of coaching and communication. For some of my teammates, their race results aren't what they want. When things don't go right, it can be human nature to make excuses and point the blame at someone. They think the coach should make them better, which isn't always the case. I've worked with all kinds of coaches during my career. The coaches are just another tool for us to learn how to use them. Luckily, I've learned how to use our coaches, tapping into their strengths to improve my riding.

FOR THE PAST 12 MONTHS, I've spent 170 days traveling, going from a comparative neophyte in snowboarding to the odds-on favorite. I try to tune out talk of my championships to eliminate any outside pressure on me. I'm still thinking of myself as an underdog, the old guy trying to show up the young bucks. But Sara will be watching TV and come upon a program with a Paralympics preview in which Carolyn Manno of NBC Sports says that Mike Schultz will be someone to watch during the Games. *He's a favorite to win gold,* she says. *He's helping people.* Sara records the segment, and when we watch together we both go cold with goosebumps and excitement as we realize the big show, the event that has been in my daily thoughts for the last three and a half years, is less than a month away.

I remain home for the final three weeks before departing for South Korea. As my teammate and best friend, Sara understands how to help me get in the proper state of mind. My experiences have equipped me to handle uncomfortable and difficult situations better, but I plan to give myself the best chance to win by being mentally strong and not getting distracted, whether by teammates, my home life, hype, or the enormity of the moment. Sara stops saying the word *gold,* simply banishing it from her vocabulary. I do, too. Around the house, Sara holds her breath, because it's when I'm humming along smoothly that mishaps tend to occur. This time she's determined that things will be different. Sara bottles up any worries and makes these final moments at home together all about me. She must be exhausted, her emotional bucket near empty, but she doesn't say so.

Sara shields me from other stressors, too. She doesn't mention when Lauren gets sick. She doesn't tell me about bills coming due, freeing me to focus on being an athlete. "Can I do anything?" she asks. Other than that, Sara asks little of me. I know she gets frustrated, but she doesn't show it each time I take off to train at Powder Ridge or the gym again. I'm on snow every day, taking runs through the gate and boardercross course we've set up on the slope. Sara picks up the slack at BioDapt, keeping the business running in my absence. She's supporting me the best she can.

With three days till it's time to depart for South Korea, my hometown of Kimball organizes a sendoff. I deliver a presentation at the Kimball elementary school that Sara and I attended. Afterward, the fire department gives me a lift in one of their engines to Kimball High School, my alma mater, where I deliver a 10-minute talk to the school in the packed auditorium and see some of my old teachers. Students have gotten together to make posters for good luck, and they hand them to me, creating a massive pile of drawings that I'll need help hauling out of there.

The next night my mom and dad, my brother and nephew, and Sara's mom and grandma all gather for a dinner with me at Powder Ridge, the ski resort so central to all our lives. We have a nice family dinner together in the lodge. In two days, I'll be on my way halfway around the globe to South Korea.

All that's left to do is pack for the Paralympics. The day prior to leaving, Lauren joins me in my workshop to help me do the final service and assembly on my two Moto Knee kits. I always bring two assembled kits with me during major competitions, in case something fails while on course. I have a back-up I can swap in a matter of minutes, kind of like a NASCAR pit stop. Lauren is so excited to help me, and I do what I can to try and make her feel helpful. I give her some extra nuts and bolts to thread together on spare frame parts. She's only four, so I have to keep an eye on her, making sure she doesn't misplace something important.

I know it will be a week before Sara joins me in South Korea. I won't see Lauren, who will stay home with her grandmothers, for three weeks. She's old enough to understand what it means now when daddy goes away. When I travel, she likes to make "good luck" cards for me using markers and crayons and slip them into my travel bag when she thinks I'm not looking. This time, she's also adamant that I pack "Lucky Bear," a foot-tall stuffed teddy bear adorned with four-leaf clovers. I explain that I don't have room in my luggage, but she won't hear it, jamming the stuffed animal into a compartment or bag every time I turn my back. This is Lauren's stubborn side. "Just like her dad," Sara says.

Finally, after going back and forth several times, I relent and promise to bring Lucky Bear to the Paralympic Games. Lauren's face lights up in a grin. "Dad," she exclaims triumphantly, "he's going to bring you extra luck!"

20

Red, White, and Blue (and Gold)

On March 2, Sara and Lauren drive with me an hour and a half to the airport in Minneapolis, and we all share emotional good-byes. I'm excited the moment is here, but also very sad knowing that we won't see each other for a long time. Then I board my flight to meet Team USA at the airport in San Francisco so that we can fly together to Seoul. We travel on United, the official airline of the team, and they allow us to board first, though we are relegated to coach class. *Are you kidding me? They are the "proud sponsor" of Team USA and they can't even upgrade us on the way to the Paralympic Games?!* The U.S. team spends hundreds of thousands of dollars on travel annually and there are no benefits to us individual athletes from United. This irks me every time I see a United ad supporting Team USA. Instead, I upgrade myself to Economy Plus class on my own dime. The airline crew has Team USA signs they hold up while announcing to the other passengers that we are on the flight en route to the Games. The applause from other passengers feels good.

Once we land in Seoul, we are ushered through team processing for an entire day at a hotel in the city, where we receive three duffel bags' worth of gear and apparel. Nike has a dedicated area, and so does Ralph Lauren. They are the official apparel providers of the Games, and they have mannequins and fitting rooms set up for us to try on dozens of outfits. We walk out with a few pairs of shoes, jackets, pants, shorts, mittens, hats, a Polo parka equipped with a heater, and Nike exercise outfits. The only thing they don't provide is underwear. Once they've outfitted all 70 of us with a comical quantity of apparel, they place hundreds of bags on a box truck that will follow our team bus on a two-hour drive out of the sprawl of Seoul and into the mountains, twisting and turning on narrow hairpin roads to the resort where we'll hold a final training camp before competition begins.

The resort, High One, resembles a fairytale castle perched halfway up a mountain. Inside, it's extravagant, with marble floors and pillars, and a gondola to whisk guests from the side of the hotel to the top of the mountain. Team Canada is lodging here, along with the U.S. Ski & Snowboard Team. The stay is ostensibly for training, but mainly we are here to have fun freeriding and to blow off steam before the pressure cooker of the Games.

Soon after we arrive, I learn that I am one of several athletes nominated to act as flag-bearer for the U.S. delegation. Athletes from other sports, such as curling, Alpine skiing, and Nordic skiing, have been likewise nominated. Mike Shea is the sport representative for snowboarding—the one designated to go to bat for me. He asks me for my credentials and biographical information to burnish my candidacy so that he can advocate for me at a meeting of the various sport representatives. I'm definitely excited about the possibility of this honor but know it may be a long shot since I have no Paralympic Games experience at this point. Many others have been on the team much longer than I have.

I am roomed with Keith Gabel, and on our final night at the resort he enters our room while I'm hunched over my laptop. I'm drafting a message to Shea with the information he has requested. "Shea just got done with the meeting with the rest of the representatives and they discussed who should be nominated to carry the flag into the stadium," Gabel says.

"Oh, shit!" I say, startled. "I was supposed to be working on getting more information to him."

"I don't think it went very good for you," Gabel says. "You probably should have put more effort into the information you gave Mike."

I'm crestfallen. I've blown my chance at a great opportunity.

Gabel can see that I'm down. He tells me Mike is across the hall in another room. "We should go see how the meeting went."

I pick myself up and mope across the hall. When Gabel opens the door, our entire U.S. Snowboard Team is waiting, sandwiched into a small hotel room. "You got it!" they yell. "You're the flag-bearer!" I'm stunned speechless. I'm surrounded by teammates sitting on the beds, desk, tables. All eyes are on me. I don't know what to say. Mike Shea delivers a few words crediting me with being a good team player, helping my teammates with equipment, and having an overall positive influence. I grow emotional hearing Shea talk.

I'm not here racing for myself. I'm not only representing our team. I will be representing our nation, the one my veteran friends honored with their sacrifices. It feels so good to be surrounded by the support of a team again, recalling my old pro snocross days, before my amputation, when we all pulled together for a single goal, something bigger than each of us.

THAT NIGHT SNOW BEGINS FALLING, light and fluffy flakes that continue until morning. We all wake a little on the tired side, but we're eager to grab first chairs and make first tracks, flowing through untouched snow. I ride the gondola with a few others over the crest of a ridge, revealing the resort on the other side, coated in a foot of fresh powder. Several hotels rise at the base. The resort features glades trails through the trees and gulleys with ribbons of deep snow snaking through for long, narrow runs. It's a beautiful scene, everything decorated in a deep coat of white. In Minnesota, we seldom get to ride powder, and I'm delighted.

The resort is equipped with a P.A. system, speakers echoing through the valley with announcements in Korean, which none of us understands. It calls to mind *The Hunger Games*, when someone is killed and their death is announced, echoing through the forest. Each time the P.A. squawks to life, we joke about who has possibly died this time, quoting lines from the movie. We're in jubilant moods. Everyone hoots and hollers. Powder days turn everyone into kids, and this is the best powder day I've ever experienced. If these first several days of the trip are a precursor to the rest of it, we are in for an epic time.

Just after lunch, the entire team and staff loads onto two charter buses, winding our way through the mountains for a ride to our accommodations in the PyeongChang Olympic Village. I hate riding on buses. I get carsick easily in the mountains, and I always seem to be sitting next to the loudest person who won't stop talking. I plug my headphones into my ears and put on some mellow music on my vintage iPod to calm me, and try not to blow chunks due to a nauseous feeling in my stomach from the serpentine roads.

Excitement rises as we approach the athlete accommodations in the Olympic Village. Today will be a scramble. We must move into our apartments, get dressed, and get to the opening ceremony. The bus rolls through a security checkpoint into a commons area that resembles airport-style security and bag checks. At the center, flagpoles are arranged in a circle, with all the nations represented. My anticipation of the ceremony tonight is building.

Departing the bus, on the right is the cafeteria building, and a wooden ramp leads to six high-rise apartment towers, constructed especially for the Games. The U.S. team has its own apartment building. The first two floors are devoted to the U.S. team staff, physical therapy, athlete support, and a commons area for medical treatment. We also have a lounge for Team USA to hang out, play video games, watch TV, and make phone calls.

There's only one elevator per building, and Team USA staff must hump all our gear up to our rooms. You can fit maybe six or seven bags on each load, so they work in a cluster, sending load after load up in the elevator. There are 74 athletes, multiplied by three or four bags each—hundreds of bags total. The process will take two hours.

We snowboarders are housed on the 12th floor, which proves to be a great warm-up exercise when we are forced to climb on foot while the elevator is occupied. I'm in a four-bedroom apartment unit with Gabel, Shea, Noah Elliott, Jimmy Sides, Mike Spivey, and my fellow Minnesotan and friend Mike Mann. As we check out our room, we're puzzled at the set-up. The building is brand-new and will be turned into apartments after the games. We only have access to our bedrooms and our bathrooms. The kitchen cabinets, the sinks, the drawers, and even the fireplace are all covered by temporary paneling. A couple of our bedrooms are separated by temporary walls in order to fit more athletes into this short-term setup. Mann and I share a room. Sides and Spivey, both Marines who each lost an arm while serving separately in Afghanistan, share a room. Gabel, Noah, and Shea have their own rooms. Each room has a closet or two for hanging all our swag, including the elaborate matching outfits we must wear to the opening ceremony in a few hours.

We must wear pants, a sweater, and a scarf, with a big heavy puffy jacket equipped with a heater inside. We must tuck the shirt in just right, and the handkerchief must be tied just so. Our socks must go over the cuff of our pants, and we must wear a pair of heavy hiking boots with red laces that were definitely not designed with amputees in mind.

During processing, we were told exactly how our gear was supposed to be worn, and none of us can remember. I don't know how to tie my handkerchief. I don't know if my pants go inside my boots, or over the top. We compare results, mocking one another, scrambling to coordinate our ensembles for the opening ceremony. I even pull up my cheat sheet that was emailed to us with directions. It still doesn't make much sense.

That's when Mike Shea steps up and says, "No, no, no, no."

Shea is Team USA's Mr. Fashion. He knows the look Ralph Lauren, official team apparel designer, wants us to achieve. With help from Shea, our in-house stylist, we get our outfits looking sharp.

Dressed and ready, we all make our way downstairs to the front of the apartment buildings. Ushers lead us in a parade of nations, in alphabetical order, placing the U.S. nearly last. As the other nations walk past, making their way onto waiting buses to whisk them to the stadium, we hoot, holler, and high-five their athletes. Many of us from rival international countries have become friends over the years while competing together on the World Cup tour.

A bus drops us outside the stadium, where we are herded under a massive tent to keep out of the fog and a slight drizzle. The air is wet with humidity and it feels like it might rain at any moment. A local South Korean volunteer force is at every corner, smiling and willing to help us any way they can. Snacks are laid out, and we mingle with athletes from other nations. Countries are led in alphabetical order once again, so we are near the end.

This is when I'm handed the flag. I think I understand flag etiquette, but am I supposed to wave it? I want to do it right, but I'm given little instruction. I'm told to follow our South Korean model into the stadium, and that the other members of the team should remain about 10 paces behind me.

We wait for 30 minutes under the tent, inching forward as the other teams take their turns on parade. I pass the time texting with Sara. She has finally made it in the stadium now, with her sister, Jillian, and Mark Mann's wife, Rachel, after 30 hours of travel on airplanes, airports, taxis, buses, and trains. Lauren is in Kimball, 10 time zones behind, where it's 5 AM, watching the ceremony with my mom and Sara's mom.

When we finally enter the doors from outside, I get a peek into the stadium. I feel a surge of emotion, shivering at the sight of the packed stands. This is it, the first steps of our week together at the Paralympics, one we've been preparing for and anticipating for the last four years.

THE EYES AND APPLAUSE wash over me as I step into the vast Olympic Stadium beneath a cold night sky. Behind me is the 74-athlete delegation of the United States team, the largest of the 49 countries on hand for this, the pinnacle of competition for adaptive athletes anywhere in the world. My teammates, my friends who've become as close as family during the past four years, grip phones and cameras to memorialize the moment as I lead them from the tunnel into the open air of the stadium, just the way I'd dreamed. A surprise twist: the American flag waving from a staff I'm clutching. I'm smiling because I'm delighted to be here, because I cannot help myself, because of the butterflies in my stomach, the goosebumps on my arms. Yes, I'm nervous.

Don't trip and fall, drop the flag, I tell myself. *Not while the world is watching.*

Over my right shoulder, there's Mike Shea and Keith Gable, who've been on the snowboard team twice as long as I have. They are my buddies. We ride together and room together on the road. They've nominated me to carry the flag and advocated for my selection. Shea's GoPro records the moment. He minds the details and relishes the chance to spiff up in our team uniforms. Gable is one of the first snowboarders I met when I began competing at Winter X Games. A competitive personality who's at home riding the untamed, treacherous terrain of the mountain backcountry, he's nevertheless always been generous with a kind word or advice. This is his second trip to the Paralympics, and he's beaming like it's his first. So is Amy Purdy, a bronze-medal winner at the 2014 Paralympic Games, and one of the key figures who introduced me to snowboarding a half-dozen years ago. A model, Amy's teased brown-and-blonde strands of hair flow from her Team USA beanie as she marches ahead, basking in the spotlight just as she had when she appeared on a season of *Dancing with the Stars.* There's Noah Elliott, the 20-year-old cancer survivor and the newest member of the team, who I've mentored, and who will be my toughest competition. He appears awed by the moment, the biggest of his young career, and the scale of the stadium. The wheelchairs are behind me, riding right up my heels in their excitement.

I'm supposed to be leading, but the team engulfs me, waving to the stands, filled to capacity with 35,000 people bathed in red, white, and blue lights. Somewhere up there are South Korea's president and first lady, mingling with U.S. dignitaries. Somewhere up there is Sara; I scan the crowd for a glimpse of her, but the colored lights and the flashes from cell phone cameras make it difficult to see. We athletes on parade are the culmination of a sophisticated, choreographed spectacle featuring song, dance, and high-tech pageantry, all broadcast live on MSNBC. Family, friends, and neighbors are watching, including back in Kimball, population 791. Millions more are tuned in across South Korea and around the globe.

This is no time to take a tumble. I concentrate on the mechanics of each step as if I'm learning to walk with an artificial leg for the first time. It's been nine years; most days I make it look smooth and natural. But not today. Our clunky leather hiking boots are too heavy, like swinging a sledgehammer with my knee. My prosthesis rebels against the boot at the bottom of my left leg.

A fall now would look ridiculous, especially in this team uniform. We are all matched from head to toe: from knit caps to Nordic sweaters to puffy red, white, and blue parkas to leather mittens thick with fringe that call to mind General George C. Custer.

Steady, Mike. Steady.

Some teammates are my biggest rivals in racing, men 10 to 15 years younger—stiff competition standing between me and my goals of a medal. Many are also clients, wearing prosthetics I've designed and built for them through my company BioDapt. It's surreal to be surrounded by snowboarders on the team riding on my equipment. I've tried to be a good teammate, and it hasn't gone unnoticed. They've voted for me to carry the Stars and Stripes, to lead our team.

I clutch the flag with my fringed leather mittens and think of the U.S. soldiers I've met and befriended. I think of friends who've lost limbs fighting under this flag, and what it represents to our team, our nation. For a patriot like me, this is the ultimate honor.

It's taken me countless steps to get here, and I've taken more falls than I want to recall. But not now—it's time to stay upright. *Keep moving, Mike, one foot in front of the other. You're so close.*

Tomorrow, official training begins on the mountain, everything I've worked for, trained for; all the scraping, sacrifice, and time spent traveling, away from home, family.

I don't want to forget to enjoy tonight with teammates, coaches, trainers. I promised myself I would soak in the moment, the sights, sounds, the flag hefted in my hands, all the sensations of the Games.

Hear that? They're cheering for you, Mike.

I'm nearly across the stadium now. There are only a few final steps to go.

THE NEXT DAY OF TEAM PRACTICE is the first of two scheduled before snowboardcross competition begins. In the morning, we take a 40-minute bus ride from the athletes' village to Jeongseon Alpine Center, on Gariwangsan, a 5,000-foot peak. One year after the World Cup test event, the venue has been transformed, with a massive hotel open for business, a blacktop parking lot, and roads with tunnels cut right into the mountain. Shipping containers stacked two high have been arranged in a 100-foot line at the base of the mountain, like a little village. Each country has its own small workshop inside, where wax techs will tune up all the riders' equipment and make repairs. The U.S. is in the first row on the second level. This is our base camp.

My teammates and I get dumped off at the athlete hospitality tent, past the hotel and gondola. We gear up and hop on the gondola for our first practice on the mountain. From the gondola, I get my first glimpse of the course, its outlines marked with blue dye on the snow, and the enormous finish line area with bleachers and a massive TV screen, located halfway up the mountain.

My heart beats faster with excitement. This will be a fun course with no real difficult technical features to make it too sketchy or unpredictable. I'm excited at the fairly simplistic features compared to some of the courses I've ridden. I can charge this setup.

We are granted about two hours each day on the course, which equates to about five runs. I want to ease into practice and not make any mistakes that could result in injury. I begin riding at about 75 to 80 percent of my pace, ramping up steadily on the second day of training, playing around with line choices, my confidence building.

On my final training run, I line up in the gates with Noah in the hopes of simulating real race conditions. Despite all my training on starts, Noah gets out of the gate faster and grabs the inside line into the first corner. I'm hot on his heels. This will be my chance to figure out how to pass on the course, so that if I'm behind in a heat, I know what I can do to make a pass.

I try to stick to Noah's tail all the way down. He begins to pull away. As we approach the end of the course, I've reeled him in again, and I'm looking to make my move. With the third-to-last turn coming, I have momentum and Noah has drifted a little wide. If I can cut some distance, I'll prepare to attempt a pass on the final turn. The second-to-last turn is a near-180-degree left-hander, and I'm on Noah now. Heading into the final turn, a right-hander, I hold an inside line and press the issue, sliding ahead and slamming the door, leaving Noah with nowhere to go. The tip of his board rides up over the tail of mine, causing me to spin and catch an edge, sending us both crashing to the snow with a thud and a spray of white.

We aren't traveling too fast and quickly pop up and finish the run, meeting at the bottom. Neither of us is hurt, but Noah is spooked. Brushing the snow off, he says, "Dude, this is just snowboarding."

I'm not sure how to respond. I have my game face on. Sure, one of us, or both, could have been injured. Still, tomorrow we will be racing for real. I need to figure out strategy for passing. "Sorry, man," I say, trying to sound convincing. "Totally pushed that one a little further than I should have."

Noah is rattled, but I try to brush off the exchange like it's no big deal. Inside, I'm thinking, *No, this is not just snowboarding. We're at the*

Paralympics, an event we've trained for the past four years. With all my racing experience on dirt bikes and snowmobiles, I know that practice is the best place to dial in your race so that you can bring the experience to the competition.

In a meeting with teammates later in the day, I stay after everyone has dispersed to talk to coaches Graham Watanabe and Cody Brown privately about my duel with Noah. They tell me that practice is for experimentation, to learn what works and what doesn't. "Yeah, Schultzy," says Graham. "That's how you know how it works."

"High-five for going for it!" Cody says.

"Neither one of you got hurt," Graham says, "Awesome!" He adds that hopefully Noah and I have learned something we can take into our races. I know I have at least.

I WAKE ON MARCH 12, race day, an hour before the sun. I'm the most nervous I've ever felt as an athlete. Before I get out of bed, I visualize my race run from top to bottom at least three times, a technique I've learned from my coaches over the years. The more times you visualize your run and the features, the less you have to think about it in the moment. I have no appetite and an upset stomach as I gather my things and get dressed in the apartment I share with the other racers. The conversation with my roommate Mark Mann is a bit different today. We are positive but quieter than usual. We are both trying to calm our nerves, knowing that we will likely duel head-to-head at some point in our race toward gold. I've sorted my dress routine; I put my mid-layer on, my black race pants with the U.S. flag on the left thigh, and my team jacket. I pack an extra mid-layer in case I get soaked from rain or sweat. I pack several snacks for throughout the day while on the mountain, which will be key to keeping my energy levels up.

Before heading out the door, I perform one last task: I rub the head of Lucky Bear, the stuffed animal adorned with shamrocks that Lauren insisted I pack. I think about my beautiful daughter back home. "Dad, you need him with you," she had said. She was right. I'm glad to have him now. I give Lucky Bear three rubs for luck, and nod at the stuffed animal, knowing it's going to be a good day.

Before boarding the bus, I stop at the cafeteria and eat breakfast, making a strong effort to get my food down. I'm still nauseous from pre-race jitters, but eating is a must if I'm going to perform well. We board the bus as a team, and I put my headphones on and tune everything out and just try to relax. Once we arrive at the competition venue, we assemble our boards and bindings. For this specific event, I have two race boards and a free-rider I use to get on and off the mountain. My boards have been freshly tuned the night before by our wax serviceman, Skiddy, who's one of my favorite characters on the team. A rancher from Oregon whose given name is Mark Kelly, Skiddy has a thick, sandy-colored beard flecked with gray, and he's fond of wearing cowboy hats and boots. He takes seriously his work making our boards fast, but he's always able to make light of difficult situations, accentuating the positive and boosting morale. He never fails to make me laugh and smile as we prep for our race days.

I don my race leg setup—my Moto Knee, Versa Foot, and socket. I put my upper body armor on, a zip-up with low-profile elbow pads, shoulder pads, spine protector, and chest pad. Lastly my red, white, and blue jersey goes over it all. Today the jersey has a weightier feel to it. The last of my gear is my red helmet and a fresh set of Oakley mirrored goggles that I got at team processing. All geared up, the butterflies and nausea persist. I need to push through distraction and the pressure of the moment. I remind myself that I must focus on riding my snowboard, launch quickly out of the gate, hit my lines, and just keep charging. I board the gondola and cruise up the mountain and get an eagle-eyed view of most of the course on the way up, still anxious as ever.

FOLLOWING MY SECOND AND FINAL practice run on the snowboardcross course that morning, I'm feeling good about my riding when I spot Sara at the finish line area. She, her sister, and Keith Gabel's wife, Heather, come blitzing across the snow as I exit the course fence.

I'm so happy to see Sara as we hug for the first time in more than a week. She's been staying in a hotel while I've been sequestered in the athletes' village. "I love you, honey," I say quickly before dashing off up the mountain to the top of the course for the first qualifier. This is it—go time.

The qualifier to determine seeding and race brackets is a timed run, and I make a mistake on a turn, skidding out and forcing me down into fifth place. Now I have to fight my way through with an extra round of racing if I want to make it to the medal rounds.

Once head-to-head heats begin, my first two races give me little problem. In my third, I face Mark Mann, my training partner, friend, and roommate in the athletes' village. This will be a nerve-wracking matchup. Mann is fast in the start section. In training we are close, and I know that a small mistake can cost me.

In our race, my practice at home pays off and I get the holeshot, seizing the lead out of the gate. We are close on the course when I wobble a bit, nearly sliding out on my toe side, putting my hand down for a moment to regain my balance. Seeing this and not wanting to get tangled up, Mann checks his speed to avoid a possible collision, rather than attempting to pass. I'm thinking, *I almost lost it there. That would have sucked!* The close call causes me to sharpen up, and the decision to be conservative rather than flying by when I was nearly down costs Mark the race, allowing me to gain position and edge him out.

Next, I face Noah, my closest competition and biggest source of worry. I've been nervous all day, more than usual on race day. Now the butterflies get worse. Noah is the one guy who's a major threat. I've got to make it happen. No mistakes. This is the semifinal bracket. The winner will advance to race for gold and can finish no worse than silver. If Noah knocks me out, the best I can do is bronze, and I may finish out of the medals altogether.

I mull my lines against Noah. I know his strengths. I sponsor him. I'm hoping I'm in his head a little, too, the result of us tangling up in practice yesterday. I'm fine with him thinking that I'm willing to send it in there with force, if needed.

WHEN WE GET TO THE TOP of the course before my showdown with Noah, there's a gate malfunction that delays the race. Organizers discuss alternatives, one of which is to cancel the competition. The other is to use the current standings to determine the final rankings. My heart sinks at the thought. If we proceed with either option, there will be no medal for me, once my poor qualifying time is factored into the standings. I want to say something, but bite my lip. My fate is outside my control, and my anxiety worsens for nearly two hours until eventually a fix for the gate is jury-rigged using bungee cords. A race official will stand between the two gates, holding the free ends of two bungee cords in each hand. The other ends are attached to the frame of the gate. When it's go-time, the official will simultaneously release each bungee cord, and we will bolt from the gate. This is no big deal to me since I grew up racing motocross with bungee cord starts. It's hardly high-tech, but at least the medals will be decided head-to-head on the course. Bring it on!

Noah and I finally prepare to line up and face off. Noah has the right to choose which gate position he wants because he finished better in time trials. He picks the right gate, the outside, and I'm thrilled. The first corner is a left-hander, and I will have the inside gate, and the inside line. All I need to do to seize control of the race is nail the holeshot, which I do once the gate drops and the race is underway.

We boom down the first straightaway, nearly bumping. I hold my line, Noah dead even with me, less than an arm's length away. I'm on the inside, he's on my toe-side, his back to me down the straightaway and around the first corner, a left turn, where I dig my heels in and edge ahead slightly. Our boards are rubbing, bumping, jockeying for position. I outweigh Noah by 40 pounds. He's not moving me. I stay strong, and he's forced to check up when I force him inside on a right-hander through turn two. Noah skids out slightly to avoid a collision, allowing me to take the lead after the second corner. The race isn't finished, though. We hurtle down the course, and after turn four, Noah attempts to reel in my lead. He knows he must make his move soon if he's going to catch me. He forces the issue, carrying too much speed into turn five, a left-hander, and skids out in a cloud of snow dust on his heel edge, a mistake that costs him valuable speed, allowing me to pull away. I make no mistakes; this is my best run of the Games, nearly flawless. I'm tight around turns, rolling through bumps. Launching from the last 45-foot jump before the finish, I land cleanly and tuck for the final few feet. Crossing the finish line first feels like 200 pounds has been lifted from my shoulders. I relax, finally allowing myself a peek over my right shoulder. Noah is nowhere in sight and I raise my right fist in triumph, guaranteed at least a silver medal.

NERVES GONE, I'M BACK AT THE TOP of the course, hooting and hollering, high-fiving everyone I encounter. I'm about to face Chris Vos of Holland in the final for the gold medal. Vos, who's about half my age, has been the most consistent rider in our class, garnering the most attention over the last couple seasons. While I was laid-up with my heel injury, he was the rider to beat. I know that even a small mistake against him will mean game over. The pressure is off, though. Lose this race and I still walk away with silver. Vos has first pick for gate position because he's got a better qualifying time than I do. When he picks the outside gate, just like Noah, I'm thinking, *No way! You just handed me the advantage. I'll take it! Thank you!* With the inside gate, I've got control of the first corner as long as I get a decent jump out, and I'm smooth through the first couple features.

When the official drops the bungee, I'm 100 percent focused on grabbing the holeshot and nailing the first straightaway, calling on the countless hours of practice on my starts back home and at Powder Ridge. I charge the start section and the opening three features. Riding as fluid and smooth as possible, I apply technique with my feet to pull my board up over the rollers, and press down on the backside of the features, accelerating me into a lead on Vos as we negotiate the next set of jumps. Vos doesn't fare as well. As I enter turn one, I hear something behind me—an off-balance Vos decking a roller and crashing—but keep my attention on the course, refusing to be distracted, hitting my lines all the way down. Three-quarters of the way down, on a tight right-hander, I glance over my right shoulder and there's no sign of Vos. My heart leaps, but I must remind myself to focus. Smooth edges. Ride it all the way home.

On the last jump, I leave the face of the six-foot-tall ramp. Airborne, my arms whirl, "rolling down the windows," and I stick the landing, tucking forward, pumping my fists as I cross the finish line. Standing upright and raising my arms in victory, I veer hard right and see Sara on the giant TV screen at the base of the run. Rendered huge and in hi-def, she's jumping up and down in the stands, clutching a small U.S. flag in her fist, tears streaming down her cheeks. The most powerful emotions I've felt as a competitor swamp me—awe, pride, happiness, a feeling of the most incredible accomplishment. All the work, effort, and sacrifice to get here—not only in the last three and a half years, but since the moment the doctor said those life-changing words, *we have to amputate*—has paid off. The roller coaster of ups and downs is over, replaced by joy. Mission accomplished.

Vos makes his way down and we share a hug. Yes, I've won a gold medal. And yes, I've beaten other snowboarders. I've conquered a new sport, too. But the most special feelings come from having hit bottom physically and emotionally multiple times and bouncing back repeatedly during the past couple years, while never failing to work toward this goal.

Organizers hold us in a corral near the finish line until the other classes finish their finals. The other competitors and I high-five and snap selfies. There's a small ceremony, with the top three finishers parading in front of the crowd. I raise my board over my head and let out a yell as they announce my name. In the corral, media can request an interview. I stand for several, and that's where Sara spots me, scaling two barriers to reach me with a huge hug over a fence. After a couple interviews, Sara calls Lauren on FaceTime back at home, where it's three in the morning. She's been awake with her grandmothers to watch me race. Lauren answers the call with a piercing, high-pitched, four-year-old scream. "Daddy!" she shrieks. "You won gold!" I have, and hearing her voice, seeing her joy, makes me shed tears of happiness.

Finally, an anti-doping handler ushers me from the media area for a mandatory drug test. As a medal winner, I'd been chosen at random. They can test me at the competition site or the medal ceremony site, down the mountain near the athlete village. Either way, I need to provide them with a urine sample. I've got on all my gear and I want to get out of my Moto Knee and into my walking leg before climbing atop the podium. I have officials drive me to the tech shed in the shipping containers at the bottom of the mountain, where I've left my walking leg. Once there I swap out my Moto Knee for my walking leg. That's when I realize I'm not going to be able to hold it till the medal ceremony, which is a 40-minute drive away. So we drive to the drug testing facility on the mountain, where technicians collect urine and blood samples. It takes longer than anticipated before I'm cleared to leave and collect my gold medal. My handler takes a call and tells me, "They're going to hold the medal ceremony for you, but we need to hurry." I'm feeling under intense pressure as I'm bundled back into a minivan and raced down the mountain, whipping around curves and crossing into the opposite lane of traffic to pass other vehicles. We're hauling ass, narrowly avoiding collisions, passing when we shouldn't. *Holy shit! Don't kill us before the medal ceremony.*

I've dreamed about standing atop the podium with the anthem playing here since joining the U.S. team almost four years ago. Now I will get to live the fantasy as we pull up and park and I rush from the minivan to the stage. Hundreds of people have gathered, including Sara and her sister, Jillian. Noah has won bronze, and he steps onto the podium first, followed by Vos. Wearing my walking leg, I step up front, center stage. Behind me there's a massive deep-blue backdrop. In front, a media contingent with cameras and the flags of Holland and the United States fluttering in the wind. South Korean women hand us our medals and Bandabi, an Asian black bear who is the Paralympics mascot in PyeongChang. Then the opening notes of the U.S. national anthem start to play and the U.S. flag rises, along with a big knot in my throat.

Tears blur my vision—red, white, and blue running together—but the clarity of the dream remains, more intense than I'd ever imagined.

THE GAMES ARE NOT OVER FOR ME. After the ceremony, Sara, Jillian, Noah, and I return to the athletes' village lounge for some snacks, but I experience an adrenaline dump that leaves me sapped of energy. I'm shot and all I want to do is climb in bed. I fall asleep with my phone pinging messages of congratulations from back home, 15 time zones away, where friends and family are waking up to the news that I've won.

The next day Sara fetches me, and we return to her hotel, which is vastly nicer than my crowded apartment. We order pizza and pick up a bottle of chardonnay for me, spending a quiet night together relaxing and falling asleep early.

There's three more days until the banked slalom competition. Rainy weather moves into the mountains, and the temperature warms to 65 degrees, cancelling the first day of training. It's still raining during practice, and overnight the temperature drops, the wet course turning to a treacherous sheet of ice. On competition day it's 25 degrees Fahrenheit and icy. The warm-up run from the top of the mountain to the top of the racecourse is the most difficult and sketchy run I've ever made. A sheet of ice you can literally ice skate on, these are definitely not ideal conditions for racing on a snowboard.

The final results will be based on the best of three timed runs. On the fast, slick course I struggle to manage my speed. My first run puts me in second place, .10 of a second off the fastest pace. My second run, I wipe out in a corner, and drop to fourth, .10 behind Vos for bronze. On my third run, I finish with a 54.42, my best. I spend the day nervously watching the times roll in. In the end, Noah throws down an incredibly fast and smooth run and beats me by 1.52 seconds to take the gold.

I have no regrets about winding up with a silver medal. Today, I'm just not fast enough to win. Each of Noah's runs bests all my times. I've developed a leg for him so that he could achieve his dreams and mentored him as he learned to snowboard. Back on the medal stand, seeing Noah atop provides its own rewards. He's the future of the sport. At 20 years old, living in Utah, and training at the Olympic training center in Colorado, he will only get faster. This will be his life now.

For me, the pressure to perform is gone, and it feels good to chill for a few days at the Games. My body and mind feel deflated. Not in a bad way; in the way that I had given everything I possibly could for the last few months, and now I can just enjoy not preparing or worrying. I sit for a couple interviews and promotions and check out some of the other competition venues. Sara and I attend the gold-medal sled hockey competition, cheering the U.S. to a win in overtime.

This moment marks the end of my snowboarding career. I'll be 40 come the next Paralympic Games, and I doubt I can hang on and find the motivation for another four years of training, traveling, and competing against athletes nearly half my age. Reflecting on all that I've overcome, the opportunities to travel the world and compete as a professional in multiple sports, I'm content knowing I've exceeded all my dreams. Most athletes never get to savor the kind of perfect finish I've achieved. Here's my chance to go out on top.

Epilogue
After the Gold Rush

Whenever anyone asks the million-dollar question—*Would you wish to have your leg back, if you could?*—I don't even have to consider my answer for a second. Yes, of course I would. I would gladly give everything up—the Paralympic and X Games medals, the snocross tour championship, the accolades, the business, everything—to have my leg back. Don't get me wrong; I've had fun as an amputee. But I hate having one leg. To put it plainly, it's a pain in the ass, literally and figuratively. At night, as I ready for bed and remove my prosthesis, I become handicapped. One of the most dangerous parts of my day comes when I go for my nightly shower, balancing on one foot on a slick, wet floor and trying to hold on while washing myself. I've fallen before and been lucky not to injure myself badly.

I'm unable to turn back time or grow a new leg (even though Lauren, now eight years old, keeps asking if I ever will). Soon after my injury I also realized that our lives are in our own hands and it's up to us to create and follow through with our chosen path (which is usually constantly evolving). We do this by setting goals, making positive decisions, and surrounding ourselves with good people—and if the goal is worth achieving, then it's worth the hard work and sacrifice needed.

After accomplishing my greatest goal as an athlete, I plan to continue in the sports I love and enjoy and continue creating better adaptive equipment to serve more sports and activities. I have so many ideas and ambitions. *Could I win another gold at age 40? Am I really ready to hang up my race gear for good? To give up those good feelings when the results arrive after hard work?* The more I think about retirement, the more my mind continues racing.

I've always told myself that I'll continue competing as long as: 1. I'm having fun; 2. It's financially worthwhile; and 3. I'm still competitive. Snowboarding still checks all three boxes for me. Although not an easy decision (involving a lot of back and forth between Sara and me), I've decided to charge hard in preparation for the 2022 Paralympic Games, held in March in Beijing. I'm going to give my best runs against Noah, Chris, and a couple new athletes wearing BioDapt prosthetic equipment I've built in my shop.

I love competition too much to quit now. My race isn't over yet.

Acknowledgments

To the people who have helped me, influenced me, and played a role in the person and athlete that I have become—a Paralympic gold and silver medalist; a 10-time X Games gold medalist; a multisport professional athlete; an inventor, business owner, and father.

Matt Higgins (coauthor): Writing this book has been a long, fun, and at times challenging project, and I couldn't be happier with the result. You were able to help capture the right words and emotion while telling my story. To have my story written in a book is my own priceless piece of history that I can forever share with my family, friends, and readers around the world. Thank you, Matt!

Sara (wife): You are the most patient and caring person I have ever met. You give me your shoulder to lean on when I need it most, you are the best cheerleader when I'm on course...even after 20 years of competing, you give me space when I need it and reel me back in when I take things too far. Since the beginning, you've always brought out the best in me. You are the one who balances me out. I wouldn't be who I am today without you in my life. I love you, babe!

Lauren (daughter): You have already become an extraordinary little person who is talented, smart, and very driven. You are much like me but so much different at the same time. You make your mom and me very proud to be your parents. I look forward to sharing many experiences and wisdom with you as you grow and begin the pursuit of making your best life. Your adventures are just beginning, and I can't wait to see what the future holds for you!

Dad: Thank you, Dad, for teaching me many of the most important things in life at an early age, including the hard work and dedication to earn what you want out of life, and for the understanding of and appreciation for the great outdoors.

Mom: Thank you, Mom, for always believing in me through every step of life. I know I've put you through a roller coaster of emotions since the beginning, and you've always supported me while chasing down my dreams no matter how uncomfortable it made you feel during all the injuries and setbacks.

Rick: Thank you, Rick, for bringing me into Mom's and your company right out of high school, which helped me grow as a person and professional early on. This opportunity helped me understand my true potential in many ways.

Chris (older brother): I look back at all the fun we had in our younger days with all the camping, hunting, four-wheelers, dirt bikes, and working on the farm. Your work ethic and attention to detail was something I always looked up to.

Luke (brother-in-law): Thank you for all the help during the years after my amputation with BioDapt, traveling to adaptive races around the country, and all the input to help with skiing and snowboarding!

Jim Wazny: Thank you for being that person who reached out to me very early on and "flipped the switch" to show me what was possible as an amputee. It's been a blast to ride with you over the years on dirt and snow.

Chris Ridgway: You started out as my archrival on the track but soon become a great friend off the track through all of our two- and four-wheel adventures. I still owe you a block pass!

Graham and Cody (Team USA snowboard coaches): Thank you for all the great insight and coaching throughout the '17–18 season while I went from just a snowboarder to Paralympic champion. I thoroughly enjoyed that season!

Skiddy (Team USA snowboard tech/serviceman): You were more than our snowboard "serviceman"; you were/are master of speed, technician, motivator, comic relief, and awesome friend in our quest for Team USA Gold. You could always make us smile or laugh or calm us down in the most stressful and uncomfortable situations during those long competitions and road trips!

Kep: I'll never forget the comment you made to me, the motorsports athlete: "I'm going to make a snowboarder out of you yet." Ha! Look at me now. Thank you for being my first snowboard coach, pushing me out of my comfort zone, and most of all, being a really rad dude to me and all the other adaptive athletes.

Snocross racing family: You were my second family—I loved to be around like-minded, hardworking, competitive, and motivated people who absolutely loved the sport of snowmobiling. The hardest part of my injury was when I thought I had to give it all up—not the racing part, but traveling the race circuit with you all. This will always be one of the highlights of my life.

Keith Gabel, Mike Shea, Nicole Roundy, Brenna Huckaby, Noah Elliott, Brittani Coury, Mark Mann, Evan Strong, Amy Purdy, and Mike Minor (Team USA Snowboarding Teammates): We've shared excitement, challenges, and adventures from all around the world in the quest to prepare and compete for gold. You've each taught me something about life, competition, and myself over the years while traveling. Most of my best experiences with you while on the team didn't really have much to do with competition at all. I'll always remember and cherish the treks through airports and cities, shredding the beautiful mountains on our boards, and finally catching a glimpse of that elusive Sasquatch in Oregon!

Dan Gale and Amy Purdy: Thank you for all that you do to help grow the adaptive sports world. Both of you were a major influence on where I am today as an adaptive athlete.

Mike Glefke and Team Avalanche crew: Even though our partnership in racing ended on the rocks, my best pro racing memories were while I was part of Team Avalanche. We had so many great moments on and off the racecourse. —*Monster Mike #5*

Chris Carlson: I'll always be thankful for your willingness to give such a large helping hand when my business (BioDapt) first got rolling.

Chip Taylor (prosthetist): Thank you, Chip, for being my "leg mechanic." You were a key player to getting me back in action so quickly and keeping me going because of your expertise and attention to detail.

Wayne Davis: You've been capturing my racing action through photography as far back as I can remember, and to now have you shoot the cover photo for this book was the perfect fit! Thank you for all the great moments you've photographed throughout my career.

Photographers (Wayne Davis, Joe Wiegele, Gary Walton, Joe Kusumoto, Mike Reis, Natasha Vos, and my wife, Sara): Thank you to all the great photographers who captured the images highlighted in this book. Many of you have taken photos of my career for many years, and some for only a couple major events, but you've all captured important moments that will now be locked into my story forever.